MARK ANTONY'S HEROES

Also by Stephen Dando-Collins

*Caesar's Legion: The Epic Saga of Julius Caesar's
Elite Tenth Legion and the Armies of Rome*

*Nero's Killing Machine: The True Story of Rome's
Remarkable Fourteenth Legion*

*Cleopatra's Kidnappers: How Caesar's Sixth Legion
Gave Egypt to Rome and Rome to Caesar*

MARK ANTONY'S HEROES

HOW THE THIRD GALLICA LEGION SAVED AN APOSTLE AND CREATED AN EMPEROR

STEPHEN DANDO-COLLINS

BICENTENNIAL
1807
WILEY
2007
BICENTENNIAL

John Wiley & Sons, Inc.

CONTENTS

ATLAS

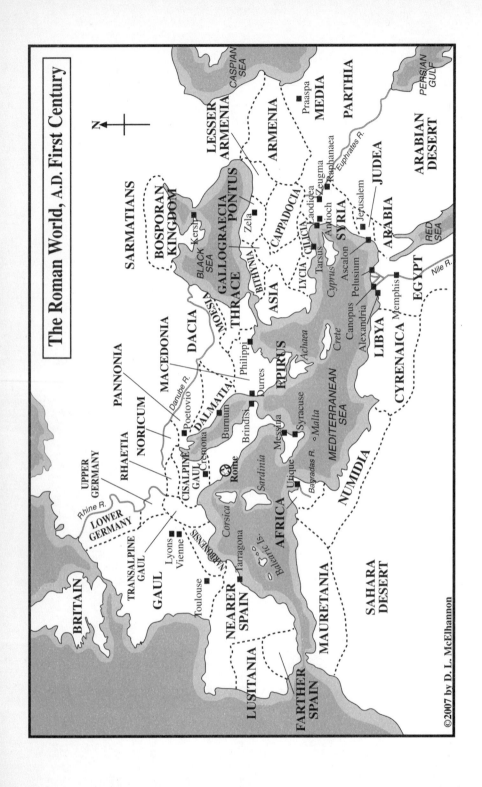

The Roman World, A.D. First Century

©2007 by D. L. McElhannon

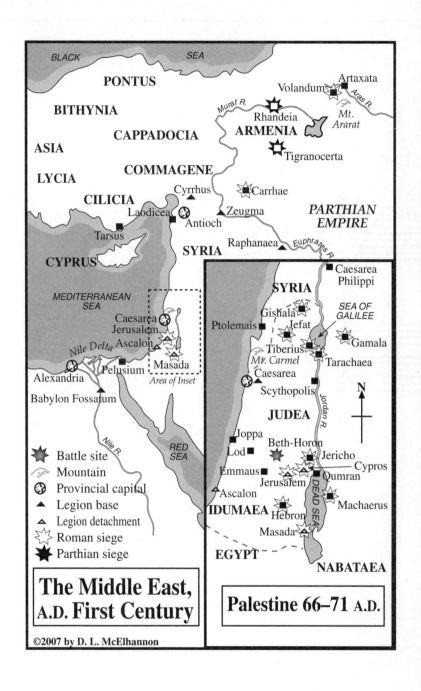

BLACK SEA

PONTUS

BITHYNIA

CAPPADOCIA

ASIA

LYCIA

COMMAGENE

CILICIA

Laodicea

Tarsus

CYPRUS

MEDITERRANEAN SEA

Caesarea
Jerusalem
Ascalon

Nile Delta

Alexandria

Babylon Fossatum

Pelusium

Masada

Area of Inset

Murat R.

Volandum

Artaxata

Aras R.

Rhandeia

ARMENIA

Mt. Ararat

Tigranocerta

Cyrrhus

Carrhae

Zeugma

Antioch

SYRIA

Raphanaea

Euphrates R.

PARTHIAN EMPIRE

Caesarea Philippi

SYRIA

Gishala

Jefat

Ptolemais

SEA OF GALILEE

Gamala

Tiberius

Mt. Carmel

Tarachaea

Caesarea

Scythopolis

JUDEA

Jordan R.

Joppa

Lod

Beth-Horon

Jericho

Cypros

Emmaus

Jerusalem

Qumran

Ascalon

DEAD SEA

Machaerus

IDUMAEA

Hebron

Masada

EGYPT

NABATAEA

Nile R.

RED SEA

N

★ Battle site
〰 Mountain
✪ Provincial capital
▲ Legion base
△ Legion detachment
☆ Roman siege
✶ Parthian siege

The Middle East, A.D. First Century

©2007 by D. L. McElhannon

Palestine 66–71 A.D.

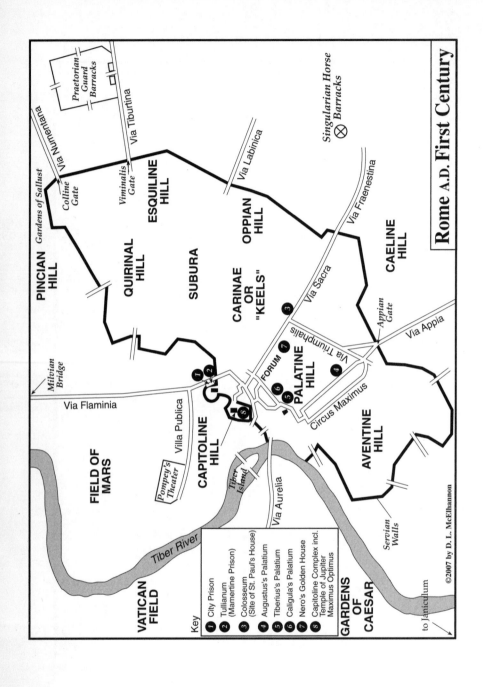

Rome A.D. First Century

Key

1. City Prison
2. Tullianum (Mamertine Prison)
3. Colosseum (Site of St. Paul's House)
4. Augustus's Palatium
5. Tiberius's Palatium
6. Caligula's Palatium
7. Nero's Golden House
8. Capitoline Complex incl. Temple of Jupiter Maximus Optimus

©2007 by D. L. McElhannon

PINCIAN HILL

QUIRINAL HILL

ESQUILINE HILL

OPPIAN HILL

CARINAE OR "KEELS"

CAELINE HILL

SUBURA

PALATINE HILL

AVENTINE HILL

CAPITOLINE HILL

FIELD OF MARS

VATICAN FIELD

GARDENS OF CAESAR

FORUM

Gardens of Sallust

Praetorian Guard Barracks

Singularian Horse Barracks

Colline Gate

Viminalis Gate

Milvian Bridge

Via Numentana

Via Tiburtina

Via Labinica

Via Fraenestina

Via Sacra

Via Triumphalis

Appian Gate

Via Appia

Via Flaminia

Villa Publica

Pompey's Theater

Tiber Island

Via Aurelia

Tiber River

Circus Maximus

Servian Walls

to Janiculum

ACKNOWLEDGMENTS

This book, the fourth in my Roman legion series, would not have been possible without the immense help provided over many years by countless staff at libraries, museums, and historic sites throughout the world. To them all, my heartfelt thanks. Neither they nor I knew at the time what my labor of love would develop into. My thanks, too, to those who have read my research material as it blossomed into manuscript form and made invaluable suggestions.

Once again, I wish to record my gratitude to several people in particular. To Stephen S. Power, senior editor with John Wiley & Sons, for his continued enthusiasm, support, and guidance. And to Wiley's patient production editor, John Simko, and copy editor Bill Drennan. To Richard Curtis, my unrelenting and all-conquering New York literary agent, who launched the campaign for these legion books and has kept me on the march ever since.

And my wife, Louise, who has been at my side through many a battle for many years. As Shakespeare has Domitius Enobarbus say of Cleopatra in *Antony and Cleopatra*: "Age cannot wither her, nor custom stale her infinite variety."

AUTHOR'S NOTE

The exploits of the 3rd Gallica Legion under the two Mark Antonys are well documented by Plutarch and Tacitus. There is no specific documentary evidence to say it was the 3rd Gallica Legion that saved the life of the apostle Paul or conducted him to Rome. That the 3rd Gallica was one of the legions of the Syria station in the first century there is no dispute. And, while some historians for many years put the view that only auxiliaries were stationed in Judea prior to A.D. 66, Josephus makes numerous references to legionaries, centurions, and their tribune commander based in Judea during this period, in both his *Jewish War* and his *Jewish Antiquities*. The Holy Bible, in Acts of the Apostles, also differentiates between foot soldiers (legionaries) and speermen (auxiliaries) stationed at both Jerusalem and Caesarea.

Acts, in describing the apostle Paul's journey under guard from Caesarea to Rome, tells us that a centurion was in charge of the military escort. Centurions generally only commanded legionaries, and only legionaries, citizen soldiers, were permitted to escort prisoners who were Roman citizens, as Paul was. Various other references led me to conclude that the legion stationed in Judea in the A.D. 60s, while still part of the overall Syria garrison, and that was involved in saving Paul's life on three separate occasions, was the 3rd Gallica.

Apart from Plutarch and Tacitus, I have referred to the works of numerous classical writers who documented the wars, campaigns, battles, skirmishes, and most importantly the men of the legions of Rome that have come down to us, Appian, Plutarch, Polybius, Cassius Dio, Josephus, Julius Caesar, Cicero, Pliny the Younger, Seneca, Livy, and Arrian among them. Without the labors of these writers the books in this series would not have been possible.

All speeches and conversations in this book are taken from dialogue and narrative in classical texts, and are faithful to those original sources. For the sake of continuity, the Roman calendar—which in republican times, until Caesar changed it in 47 B.C., varied by some two months from our own (it was a difference of sixty-seven days by 46 B.C., when Caesar corrected the calendar)—is used throughout.

Place names are generally first referred to in their original form and thereafter by the modern name, where known, to permit readers to readily identify locations involved. Personal names created by English writers of more recent times and familiar to modern readers have been used instead of those technically correct—Mark Antony instead of Marcus Antonius, Julius Caesar for Gaius Julius Caesar, Octavian for Caesar Octavianus, Pompey for Pompeius, Caligula for Gaius, Vespasian for Vespasianus, Trajan for Traianus, Hadrian for Hadrianus, and so on.

In the nineteenth and twentieth centuries it was fashionable for some authors to refer to legions as regiments, cohorts as battalions, maniples as companies, centurions as captains, tribunes as colonels, and legates as generals. In this work, Roman military terms such as legion, cohort, maniple, and centurion have been retained, as it's felt they will be familiar to most readers and convey more of a flavor of the time. Because of a lack of popular familiarity with the term legate, "general" and/or "brigadier general" is used here. "Colonel" and tribune are both used, to give a sense of relative status.

Likewise, so that readers can relate in comparison to today's military, when referred to in the military sense praetors are given as "major generals" and consuls and proconsuls as "lieutenant generals." In this way, reference to a lieutenant general, for example, will immediately tell the reader that the figure concerned is or has been a consul. I am aware this is akin to having a foot in two camps and may not please purists, but my aim is to make these books broadly accessible.

So once again I set you on the march with the men of a Roman legion, and lead you through hundreds of years of grueling campaigning. This time I tell the story of a unit that made a name for itself under Mark Antony, only for its early glory to fade. Then, bloodied and withdrawn from the fray, it turned its fortunes around, put an emperor on the throne, marching, ironically, behind another man named Mark Antony, to become dreaded by friend and foe alike. Most of these men were conscripts. Their life was extraordinarily tough. With a strong chance of being killed in action, they marched from one end of the Roman Empire to the other to fight enemies ranging from Parthians to Sarmatians, as well as their fellow Romans in various civil wars.

These are the men who made Rome great—one or two extraordinary men, and many more ordinary men who did often extraordinary things. I hope that via these pages I can help you come to know them.

I

GET UP AND FIGHT!

he sun would soon rise over the body-strewn battlefield, and victory looked no closer than it had when the fighting had begun
seventeen hours before. Two Roman armies made up of thirteen
legions, plus cohorts of the Praetorian Guard, numerous auxiliary units,
and thousands of cavalry, had fought each other to a standstill through
half the previous day and all through the night. The soldiers of the 3rd
Gallica Legion were covered in blood. From head to toe, their muscles
and joints ached. They were hungry, thirsty, utterly wearied, and frustrated
after being repelled time and again by the other side. Losing heart,
legionaries of the 3rd Gallica began to flop on the ground alongside the
equally exhausted troops of the Praetorian Guard and other units that had
withdrawn from the battle. And they refused to return to the fight.

The year is A.D. 69. The month is October. In little more than twelve
tumultuous months, Rome has had four emperors. Nero, who disappeared
and is presumed dead. Galba, assassinated in the Roman Forum. Otho,
who committed suicide after his army was defeated. And Vitellius, current
emperor, who deposed Otho after a bloody battle at Bedriacum—not far
from this very spot where these thirty-five hundred soldiers of the 3rd
Gallica Legion are sprawling on the grass and sitting on low stone fences
that border roads, fields, and vineyards. Now there is a new contender for
the throne, Lieutenant General Titus Flavius Vespasian, military commander in the Roman East. The legionaries of the 3rd Gallica, who previously served under General Vespasian, have led an army into Italy to
overthrow Vitellius and install Vespasian on the throne of the Caesars in
his place.

The men of the 3rd Gallica, veterans of the Jewish Revolt, famous
overnight for wiping out thousands of invading Sarmatian cavalry on the
Danube the previous year, had fought skirmishes on their march down to

1

the wealthy northern Italian city of Cremona. But here, outside Cremona, Vitellius's army has stopped them in their tracks. Here, after hours of fruitless struggle, the 3rd Gallica and its fellow Vespasianist legions are ready to quit. Even the 3rd Gallica's influential chief centurion, Arrius Varus, who had assumed the role of second in command of the Vespasianist army, had been unable to motivate his men to throw themselves back into the fray. Now, fatigued 3rd Gallica soldiers such as Legionary Gaius Volusius look up as the army's commander comes striding purposefully toward them in the moonlight.

Brigadier General Marcus Antonius Primus is a notorious figure, a courageous rogue described by the Roman historian Tacitus as the worst of citizens during peacetime but the best of allies in war. Ten years back, during the reign of Nero, Primus had been convicted of fraud and sent into exile. Nero's successor as emperor, Sulpicius Galba, had recalled Primus and given him his first military command, that of a new legion raised by Galba in Spain on his way to claiming Nero's throne for himself—the 7th Galbiana Legion, or Galba's 7th. Historian Tacitus seems to have met Primus when in his youth. Considering him audacious in the extreme, he would describe the general as "brave in battle, a ready speaker, talented at generating hatred against other men, powerful in the middle of civil strife and rebellion," yet also "greedy, a spendthrift."

This was the general who now climbed onto a mound and looked around at the men of the 3rd Gallica Legion and the Praetorian Guard who lounged before him. Tall, well built, in his early forties, Primus had already moved among the men of the legions that had followed him from their bases in Pannonia to invade Italy. The men of the 3rd Gallica have heard those troops respond to the words of General Primus with shouts and cheers. Those legions had failed to keep the previous emperor, Otho, on his throne; Primus has goaded them with that failure. And they roared and came to their feet as Primus pointed the way back to the battlefield. The general had then turned to the legionaries who have marched from their bases in the province of Moesia, modern Bulgaria, and scoffed at their boasts just the previous day that they would whip Vitellius's legions. Stung by his rhetoric, the men of these legions had risen to prove to the general that they could fight as well as boast.

Now, from his elevated position, Primus looked at the troops of the Praetorian Guard as they mingled with the 3rd Gallica. These guardsmen had been dismissed from service by the new emperor, Vitellius, because they had loyally served his predecessor Otho. They had flooded to Vespasian's banner, declaring they wanted to get even with Vitellius. Now, with hands on hips, Primus glared at the Praetorians. He'd had enough of them, these elite Italian troops who had the best pay and best conditions in the Roman army, troops who boasted of their superiority over common legionaries.

"Clowns!" Primus called to the Praetorians, according to Tacitus. He pointed to the standards of the Praetorian cohorts planted in the earth, and the shields and javelins stacked untidily all around, and told them where their honor and their future lay—out there on the battlefield. Angrily, the Praetorians declared that they would show the general that they have yet to finish the fight.

But for the soldiers of the 3rd Gallica, his most elite legion, General Primus took a different approach. These men had been recruited in the Roman province of Syria. All were Roman citizens, and some were descendants of legionaries from Spain, Italy, and France who had settled in Syria over the past hundred years or so after retiring from the Roman army. Their legion had gained fame when, a century before, in 36 B.C., it had saved Mark Antony from defeat and death in a bloody campaign against the Parthian Empire in the East. As the legion's "Gallica" title implied, back then the men of the 3rd Gallica had been recruited in Gaul. Under Antony, when the legion's Gallic veterans had retired in Syria, the unit had subsequently been filled with local Syrian recruits, as it had been ever since. Irrespective of that change in recruiting ground, down through the decades the reputation gained by the original 3rd Gallica as the saviors of Mark Antony marched with the unit wherever it had taken the field.

"Under Mark Antony, you defeated the Parthians," Tacitus says General Primus declared, looking now at the men of the Gallica. "Under General Corbulo you whipped the Armenians. And lately, you have discomforted the Sarmatians."

"Discomforted" the Sarmatians? This latter comment would have brought a wry smile to the lips of many a 3rd Gallica legionary. As Primus knew, the Gallicans had slaughtered the Sarmatians in their thousands, with hardly a casualty of their own.

Now, Primus urged the 3rd Gallica to live up to its fearsome reputation, to go against the enemy one more time, to show the remainder of the army how to fight, and to lead the way to victory for Vespasian. On the 3rd Gallica hinged the outcome of the battle, and the civil war. Would they rise to their general's challenge?

FOR POMPEY, CAESAR, AND ANTONY

O riginally, in the time of the Roman Republic, Legio III, the 3rd Legion, was one of four legions, or regiments, raised at Rome by the two most senior elected officials, the consuls, who were in effect a pair of presidents. Back then, the 3rd Legion had been made up of six thousand men, a mixture of light infantry and heavy infantry. They were draftees from all walks of life—*legio* means levy, or draft. Every March, the recruits, Roman citizens all, had been conscripted in Rome for six months of military service. The rank-and-file citizen-soldiers had elected their centurions from among them, while the six young tribunes, or colonels of each legion, had been chosen by the consuls from Rome's elite families. The tribunes commanded the legion among them, on rotation, two months at a time. In the field, each consul had led an army made up of two of the four Roman legions plus legions provided by Rome's allies throughout southern and central Italy and gentlemen cavalry who provided their own horses. In those early times Rome was a city-state; her control of Italy was still some time off. Italy north of the Po River was then part of Gaul. And the Gauls had been Rome's fierce enemies, even sacking Rome on occasion. By the first century B.C., Italy north of the Po—or Cisalpine Gaul, as the Romans called it—had been incorporated into the Roman Empire. So, too, had southern France. It was there, in Transalpine Gaul, a province of Rome, that Gnaeus Pompeius Magnus— Pompey the Great, a powerful Roman consul and all-conquering general—had conscripted a new enlistment of the 3rd Legion in 65 B.C.

For some time, Pompey had maintained several legions in southern Italy—his 1st and 2nd Legions, units he had personally raised and paid for in his home region of Picenum in eastern Italy when he was just twenty-three years of age. These 1st and 2nd Legions had become his elite units, in effect his bodyguards, as he first helped the dictator Sulla win a civil war, then retook Sicily and North Africa and conquered the East for Rome, creating his great fame and his great wealth. Backed by the renowned and feared 1st and 2nd Legions, he had then asserted his will back at Rome.

Pompey was voted power by the Senate to recruit large numbers of new legions to combat enemies threatening Rome's interests abroad, including tens of thousands of Cilician pirates in the eastern Mediterranean. There was now a conscious effort by the Roman leadership to ease the manpower drain on the capital and use provincials to fight Rome's battles for her. So the first new unit raised by Pompey was this fresh enlistment of the old 3rd Legion, conscripted not at Rome but from Roman citizens in Transalpine Gaul. Pompey also enlisted new 4th, 5th, 6th, 7th, 8th, and 9th Legions during this period, in the Gallic provinces and in the two Spanish provinces.

Under Pompey, the new 3rd Legion went on to fight the rebel Roman governor of Spain, Quintus Sertorius, and had participated in the defeat of the rebel army of the escaped slave Sparticus, in Italy. With Spain thereafter given over by the Senate to Pompey's rule, his 3rd Legion had subsequently been stationed there and took part in grueling campaigns to bring western Spain and Portugal under Roman rule. Under a fiery young general, Marcus Petreius, they achieved considerable success against wild tribes and hilltop fortresses by employing unorthodox tactics.

By January 49 B.C. the men of the 3rd Legion were preparing to go into retirement, having served their contracted sixteen years in the Roman army. But on the thirteenth of that month, renegade Roman general Julius Caesar crossed the Po River and invaded Italy, and was declared an enemy of the state by the Senate. The men of the 3rd retained their loyalty to Pompey, father of the legion, who had been appointed to command the Senate's forces in the civil war against Caesar. But Caesar had caught the Senate unprepared, and Pompey was forced to evacuate to Greece, leaving Italy to Caesar after limited fighting. With Pompey retaining control of Roman naval forces, Caesar, instead of following him across the Adriatic, turned around and advanced his legions into Spain, which was controlled for Pompey and the Senate by seven legions, including the 3rd.

There, the 3rd Legion experienced unusual phenomena—defeat and surrender. After Caesar bottled up the senatorial forces at Lérida in northeastern Spain, the unimaginative senatorial generals Petreius and Lucius Afranius broke out and led most of their starving troops, including the men of the 3rd Legion, north toward the mountains. They were hoping to gain supplies from friendly Spanish tribes, but Caesar gave chase, overhauled them, and cut them off. Afranius and Petreius had begrudgingly surrendered. As part of the surrender deal, Caesar gave the five senatorial legions their discharges. For soldiers of the 3rd such as Legionary Gaius Aiedius, the humiliation of surrendering and disarming after sixteen years of glory-filled service for Pompey and Rome was tempered by this honorable discharge. After all, they had been due to go into retirement anyway at the time the civil war broke out. Caesar even paid them their overdue wages, although he was so broke he had to borrow from his own officers to do it.

Escorted by Caesar's 7th and 9th Legions, the unarmed men of the 3rd and Valeria Legions marched to the Var River, beyond which lay the 3rd's home territory of Transalpine Gaul. There they were allowed to go home, as the 7th and the 9th marched to Piacenza to join young general Mark Antony, who was in charge of Italy in Caesar's absence. Legionary Aiedius of the 3rd eventually found his way to the prosperous town of Aquinum, modern Aquino, in south-central Italy; within a decade Aquinum would sport a triumphal arch dedicated to Mark Antony. Here Legionary Aiedius settled, and ended his days. His tombstone, built into the walls of a later Christian church, survives to the present day.

Over the twelve months following the discharge of the 3rd Legion, Caesar raised more than twenty new legions to carry the war to the senatorial forces in Greece, Macedonia, North Africa, and Spain. Most of these units were recruited in Italy and Cisalpine Gaul, some in Transalpine Gaul. Caesar also raised a new enlistment of the 3rd Legion, and some of the 3rd's former men would have been recalled from retirement. The bulk of the six thousand men now filling the legion's ranks were recruited in Transalpine Gaul.

For most of the next five years the 3rd Legion was stationed in Gaul. It was one of the handful of legions, including the 16th, which kept a watchful eye on the tribes in Belgium and central and northern France— "Longhaired Gaul," as the Romans called it, in reference to the shoulder-length hair of these tribesmen, who had been conquered by Caesar between 58 and 50 B.C. By this time, the 3rd was being called the 3rd Gallica Legion—Gallica meaning "of Gaul." Why? Just before the civil war broke out, Pompey had gained control of Caesar's 15th Legion, which had taken part in Caesar's conquest of Gaul. The 15th had been among the units evacuated by Pompey to Greece. In his memoirs, Caesar refers to the 15th at Pharsalus as the 3rd Legion. We have no explanation why. It is possible that knowing that Caesar had disbanded Pompey's 3rd Legion at the Var River, Pompey had renamed the 15th the 3rd. Apparently, in response to this, and to differentiate the two units, the new 3rd Legion in Gaul became known as the 3rd Gallica.

By 45 B.C. Caesar had defeated Pompey in Greece and the senatorial armies in North Africa, then conquered Egypt. In the process he also conquered Queen Cleopatra of Egypt, but in an entirely different way. Just when Caesar thought he had gained control of the Roman Empire, Pompey's sons Gnaeus and Sextus began an uprising in Spain that soon had most of the people of the Iberian Peninsula behind them and that saw five of Caesar's legions desert to the Pompey brothers.

Caesar ordered the 3rd Gallica to march from Gaul to join the only other legions in Spain that had remained loyal to him, the 21st and the 30th, both relatively new units that had been raised by Caesar in 49 B.C. In all probability the 3rd had been stationed just over the Pyrenees Mountains in the Gallic province of Aquitania, today's French region of Aquitaine, and this proximity was why it was sent to join Caesar's forces in Spain. Caesar ordered other hardened units to march to Spain from Italy and southwestern France, while he himself hurried there by land and sea to take command.

In Spain the inexperienced troops of the 3rd Gallica enlistment joined the 5th Legion, remnants of the 6th, plus the 7th, 10th, 21st, and 30th Legions, to form an army that battled Gnaeus Pompey's larger but less experienced army outside the hill town of Munda on March 17, 45 B.C. Charging uphill, Caesar's troops faltered, then stopped. It took Caesar to go out in front of them and lead a renewed attack before the men of the 3rd and their comrades won the day. Young Pompey was soon tracked down and killed. His senior generals and forty thousand of his men died on the battlefield.

Among those dead generals was Titus Labienus. He had been Caesar's astute and loyal deputy for the nine years of the Gallic conquest but had changed sides and supported Pompey and the Senate in the civil war. Labienus and Pompey came from the same region, Picenum in northeastern Italy, and this had some influence on his decision to defect. But the main reason for Labienus's change of sides was apparently because he could see that Caesar was intent on destroying the Roman Republic.

General Labienus had a son, Quintus, who within a decade and a half would figure prominently in the affairs of the 3rd Legion. It seems that young Quintus was not yet of age—Roman men officially came of age in their fifteenth year—and took no active part in the civil war. He probably would have sat out his father's last years with his mother, at Rome or in his home region of Picenum. The wives and children of thousands of other opponents of Caesar remained safely in territory controlled by him throughout the Civil War, protected by the conventions of the day.

Munda, the battle in which Titus Labienus died, was the last major battle of the civil war. But Caesar was not to enjoy control of the Roman Empire for long. Almost exactly twelve months to the day later, on March 15, 44 B.C., the Ides of March, Caesar was assassinated at Rome. The 3rd Gallica Legion, left in Spain under one of Caesar's generals, sided with Mark Antony in the tumult that followed Caesar's murder. Antony emerged as one of the three leading figures, along with Caesar's great-nephew and heir Marcus Octavianus, or Octavian as we have come to know him, and Marcus Lepidus, another of Caesar's former deputies. The trio divided the Roman Empire among them, forming the Board of Three for the Ordering of State, the so-called Second Triumvirate. Antony took the East as his area of control.

But the East had come under the control of Marcus Brutus and Gaius Cassius, leaders of the plot to assassinate Caesar, who were determined to overthrow the triumvirs and restore the Republic. Cassius had brought all the legions in Syria and Egypt under his control. Brutus had recruited a number of new units in Macedonia. Early in 42 B.C. they concentrated their twenty legions at Philippi in Macedonia. Leaving Lepidus in charge in Italy, Antony and Octavian took twenty-nine legions to Macedonia to confront the Liberators—as Brutus and Cassius were styled by their many supporters. The 3rd Gallica Legion was one of the units under Antony's command.

In the first week of October 42 B.C., Antony launched an attack against the Liberators. The First Battle of Philippi lasted all afternoon and resulted in a stalemate. Antony and Octavian lost sixteen thousand men, the Liberators lost only eight thousand, but Cassius was dead. Three weeks later, Brutus allowed himself to be talked into the Second Battle of Philippi. When his forces were routed, he committed suicide. The triumvirs now controlled the Roman Empire. A number of the units involved in the Philippi battles on both sides were disbanded or amalgamated following the two battles, and tens of thousands of legionaries retired. Retirees from the victors' side were given land at new military retirement colonies, many of which were founded in Italy and southern France. Veterans who had served in the Praetorian Guard cohorts that had marched for Antony and Octavian were given land grants at Philippi itself. The remaining legions were divided among the triumvirs.

As Octavian returned to Italy with several legions, Antony marched with the units retained by him, heading east, out of Macedonia and toward the Hellespont. Antony's force numbered some seven legions, including the 3rd Gallica. With most of the 3rd's men just eight years into their sixteen-year enlistments, they still had half their time to serve. As they headed to the East with Antony, the Gallicans were accompanied by the most famous legion of its day, the 6th Ferrata, which had led Caesar's conquest of Egypt. There was also the 3rd Cyrenaica, the 4th Scythica, and the 22nd Deiotariana. Antony's legions marched with enthusiasm—their commander had promised each man in his army a reward of 5,000 sesterces on the completion of their next campaign. To men whose salary was 900 sesterces a year, this was an incentive that generated loyalty, obedience, and anticipation.

Marching with them were a few thousand men who had previously served in the Liberators' army. Antony was sending them back to Syria, where they'd been stationed prior to the Philippi battles, to provide garrisons for the major cities there. Roman historian Cassius Dio says this was because these men knew Syria well. It would allow Antony to keep his best troops in the Near East, within striking distance of the Middle East yet capable of turning around and heading for the West should the need arise.

Ferried across the Dardanelles to the province of Asia, Antony's army marched slowly through the region, as Antony lived up to his reputation as a man who loved bacchanalian feasts, drinking, and a good time. He partied at every city he came to. The locals, wearied of the rough rule of the Liberator Cassius, welcomed Antony with crowds and celebrations as he in turn honored many cities and returned lands that had been confiscated by Cassius. Knowing that control of the eastern Mediterranean would depend on sea power, Antony ordered the cities of Asia to build and crew a fleet of two hundred warships, to be delivered the following spring. The communities of Asia competed with each other to build the finest vessels in the fastest time. But the Asians soon began to tire of Antony's tax gatherers, and, according to Cassius Dio, of the habit of Antony's subordinates to sell positions of influence to the highest bidders. With Antony ordering them to raise as much as they could as quickly as they could to fund his military plans, his officials also confiscated the property of wealthy locals and demanded that towns and cities pay twice the usual annual "tribute," or tax.

Historian Plutarch says that one local official, named Hybreas, boldly complained to Antony, "If you can take two yearly tributes, you can no doubt give us a couple of summers and double the harvests."

Instead of being angry, Antony was surprised. He took no interest in the finer details of government and had no idea how exacting his staff were being when it came to raising funds. Plutarch says that Antony was touched to the quick by Hybreas's remarks, because he was ignorant of most things done in his name by subordinates.

At the famous temple city of Ephesus in Asia, Antony was met by ambassadors from John Hyrcanus, Jewish high priest at Jerusalem. Hyrcanus had been confirmed in his position by Julius Caesar after Hyrcanus had supported the hard-pressed Caesar during his war in Egypt, helping him win control there in 47 B.C. Antony accepted Hyrcanus's pledge of loyalty and reconfirmed him in his post as high priest.

In the province of Bithynia, Antony encamped his legions, quite probably at the base established there by Caesar in 45–44 B.C. as a prelude to his planned Parthian operation. In 42 B.C. this camp had housed three legions that subsequently went over to the Liberators. Here, surrounded by his best troops, Antony received deputations from throughout the East. Among the many potentates who courted him here were thirty-two-year-old Herod of Judea—who was to become famous as Herod the Great—and his elder brother Phasaelus. Both were Jews, with Arab blood. They were the sons of the late Jewish leader Antipater, who had been made governor of Judea by Julius Caesar after Antipater had led a Jewish contingent in the army that reinforced Caesar in Egypt in 47 B.C. In 43 B.C. Antipater had been poisoned by opponents, and now his sons were seeking confirmation of the appointments he had previously given them—Herod as tetrarch, or governor, of Galilee, and Phasaelus as tetrarch of the Idumaea region south of Jerusalem. Antony made no appointments, but he received Herod and his brother warmly, accepted the gift of money, and sent away their opponents unheard.

As winter loomed, Antony left his legions in their camp in Bithynia and headed for Syria, taking his one-thousand-man Praetorian Guard bodyguard and the former Liberators' troops with him. In Syria he resided at a former Seleucid palace at Daphne, near Antioch, the Syrian capital. Here countless Syrian nobles came to pledge their loyalty to him. But some had reputations as oppressive rulers of their cities and regions, and others were friendly with the Parthian Empire beyond the Euphrates. Antony removed a number from power. Others took the hint and fled to Parthia. To Daphne, too, came a party of one hundred Jews to make a case against Herod and Phasaelus, declaring to Antony that while High Priest Hyrcanus seemed to be running Jewish affairs, it was Herod and his brother who were really in control. Again, Antony sided with Herod and sent his opponents away.

When another party, of a thousand Jews, met Antony after he arrived at the key port city of Tyre and made a case against Herod, Antony lost his patience. Herod had recovered Galilee from Marion, the commander left in charge there by the Liberator Cassius. He had taken control of Tyre. He had allied himself with the triumvirs. Herod was capable, he had proven his loyalty to Antony, and he had contributed a large sum to his finances. All Herod's Jewish adversaries offered were complaints. Executing opponents of Herod and Phasaelus, Antony now reconfirmed the brothers' governorships. Antony and Herod would remain firm friends for the rest of their days.

Antony also sent letters to all the chief cities of the region, including Tyre, Antioch, and Sidon, and to regional leaders in Arabia. He ordered them to free every person who had been consigned to slavery by Cassius, and restored to the rightful owners the property seized by Cassius during his short reign. "Since we have overcome his [Cassius's] madness by arms," Antony wrote, the Jewish historian Josephus records, "we now correct by our decrees and judicial determinations what he has laid waste." Then, once he had settled affairs in the region to his satisfaction, and leaving the former Liberators' legionaries to garrison the major Syrian centers, Antony withdrew to the wealthy city of Tarsus, capital of the province of Cilicia, where he would winter in comfort.

As the men of the 3rd Gallica settled into their camp in Bithynia for the winter, they learned that they were to prepare for a major operation to be undertaken by Mark Antony the following spring. This would be the operation that Julius Caesar had been planning at the time of his assassination—the invasion of Parthia.

III

THE PARTHIAN
INVASION

Forty-one-year-old Mark Antony stood on the terrace of the palace at Tarsus and watched with growing anticipation as the huge barge rowed slowly up the Cydnus River from the nearby Mediterranean harbor at Rhegma. A beautiful child, Antony had grown into a handsome and impressive man, with broad shoulders and a large chest. His neck was as thick as a wrestler's. His jaw was square and set, his mouth large, his nose well defined, his eyes hooded. Yet, for a man with his reputation as a fearsome fighter in battle, he could be quite vain, and fashionably wore his hair curled into ringlets by curling tongs.

Around Antony there were smiles on the faces of his generals and the freedmen on his staff, as all eyes followed the slow course of the glittering Egyptian barge coming up the river. After much prevarication, Cleopatra, the twenty-eight-year-old queen of Egypt, had finally succumbed to Mark Antony's summonses and had sailed from Egypt to meet with him here in Cilicia.

The capital of the Roman province of Cilicia, Tarsus was a center of government, commerce, and learning—its university was famed for its Greek philosophers. Tarsus had grown prosperous since its foundation 650 years before, courtesy of the flax plantations of Cilicia's fertile interior. These provided the raw material for the linen and canvas factories and ropemakers of Tarsus, whose products were exported the length and breadth of the Roman Empire. The town was also strategically placed, being not far from the Cilician Gates, the only major pass in the Taurus Mountains just to the east. Rome's longtime enemy the Parthian Empire, whose homeland occupied modern Iran and Iraq, lay beyond those mountains. Julius Caesar had based himself in Tarsus in 47 B.C. following his conquest of Egypt. And during this stay, Caesar had apparently granted Roman citizenship to the free residents of Tarsus. Antony, since his arrival, had added to the honors, making Tarsus a free city by removing all taxes on its citizens, and also freed all those who had been sold into slavery in the city.

Word had reached Antony that Cleopatra was on her way when her fleet was sighted sailing up the Syrian coast. For a long time it had seemed that she would not come. She had ignored several letters, from Antony and from friends, urging her to meet Antony in Cilicia. So, the previous fall, Antony had sent Quintus Dellius, a member of his entourage, to the Egyptian capital to personally require Cleopatra to meet him in Cilicia and answer the accusation that she had provided financial support to Cassius the Liberator. Dellius was a good choice as envoy. A renowned historian, he was as wise as he was diplomatic. In Alexandria he had found Cleopatra very wary of Antony. She had met Antony once, at Alexandria, when she was fourteen and he was a young cavalry colonel in the army of Roman general Aulus Gabinius. General Gabinius had brought his army down from Syria to reinstate Cleopatra's father, Ptolemy XII, on the Egyptian throne after he had been deposed by his own people. Even in those times Antony had a fearsome reputation as a soldier. Only recently he had taken a rebel Jewish stronghold in Judea, while in the weeks prior to arriving in Alexandria he had led General Gabinius's cavalry advance guard in swiftly seizing the Egyptian fortress of Pelusium.

During the fourteen years since that brief encounter between princess and colonel, Antony's military reputation had multiplied. By the time that Dellius arrived at Cleopatra's court, the queen had heard how Antony dealt with opponents: he'd had hundreds, including famous orator Cicero, beheaded following Caesar's murder. And after the Battles of Philippi, he had executed the officer responsible for the death of his brother Gaius, on Gaius's tomb. Realizing this, Dellius had assured Cleopatra that she had nothing to fear from his master. Antony, said Dellius, so Plutarch records, was "the gentlest and kindest of soldiers." Dellius even advised Cleopatra to go to the Roman general in her best attire, to impress him. Cleopatra, says Plutarch, had some faith in Dellius's assurances, but had more faith in her own attractions. As Plutarch points out, those attractions had won her the hearts and support of Julius Caesar, and before him, of the Roman military commander in Egypt, Pompey the Great's eldest son, Gnaeus Pompey. And now Cleopatra, Queen of Egypt, consort of the later dictator Caesar and mother of his son Caesarion, was coming to Antony, the latest Roman strongman, intent on dazzling him.

The Egyptians, the best shipbuilders of the age, were famous for creating massive pleasure barges for their sovereigns, and the craft that brought Cleopatra up the Cydnus was no exception. Its stern was gilded with gold, and the billowing sails were made from purple, the rarest and most valuable of cloths. The oars jutting from the outriggers on either side of the barge were of shining silver; they dipped and rose in perfect harmony to the tune of flutes, fifes, and harps. Cleopatra herself lay on a bed on the deck, beneath a canopy of gold cloth, dressed as the goddess Venus. Around her were pretty young boys costumed as Cupids. The queen's female attendants, dressed as sea nymphs and graces, steered the barge's rudder and hauled on ropes to bring in the sails. The awestruck people of Tarsus had never seen anything like it. Crowding along both riverbanks, thousands of locals kept pace with the huge, slow-moving barge as it came upstream.

Antony decided that he would receive Cleopatra seated on the raised tribunal, or judge's platform, in the Forum of Tarsus. When he arrived with his entourage to take his place on the tribunal, his Praetorian Guard bodyguard spread around the city marketplace to secure it. They found the place deserted—everyone had gone to see Queen Cleopatra. Shakespeare was to write that the very air left the marketplace, such was her attraction. Once the barge docked, Antony sent a message to Cleopatra, inviting her to dine with him. Cleopatra sent back a message of her own, inviting Antony to instead dine with her aboard her pleasure barge. Intrigued, Antony accepted the queen's invitation. According to Plutarch, it was said by the Tarsians that this would be like a meeting of the gods—that it was as if Venus had come to feast with Bacchus.

Antony arrived at the barge to find that sumptuous preparations had been made. Most magnificent of all were the illuminations. As he stepped aboard, tree branches were let down bearing glowing lamps forming patterns, some in squares, some in circles. "The whole thing was a spectacle rarely equaled for beauty," Plutarch was to comment.

Now Antony was greeted by the diminutive, elegantly attired Egyptian queen. Her olive skin was as smooth as silk. Her jet black hair had been elaborately braided by personal hairdressers who worked on her coiffure for hours every day. An asp of solid gold, her royal symbol, projected from the front of a golden diadem on her head. Her elaborately decorated dress was almost skin-tight, and accentuated her figure. A picture to behold, she was unlike any woman Antony had previously seen. By all accounts Cleopatra was not an incomparable beauty. She was petite and plain. But she had a charisma that struck all who met her. The attraction of her person and the charm of her conversation were bewitching, says Plutarch. According to Roman historian Appian, Antony fell in love with her at first sight. That first night Antony was polite, and enjoyed Cleopatra's hospitality, although at this first meeting both were restrained, as the young queen explained all that she had contributed to the fight against Cassius the Liberator. Antony never raised the subject of Cassius again.

On the day following the dinner on the barge, Cleopatra went to dine with Antony in Tarsus. He strove to emulate or even outdo her but could not match the magnificence of her reception. And he found himself trailing in the wake of her conversation. She could speak numerous languages fluently and was highly intelligent. According to later Arab writers, to add to her many attributes Cleopatra was a learned scholar. Antony, in comparison, was a man without gloss, or pretense. He was a soldier, and what you saw was what you got. As Cleopatra shared his table, he was the first to poke fun at his own lack of refined wit or sophistication. He was more comfortable with hard-drinking men friends, telling bawdy barracks jokes. It was then that Cleopatra demonstrated how clever she truly was. She began to tell Antony dirty jokes—"without any reluctance or reserve," says Plutarch. And by lowering herself to Antony's level, she captivated him. Here was a woman who could drink, tell crude jokes, and gamble like a man, yet was still a sexual temptress. He fell head over heels in love with her. Appian was to say, "He became her captive as if he were a young man."

After that, says Cassius Dio, Antony gave no thought to honor but became Cleopatra's slave, and devoted his time to his passion for her. Abandoning his plans to invade Parthia, Antony accepted Cleopatra's invitation to return to Egypt with her. They promptly sailed to Alexandria. There, Antony, Cleopatra, and the members of their entourages entertained each other day in, day out, sparing no expenditure, calling themselves the Inimitable Livers. Plutarch tells the story that during this period a friend of his own grandfather visited the kitchens of the royal palace at Alexandria and found eight wild boars in various stages of roasting on the spit. The visitor remarked that the queen must be entertaining a large crowd, but the cook replied that apart from Cleopatra and Antony there were only ten other dinner guests. Not knowing when Antony would call for food to be served, the cook was preparing the same meal, time and again, so that when the call came, the meat would go to the guests perfectly cooked.

According to Appian, himself a native of Alexandria, Antony dispensed with his military uniform and his general's insignia, and wore a square-cut Greek tunic and white Attic boots. His family claimed descent from the mythological Greek figure Hercules, and now that he was wooing Cleopatra, who was herself of Greek heritage, he took every opportunity to advertise his Greek connections. And, totally trusting of Cleopatra, he let his bodyguards idle in their quarters and went about without an escort.

Cleopatra was with Antony day and night. She drank and ate with him, she played dice with him, she hunted and fished with him, and when he undertook his daily weapons training she was there, watching and admiring. She quickly talked him out of his plan to invade Parthia. Cleopatra was looking for a new Caesar, a man alongside whom she could rule the world. What Antony needed to concentrate on, she told him, was overthrowing the other triumvirs and gaining control of the Roman Empire for himself. Marcus Lepidus, Antony knew, could easily be elbowed aside; he had only been brought into the triumvirate for the sake of appearances. But the powerful young Octavian was a much more difficult opponent. In 44 b.c. Antony had made the mistake of underestimating the then eighteen-year-old Octavian when the youth had turned up at Rome to claim his inheritance from the assassinated Caesar. Octavian was wiser and more cunning than men three times his age, and Antony's initial grab for power at Rome had failed because of the young man's maneuvering. Antony had been forced to settle for the three-way sharing of power with Octavian and Lepidus. But now, at Cleopatra's urging, Antony began to see a singular role for himself.

Ignoring reports that Parthian forces were massing in Mesopotamia to the east of Syria—assuming this was merely in response to rumors of Antony's planned invasion of Parthia—Antony focused on Italy and Octavian. The officers on Antony's staff advised against opposing Octavian, and warned him of the danger posed by the Parthian buildup in Mesopotamia. But he ignored them; Antony had ears only for Cleopatra. Antony's quaestor—his quartermaster and chief financial officer—Lucius Philippus Barbatius, was so disgusted with his commander that he quit his post and sailed for Italy, where he would work against Antony's interests. Meanwhile, Antony's legions, including the 3rd Gallica, maintained their positions in Bithynia. From there they could march on Italy if the need arose, to support Antony's latest bid for power.

General Quintus Labienus sat in the old Seleucid palace at Antioch, capital of Syria, posing for a Greek portraitist who was sketching his profile. Not so long ago Labienus had been a stateless youth, a man with a price on his head, on the run from Mark Antony. Now he was the conqueror of

Syria, and his troops had hailed him *imperator*. This ancient title, which literally meant "chief" or "master," had much symbolic meaning. In time mutating into the word "emperor," it was a title bestowed on victorious Roman generals by their troops. Both Pompey and Caesar had been awarded the honor. So, too, had Mark Antony, who began his letters with the title. And now Labienus, only in his twenties, had the title and the victory to match Antony. Now that he occupied Antioch, young Labienus ordered his treasurer to mint gold coins for his troops when the time came to pay them in October. On those coins would be stamped young Labienus's image, from the sketch now being drawn, and his name, added to which would be two titles: "*IMP*," for *imperator*, and "Parthicus." At any other time, the Parthicus title would signify a Roman general who had defeated the Parthians. But Labienus had just succeeded in taking Syria from Mark Antony—at the head of a Parthian army.

The previous fall, just before the Battles of Philippi, young Quintus Labienus, then a mere Roman tribune on the staff of Liberators Brutus and Cassius, had crossed the Euphrates River in search of Orodes II, king of the Parthians. The Parthians were a nation that had grown out of the Parni, a tribe of nomadic horsemen who had built a rich empire astride most of the trade routes from the Far East to the Roman world. Labienus had been sent by the Liberators to plead for more military aid against Antony, Octavian, and Lepidus. Orodes, a member of the ruling Arsacid royal house, had previously permitted a contingent of Parthian horse archers to join the Liberators, and they were among four thousand mounted archers from Media, Arabia, and Parthia riding for brothers-in-law Brutus and Cassius by the summer of 41 B.C. But the Liberators, knowing how devastatingly effective the Parthian horse archers could be, after Cassius had faced them during the famous defeat at Carrhae, wanted many more of them.

Although he was young—only about twenty-two at that time—Colonel Labienus was an excellent choice for the mission to Parthia. With a long nose; thick, curly hair; and a beetled brow, Labienus was not handsome, but he was bright and energetic. More importantly, he had a famous father—Major General Titus Labienus, Caesar's brilliant and brave second in command, and later Pompey's general of cavalry after Labienus changed sides early in the civil war. Both Pompey and Labienus Sr. had been feared and respected by the Parthians. When young Quintus Labienus was escorted into the presence of the Parthian king, old Orodes had given the young Roman a hearing—he knew that Brutus and Cassius might end up controlling the Roman Empire. Orodes kept Labienus waiting frustrating weeks at his court without answering him. And then, in November, crushing news had reached Parthia, telling of the defeat of Cassius and Brutus in the Philippi battles.

Aware that Labienus would be a wanted man in Roman territory, Orodes had subsequently given the young Roman sanctuary at his court. In early 40 B.C., once he learned that Antony had fallen for Cleopatra and had withdrawn to Egypt, and with news coming of conflict between Antony's family and Octavian in Italy, Labienus had begun to work on the Parthian monarch, suggesting a very bold plan. Throughout their history, the Parthians had never shown an interest in conquering the Romans, or even of taking large slices of Roman territory for themselves. But they were constantly made nervous by the aggressive Romans, and never failed to fight them if they threatened Parthian territory. As recently as 53 B.C. they had destroyed a Roman army under the consul Marcus Crassus when he invaded Parthia, and two years later they had made a brief incursion into Syria. They were always looking to control states that bordered Parthian territory, to create a buffer zone between themselves and the Romans. Now, Labienus suggested, with Antony distracted and with only small Roman garrisons in Syria, here was an opportunity to seize Syria and other Roman provinces in the East, creating a massive buffer against Roman expansion.

Appreciating the opportunity, Orodes had assembled an army in Mesopotamia under the command of his eldest son, Pacorus. This Parthian prince was apparently in his thirties. Pacorus had been involved in a major military expedition in his twenties and was an excellent soldier. He was also extremely well liked by all classes for his pleasant manner and sense of fairness, and was the apple of his father's eye. Realizing that to win popular support in the Roman provinces the invaders must be seen to have a Roman leader, Orodes appointed young Quintus Labienus, sponsor of the idea, joint commander with Pacorus. This Parthian invasion force led by Pacorus and Labienus consisted entirely of mounted troops. It numbered about ten thousand men, the same size as the army that had defeated Crassus's legions thirteen years before.

In the spring of 40 B.C., this Parthian army had crossed the Euphrates River at Zeugma, east of the Syrian city of Apamea, unopposed. The town of Zeugma straddled the Euphrates at a narrow canyon, with its administrative center on the Syrian side and suburbs on the Parthian side. With the aid of local boatmen, the Parthian army was quickly ferried across. Taking the province entirely by surprise, the Parthians quickly surrounded Apamea, a 260-year-old garrison city and eastern crossroads, which sat on the right bank of the Orontes River overlooking the Ghab Valley. The

Roman commander at Apamea was the quaestor Decidius Saxa, younger brother of Mark Antony's governor of Syria, Major General Lucius Decidius Saxa. The younger Saxa, in his early thirties and serving as financial deputy to his brother, closed the city gates and refused to surrender Apamea when Labienus demanded its submission.

The governor, General Saxa, who had been one of two generals commanding Antony and Octavian's advance force in Macedonia at the time of the Philippi battles, marched from Antioch, which lay farther west on the Orontes. He arrived with a force of infantry and cavalry, and met Labienus in a pitched battle in open country. Saxa attempted to use his auxiliary cavalry against Labienus's Parthians. But his mounted troops were no match for the Parthian cavalry. Labienus's horse archers drilled their opponents with arrows; then the heavy cavalry moved in for the kill and mowed them down. Saxa and his infantry retreated behind the walls and trenches of their marching camp. In the night, Labienus had Parthian bowmen send thousands of leaflets flying into the camp attached to arrows. Those leaflets urged the Romans to come over to Labienus's side, and when General Saxa saw the mood of his surrounded men change in favor of Labienus, he broke out of the camp in the darkness. With a few supporters, Saxa fled back to Antioch. Behind him, his men went over to young Labienus.

Labienus returned to Apamea, which Pacorus was still besieging. The Roman garrison, now thinking General Saxa dead, went over to Labienus. Saxa's defiant younger brother was handed over to the Parthians and executed. Labienus then advanced along the Orontes and surrounded Antioch. When the city agreed to peace terms, General Saxa again fled, this time heading northwest, toward Cilicia. The Antioch garrison then also joined Labienus. Every city and town in Syria but one had soon gone over to the invaders. The exception was Tyre. Here, Antony's last supporters and loyal Tyrians combined to stubbornly hold out. Because the Parthian besiegers had no naval support, the Tyre garrison was able to get in fresh supplies by sea. Sending a ship to Antony in Alexandria pleading for him to come to their aid, they prepared for a long siege.

Now, with Labienus resident at the palace of the Seleucid monarchs at Antioch and enjoying his newly won power, a message from Jerusalem reached his cocommander, the Parthian prince Pacorus. It was from Antigonus, ambitious nephew of Hyrcanus, Jewish high priest. Antigonus promised a vast sum in gold and five hundred Jewish women to Pacorus if he used his forces to depose Hyrcanus.

Pacorus and Labienus now agreed on their tactics. The Parthian army was divided in three. One part would accompany Labienus and the foot soldiers he had won over in Syria as he advanced northwest into Cilicia. His objective was to roll up all the Roman provinces east of Greece, hoping that the garrisons in his path would come over to him as those in Syria had done. Antony's legions, including the 3rd Gallica, were the only unknown quantity as far as Labienus was concerned. Sitting immobile in Bithynia while their commander in chief caroused in Egypt, they represented the most powerful card in the game. Labienus was hoping that he would be able to convince Antony's legions to abandon him the way he had abandoned them for Cleopatra.

The second force, made up entirely of cavalry under Prince Pacorus, was to advance down Judea's Maritime Plain. At Joppa it would swing up into the hills and advance on Jerusalem from the northwest. The third force, also made up of Parthian cavalry and led by the Parthian general Barzaphanes, would sweep down through central Judea, follow the Jordan River as far as Jericho, then advance on Jerusalem through the hills from the northeast. The two Parthian forces would then link up outside Jerusalem and occupy the city, bringing Judea into the Parthian fold and installing Antigonus as their puppet ruler there. With the invasion just weeks old and Syria now under Parthian control, the three forces moved off on their individual missions. With news of civil war and chaos in Italy, and with Mark Antony still partying with Cleopatra in Egypt, the cocommanders were confident of success.

Meanwhile, the men of the 3rd Gallica Legion, sitting idly at their camp in Bithynia, as they had been for months, with orders to stay where they were, wanted to know what was going on. They had heard that the Parthians had invaded Syria and Judea and had won swift victories. It hadn't been meant to be like that—it was supposed to be the other way around, with the 3rd Gallica and its brother legions marching into Parthia with Mark Antony. Now Quintus Labienus was marching into Cilicia and drawing closer by the day. Why weren't Antony's legions being ordered to prepare to confront the invading upstart Labienus? And where in the name of Jove was Antony himself?

Two messages reached Mark Antony as he relaxed in Alexandria in the early spring of 40 B.C. Both made him sit up with a start. He already knew that the previous fall his brother Lucius had set off a revolt in Italy, urged on by Antony's ambitious wife, Fulvia. After initially occupying Rome, being hailed by the populace, and being joined by thousands of retired soldiers from Antony's former legions and many raw levies, Lucius had been bottled up in Perusia, modern Perugia in central Italy, north of Rome, by Octavian's forces. While Octavian himself would say in his memoirs that he felt Lucius was doing Antony's bidding, ancient authorities were convinced that Antony had no prior knowledge of Lucius's uprising. But if Lucius were to overthrow Octavian, Antony would not have objected. Antony had learned that generals staunchly loyal to the memory of Julius Caesar, and to Antony, including Publius Ventidius and Gaius Asinius Pollio, had led thirteen legions to Italy from Gaul, aiming to support Lucius.

But this latest news was not good. The relief forces had been prevented from getting through to Lucius by Octavian's eleven legions. With the men of Lucius's legions starving and unable to break through Octavian's complex entrenchments surrounding Puglia after months of fighting, Lucius had surrendered, and the so-called Perusian War had come to an end. Octavian had pardoned Lucius Antony, and had sent him to command on his behalf in Spain. Fulvia had fled from Italy to Athens in Greece. And Lucius's six legions were being shipped to North Africa.

The second dispatch informed Antony that the Parthian invasion of the Roman East was achieving spectacular success. The Parthian prince Pacorus had entered Jerusalem and installed Antigonus as high priest. Antigonus had sliced off the ears of his uncle, Hyrcanus, and sent him into captivity in Parthia. Herod and his brother Phasaelus had been taken prisoner; Phasaelus had committed suicide, but Herod and his family had escaped. Quintus Labienus's forces, meanwhile, had marched through Cilicia and as far as Ionia and Lydia, with Greece tantalizingly close. Most cities and towns on his route had surrendered without a fight. Only the island city of Stratonicea was resisting, and was under siege by Labienus. General Saxa, Antony's fugitive governor of Syria, had been tracked down by Labienus, captured, and executed.

Now Antony finally stirred himself into action. Provided with five warships by Cleopatra, he bade her good-bye and sailed for Syria, ostensibly to help the port city of Tyre, which was still holding out against Parthian siege. But as he was only accompanied by the one thousand men of his Praetorian Guard bodyguard cohort, he bypassed Tyre and left the Tyrians to their fate. Sailing on, Antony put in at Rhodes and then Cyprus, where he learned that Labienus was plundering cities and temples in the territories he had occupied to raise the gold to pay his troops. Still Antony's eyes were on Italy. Ignoring Labienus and the Parthians, he sailed on and landed in northern Asia. There he sent for the two hundred warships he had ordered built the previous year. Once the ships arrived, Antony took some of his legionaries from Bithynia on board, but the bulk of his troops he ordered to cross the Hellespont to Macedonia, away from

Labienus and the Parthians, to await further orders there. It is likely that his six legions were sent to a base Caesar had created in Macedonia in 45–44 B.C. in preparation for his aborted Parthian campaign. Antony himself sailed to Greece with his massive fleet, then proceeded overland to Athens.

Antony's wife, Fulvia, was waiting for him at Athens, and we can only imagine the confrontation when they met. Ancient authorities say that the ambitious Fulvia had encouraged Lucius to revolt because she was jealous of Cleopatra's influence over Antony, and had been determined to become the major power broker, and sideline Cleopatra. Antony, meanwhile, blamed Fulvia for Lucius's failed revolt, which reflected badly on him. Exploding into a rage, Antony is reputed by ancient authorities to have vented his anger on his wife. In Athens, Antony was joined by Julia, his influential mother. After her son Lucius's surrender, Julia had initially fled to Sicily, which had been taken over by Sextus Pompey, youngest and only surviving son of Pompey the Great. Sextus had provided ships to take her to Greece, and senior members of Sextus's staff who accompanied her told Antony that their master was prepared to enter into an alliance with him against Octavian. Antony responded that if he did go to war against Octavian he would indeed ally himself with young Pompey.

As Antony spent the summer in Athens, a number of Antony's supporters flooded to him from Italy. They brought news that Generals Ventidius and Pollio had assembled their legions at strategic coastal cities in Italy and were urging Antony to come and launch his own bid to overthrow Octavian. At the beginning of spring, Fulvia suddenly took ill. Leaving her in Greece, Antony sailed from the island of Corfu with his two hundred warships, bound for Italy and a showdown with Octavian. In the Adriatic he was met by Admiral Domitius Ahenobarbus, who had previously fought for the Liberators and had been something of a pirate since their deaths. Won over to Antony's side by General Ventidius, Ahenobarbus now allied his ships and troops to Antony. Landing at the key naval city of Brundisium, modern Brindisi, Antony linked up with friendly troops waiting nearby and lay siege to Brindisi, also sending forces along the Italian coast to seize other cities. At the same time he sent word to Sextus Pompey to act in accordance with their agreement. In response, Sextus's forces landed on Sardinia and wrested it from the two legions holding the island for Octavian, and Sextus himself commenced operations against Italy's southwestern coast from bases he had established on Sicily.

As Antony continued the siege of Brindisi, he sent orders to Macedonia for his legions, including the 3rd Gallica, to hurry across Greece to the

Adriatic coast, where his warships would ferry them over the Otranto Strait to join him. As Octavian closed around Brindisi with forces that substantially outnumbered Antony's, and with Octavian's best general, Marcus Agrippa, forcing Antony's troops to retreat elsewhere, Antony resorted to subterfuge. Each night he sent ships away from Brindisi in the darkness carrying civilian passengers. Next day those ships would return and land the civilians, armed and dressed as soldiers, to let Octavian's troops at Brindisi think that he was progressively receiving his best troops from Macedonia.

News now arrived from Greece that Fulvia had died. According to the Roman historian Appian, she had fallen sick because she could not endure Antony's anger with her and had subsequently wasted away with grief because he had refused to see her on her sickbed. Shortly after Fulvia's death, an intermediary from Octavian went to Antony's mother, Julia, at Athens, and urged her to have her son come to the peace table with Octavian. The intermediary went to Antony with the same proposal, and when his mother supported the approach, Antony agreed. Now beyond Cleopatra's influence, Antony concluded that Octavian had far too much support in Italy for him to overthrow him, and contented himself with sharing power and ruling the East.

Sending Admiral Ahenobarbus, who was despised by Octavian, away to Bithynia to become its governor, and telling Sextus Pompey to withdraw to Sicily and let him sort out matters with Octavian, Antony met Octavian at Brindisi. Together they ironed out a new five-year triumval agreement. Octavian would control the Roman empire in the West, Antony all the empire east of today's Albania. Marcus Lepidus was left with just two provinces in North Africa. Octavian and Antony next met with Sextus Pompey at Misenum and sealed a peace deal that gave him control of Sicily, Sardinia, and Achaea in Greece, and promised him a consulship. In return, Sextus promised to marry his young daughter to Octavian's nephew once she was of marrying age.

Now, to cement their alliance, Octavian betrothed his elder sister Octavia to Antony. Octavia, whose husband had recently died, was apparently no beauty, but she was an intelligent and honorable woman, and it seems Antony genuinely had affection for her. They quickly married, and Octavia promptly fell pregnant. Now, as Antony and Octavian were feted in Rome for their peace deal, Antony set the ball rolling to recover his eastern domains. Now that Herod had arrived from Judea after escaping the Parthians, he had the Senate decree Herod king of Judea and declare Antigonus, self-proclaimed Jewish high priest at Jerusalem, an enemy of

Rome. Herod was then provided with a ship to take him back to the Middle East so he could raise a local force against Antigonus. Anthony's handy envoy Quintus Dellius went along as a Roman adviser.

Now, too, Antony ordered Publius Ventidius, his finest general and loyal friend, to take the best Antonian legions, including the 3rd Gallica, and throw Labienus and the Parthians out of Rome's eastern provinces and install Herod as king of Judea in accordance with the Senate's decree. Ventidius quickly sailed for Greece. The 3rd Gallica Legion, marching west along the Egnatian Way across northern Greece with five fellow Antonian legions to join Antony in Italy, was met on the march by Ventidius. He ordered them to turn around and head for Asia, with him at their head. The men of the Gallica would at last get their opportunity to fight the Parthians.

IV

ROUTING THE PARTHIANS

After being ferried across the Hellespont by the small craft that plied the narrow strait between Thrace and Asia, and ignoring the winter weather, the men of the 3rd Gallica were pushing down through the valleys of the province of Asia at a steady eighteen to twenty miles a day. They had been spoiling for a fight for close to twelve months, chafing to go after the traitor Quintus Labienus and his Parthian friends and reclaim the East for Rome, and soon they would come to grips with both.

The legion's numbers had been reduced by casualties in the Philippi battles and by sickness, so it was down on its original strength of six thousand men. There were four thousand to five thousand of them now, in ten cohorts, or companies, led by six young tribunes. Real power within the legion was vested in its sixty centurions, midranking officers promoted through the ranks after years of service. Many of the 3rd Gallica's centurions had served in the previous enlistment of the legion, Pompey's 3rd Legion, and had seen plenty of bloody battles in Portugal and Spain and piled up a small fortune in pay, bonuses, and booty before Julius Caesar paid them off in 49 B.C. Now, ten years later, these centurions were still fit, and ready for a fight. Some were in their fifties, having previously served Pompey in other units, in other wars. Others were in their thirties and forties. Most of the rank and file were in their late twenties or early thirties. The youngest of them had joined the legion at age seventeen and now were approaching twenty-seven. They were a colorful mixture: farm boys and fishermen, unemployed workmen and petty thieves, cobblers, boat builders, tailors, carpenters, blacksmiths; they had all brought their peacetime skills to the legion, and all had gone through tough training at the hands of even tougher centurions.

Now they all looked the same, clad in the blood-red woolen tunic and red cloak worn by all Rome's legionaries. Every man was equipped with the familiar Roman helmet that looked like a modern-day jockey's cap, with the addition of a plume of yellow horsehair. On the march, it was slung around the neck. Every man sported a thick leather vest covered by thousands of ringlets of iron mail that extended to the knees. This mail was weighty, and contributed to the description of legionaries as "heavy infantry." Slung over their left shoulders were their shields—wooden, rectangular, curved, almost as big as a man, and reinforced with iron. Every shield of the 3rd Gallica carried the legion's symbol, the charging bull. The bull was a symbol common to legions that had served Julius Caesar, and this enlistment of the legion had been raised by Caesar's recruiting officers. On their waist hung their "short" weapons, the twenty-inch *gladius*, a short sword with a pointed end, in a scabbard on the right hip, and a *puglio*, or dagger, on the left. Over their right shoulders they carried poles from which hung their packs, containing entrenching tools, personal items, bravery decorations, and rations. Strapped to each carrying pole were several javelins and two sharp wooden pickets. The thousands of pickets carried by the men of the legion were used to top the earthen wall surrounding the marching camp the legion built every night when they were on the march and were retrieved the next morning when the legion "upped stakes" and moved on.

Ahead and behind them marched the other legions of Mark Antony's eastern army—the 3rd Cyrenaica, the 4th Macedonica, the 5th Macedonica, the 10th, and the most famous of them all, the 6th Ferrata. *Ferrata* means "ironclad"—it was a title the men of the last enlistment of the 6th had given themselves after winning battle after battle for Julius Caesar. They had conquered Egypt for him, and defeated the Bosporan army of King Pharnaces at Zela, after which Caesar was to say that he came, he saw, and he conquered.

Antony's troops were in good spirits. They were finally going after the Parthians who had invaded the Roman East and shamed Romans everywhere. And their general was a man they identified with. Unlike most Roman generals, who came from aristocratic families, Lieutenant General Publius Ventidius's background was as humble as that of the soldiers he led. Now close to seventy years of age, Ventidius had been born in Asculum Picenum, today's Ascoli Piceno in eastern Italy, to a family of commoners. Between 90 and 88 B.C., when he was a young man, the Social War had been waged against Rome by her allies in Italy, and Ventidius had served in the ranks of forces sent against Rome by his hometown. Captured by Roman general Pompeius Strabo, father of Pompey the Great, young Ventidius had been paraded through the streets of Rome in Strabo's subsequent Triumph. As it turned out, the war proved beneficial to Ventidius. Freed in the amnesty following the war's end, Ventidius had found himself a Roman citizen, for, among the peace terms, Rome granted Roman citizenship to the allied states, a move that brought all of Italy south of the Po River into the Roman fold.

For a number of years Ventidius made a tidy living selling mules to the Roman army—later, his detractors would call him "the muleteer." He sided with Julius Caesar during the civil war, and in 44 B.C. Caesar appointed him a praetor, a judge with the equivalent military rank of a major general, for the coming year. Immediately after Caesar's murder, Ventidius had supported Anthony, putting together a force of three legions for him in Italy. That support had never wavered, and had earned him a consulship at Antony's behest and his current military appointment.

Now Ventidius was scouting well ahead of the main column, heading south with the cavalry and auxiliary light infantry as he looked for Quintus Labienus. The exact numbers in General Ventidius's advance force are unknown, but three years later Mark Antony would have six thousand auxiliary cavalry from Gaul and Spain under his command in the East. A good part of that force was almost certainly here with Ventidius now as he drove down through Asia. These troopers had been riding for Rome for years. Recruited by Caesar, they were not Roman citizens. They served under tribal obligation to Rome, and for pay. Some had fought for both Caesar and Pompey during the civil war, some had even ridden with Quintus Labienus's father. All had fought at Philippi and were experienced horsemen and fighters. The noncitizen auxiliaries of the light infantry, who included archers and slingers, were locals from Greece, Crete, Cyprus, Asia, and Syria numbering two thousand or three thousand.

As the advance force forged ahead, the men of the 3rd Gallica and the five other legions were coming along behind with the baggage train. This was made up of thousands of pack mules—a minimum of one for every ten legionaries, and hundreds of wagons carrying the army's heavy equipment, from tents to artillery, ammunition, grinding stones, and carpentry tools as well as water clocks and the officers' furniture and silver dining plate.

The target of their operation, young Quintus Labienus, was in Cilicia. When the winter of 40–39 B.C. arrived, the youthful conqueror had pulled out of the siege of Stratonicea and taken up residence in Cilicia, intending to remain there until the spring. As his troops likewise went into winter camp at their various garrisons and hung up sword and shield until the next spring, his Parthian allies had withdrawn into Syria.

The sudden news that General Ventidius and a Roman flying column were pushing into Cilicia shocked Labienus to the core. The last he had heard, Ventidius had been in Italy, embroiled in the turmoil involving Antony, Octavian, and Sextus Pompey. With only his own local troops to rely on, Labienus packed up and left, withdrawing ahead of Ventidius, summoning his men from their various garrisons throughout the region, and sending messengers galloping into Syria to bring Parthian cavalry to his support.

As Labienus camped at Mount Amanus and waited for Parthian reinforcements from east of the Taurus Mountains, Ventidius arrived with his advance force and made camp nearby on high, sloping ground. Now Ventidius also waited—for the arrival of the 3rd Gallica and his other legions. There, in the hills, the two forces passed several nervous days, eyeing each other from their camps.

When the six Roman legions came marching up the valley and linked with their general, their troops began unloading their equipment at the campsite marked out beside Ventidius's advance camp. A legion camp was dug by its legionaries, who carried entrenching tools for the job. No slaves or auxiliaries were permitted to be involved. An advance surveying party led by a tribune had found the best location for the camp, and set out marker flags indicating the grid pattern streets of the camp and exactly where every line of tents was to be erected when the legions arrived. On General Ventidius's orders, to make it difficult for Parthian heavy cavalry to get to them, this Mount Amanus campsite was on high ground, surrounded by angling slopes.

The legionaries were soon hard at work constructing their camp, some digging, some working with timber. "No matter where this is done," wrote 2nd century B.C. Greek historian Polybius, who documented Roman legion habits, "one simple formula for a camp is employed." The square or rectangular camp was surrounded by a trench dug by the legionaries; it was typically ten feet deep and three feet across. The earth from the trench was used to create a ten-foot wall inside the trench, and on top of this were planted the pointed stakes carried by every man. The legions' artillery—light, arrow-throwing catapults and heavier, stone-throwing "engines"—was mounted on the walls. There was a gate in each of the four walls. The main gate, the "decuman gate," faced away from the enemy. Wooden guard towers rose beside each wooden gate. One cohort from each of the six legions was assigned to guard duty, and at sunset every night a password for the next twenty-four hours was issued by the army commander. In the night, the watch changed precisely every three hours at the sound of a trumpet call.

In the afternoon, while the legions worked on their camp, a large force of Parthian cavalry arrived from the east and set up a camp separate from Quintus Labienus's camp. The identity of the Parthian commander here is unknown, but it wasn't Prince Pacorus; he was still back in Syria. Likewise, the number of Parthian cavalrymen in this force is not known, but according to Roman historian Cassius Dio, they held the Roman troops in contempt because of their own vast number. We know that Pacorus had left just two hundred of his cavalrymen stationed at Jerusalem, which, being twenty-five hundred feet above sea level, was frequently snow-covered in winter. The vast majority of the men in the Parthian occupying army were down in Syria over this winter, enjoying the milder climate beside the Jordan River. Allowing for some men remaining with Pacorus in Syria, the size of the force that joined Labienus would have numbered five thousand to eight thousand cavalrymen.

Far from quaking at the sight, the men of the 3rd Gallica, sweating as they dug their trenches and erected the tents and other facilities of the camp, would have smiled to themselves. This was what they had been waiting for, a chance to come to grips with the Parthians, the old enemy who had humiliated Rome at Carrhae fourteen years before. These were not the wastelands of Mesopotamia, where Crassus and twenty thousand of his men had died and ten thousand had been taken prisoner. This was mountain country, a different battleground altogether, terrain where legionaries were at no disadvantage. Knowing what the next day was likely to bring, they would have gone to their beds that night keyed up and expectant. Some, lying on bedrolls on the hard ground in their ten-man tents, would not have slept a wink as they thought about the difficulties entailed in taking on the Parthian cavalry the next day. But the Romans had a saying "Nothing is difficult to the brave and the faithful," and many more legionaries, believing in their own courage and ability and in their general, would have snored all night.

Well before dawn the next day, the general's trumpeter had sounded reveille, and the call was swiftly repeated by all the trumpeters of all the cohorts of the legions. "Assembly" was sounded soon after, summoning the legionaries. They had slept in their equipment, and only had to take a sip of water and pull on helmets and take up shields and javelins from the weapons stacks outside their tent doors before they formed up at attention in their units on the parade square. "At ease," sounded the trumpets. General Ventidius climbed the few steps onto the camp's raised tribunal, built from layers of turf, in front of his assembled legions. His adjutant, the *nuntius*—literally the "announcer"—took his place to the general's right.

"Hail, General!" bellowed thousands of legionaries. Many men also applauded.

There, in the light of flickering lamps, Ventidius informed his troops that today they would go against the Parthians, as they had expected, and today they would be victorious and make the enemy from the East pay for the humiliation at Carrhae. The legions roared their approval. In Daily Orders announced by the general's adjutant, the legions learned precisely where they were to go in Ventidius's battle formation, and of the tactics Ventidius planned for the day, of the signals they should expect, and when.

As the sun rose over the mountains, the legions silently marched from camp behind their standards, and drew up in the ordained battle order on uneven but open ground outside the camp walls. Following Julius Caesar's practice, their battle formation would have involved three lines, with every legion's ten cohorts or companies split through the line, with four cohorts in the first line and three in each of the two lines behind, with a gap between each line. Each century within each cohort lined up with ten men to the front, and its centurion on the extreme left of the very first rank. The remaining members of the century lined up directly behind each man in front. If the cohort was at full strength, the century was ten men deep. The eagle-bearer of the 3rd Gallica, proudly carrying aloft the silver eagle standard of the legion, retired to the open space between the first and second lines, where he was joined by the boy trumpeters of the first-line cohorts. Every soldier in the ranks who had earned a bravery decoration during his career was probably wearing it—Caesar had liked his men to wear their decorations into battle, to inspire them and to awe the enemy.

Ventidius seems to have assigned his auxiliary light infantry the task of guarding his camp. Having heard how General Saxa had so disastrously thrown his cavalry at the Parthians in Syria the previous year, Ventidius ordered his cavalry commander, Brigadier General Quintus Pompaedius Silo, to hold his cavalry on the wings of the infantry battle lines and let their infantry blunt the enemy attack.

In the Parthian camp, the cavalry mounted as the sun began to rise. The Parthians employed two types of cavalry—heavy and light. Their heavy cavalrymen, called *cataphracts* by the Greeks, were bearded noblemen. They wore armor that covered their entire bodies. On arms and legs it was made up of overlapping leather segments wrapped around the limb. On the torso it consisted of a sleeveless jacket onto which were sewn pieces of metal. In some cases these were chain mail vests not dissimilar to those worn by Rome's legionaries. Some noblemen could afford even more elaborate armor, with their jackets covered with overlapping "fish scales" of bronze and iron. On their heads they wore a pointy-topped metal helmet that usually trailed a streamer or two. The cataphract's principal weapon was the *kontos*, a lance some nine feet long. On his belt he wore a sheathed sword, or an ax, and many cataphracts also carried a small bow in a quiver slung over the back. Not only was the rider armored, his horse also was covered in a coat of leather onto which was sewn fish scale bronze or iron armor. The horse armor, which extended almost to the ground, covered most of the animal's head; only the ears, nose, and mouth were exposed. Even the horse's eyes had small iron grids over them for protection. Not surprisingly, the cataphract's horse had to be large and strong to carry both its own armor and its armored rider.

Numerically, horse-archers made up the largest component of the Parthian cavalry army. At the Battle of Carrhae there had been eight horse archers to each heavy cavalryman, and the balance was much the same here at Mount Amanus. Parthian horse archer ranks were made up of the servants of nobles and also of slaves. They wore no armor, just highly embroidered jackets and baggy leggings, a cloth cap, and solid leather boots. Each was armed with two short swords, with one strapped to each leg, and a bow made from a composite of bone and wood. Hanging on his horse's left side was an ornate quiver filled with arrows about three feet long. His horse, which carried no protection, was small and fast.

The Parthian cavalry formed in loose formation outside their camp, with horse archers to the front and cataphracts in the rear. Horses, made restless by riders who were by turns nervous and excited, pawed the ground, neighed, and had to be reassured and calmed. Seeing that Quintus Labienus's troops were slow to come out of their camp to join them, and seeing General Ventidius's legions formed on the hilltop and waiting for them, the Parthians did not bother to wait to join forces with Labienus's infantry. Although the Parthians did possess militia foot soldiers back home, the cavalry were accustomed to operating without infantry support. Besides, they had little respect for Labienus's infantry, being both Romans and turncoats. Instead, the Parthians moved out and rode to the base of the hill where, above, Ventidius's Romans stood silently in their ranks. The morning breeze wafted the Roman helmet crests and ruffled the purple cloth consular standard of their general.

Skirting around to the side of the hill that offered the easiest access, to the southwest, the exuberant Parthians urged each other to great deeds this day and prepared to charge. In the Parthians' rear, mounted drummers began to pound out an ominous beat. Despite all the Hollywood movies showing Roman armies and parade participants marching to beating drums, apart from small hand-held drums used by women in religious festivals the Romans never employed drums for military or ceremonial purposes. The Parthians, on the other hand, were famed for their war drums. Up on the hill, the men of the 3rd Gallica heard the booming enemy drums, and their heart rate increased a little. Around the campfires outside every tent the night before they had boasted of how they would revenge Crassus and his legions. The moment of truth was drawing nearer by the minute.

We don't know the positions of individual legions in Ventidius's battle formation. He probably gave the famous 6th Ferrata the honored right wing. Honored it may have been, but it was also the most dangerous location—legionaries held their shields on their left side, exposing their right, and many a general attacked the opposition's right wing as a consequence. The 3rd Gallica was either on the left wing or was one of the four legions in the middle of the line.

The legionaries knew what to expect from the Parthians. Cassius, the late Liberator, had been Crassus's quaestor at Carrhae and had led ten thousand survivors of the Carrhae disaster back to safety in Syria in 53 B.C. One or two centurions now in Ventidius's army would have been among those survivors, and they would have briefed their comrades on Parthian cavalry tactics. The horse archers would charge, firing arrows as they came. Fifty feet from the Roman front line they would turn right, and, riding along the front line, they would continue firing before turning away at the completion of their attack run. They would always turn right, because the Parthian always fired his bow from his left. The Gallicans would have been warned not to relax when the horse archer turned away—he was expert at turning in the saddle and firing behind him as he withdrew. This was the famous Parthian Shot. Once the horse archers had softened up the Romans, the heavy cavalry would advance and engage them with their lances. In his Daily Orders, General Ventidius had issued specific orders on how he wanted his men to counter the Parthian tactics. Now the legionaries waited impatiently to employ those tactics.

The Parthians, milling at the bottom of the hill with rising excitement as their drums pounded, had expected Ventidius's legions to come down the hill to meet them. But the legionaries were as immobile as statues. The Parthians were brimming with confidence. Many of them had fought at Carrhae. Then, there had been ten thousand of them, against forty thousand Romans. Here, the Roman legions numbered only twenty-five thousand to thirty thousand men, while they themselves had almost as many cavalry as at Carrhae. And here the legions were led by an old man of no military repute, an old man whom the Romans themselves called "the mule-driver." Victory seemed assured. As the drums continued to beat behind them, their commander gave an order and the first waves of the thousands of Parthian horses archers urged their horse forward and began to make their way up the slope.

On the hilltop, astride a horse, General Ventidius issued an order of his own. His trumpeter blew "Ready." All through the battle lines, sixty cohort trumpets repeated the signal. Legionaries in the front line planted one javelin in the ground in front of them, took a grip on a second with their right hand, and planted their feet in a throwing stance as the first horsemen came up the hill toward them.

The Parthian archers came with bows ready and several arrows in hand, riding in a vast, loose wedge formation, which, ironically, was one of the formations the Roman legions used against cavalry attack. One hundred yards from the Roman front line the horsemen kicked their steeds into a gallop. The thousands of horse archers charged, the leading riders firing as they came. The charge made the ground vibrate beneath the feet of the legionaries. Holding their positions, the Romans raised their shields to receive the showers of arrows. Parthian bows had such firepower that at close range their arrows could pin a legionary's foot to the ground or pass through a shield the thickness of a man's hand.

And then trumpets were signaling "Loose." The Roman front line launched their javelins down the hill. "Loose" was sounded a second time. A second wave of javelins flew. Then "Close order" sounded, and the legionaries of the front line closed the gaps between them. It was methodical, it was machinelike.

Fifty yards from the Roman lines, as a plague of javelins landed in the earth just ahead of them, the first horse archers were turning right and running along the battlefront, firing as they went. Then they were arcing away. Suddenly General Ventidius's standard dipped and his trumpet sounded. Roman trumpets behind the front line blared the same signal in unison: "Charge." It was a command the legionaries had been expecting. With a roar, the front line dashed forward. The downhill run increased their speed and their impetus. With a clash of metal, leather, wood, and flesh they collided with surprised horse archers on the run. The two sides were suddenly locked together. Legionaries bent and slashed with their swords, hamstringing enemy horses. Riders were cut down, knocked flying by shields, or pulled from their steeds. In some instances, Roman legionaries lifted small Parthian riders from the backs of their horses and threw them back down the hillside into riders behind them.

Desperately, Parthians cast aside bows, which were useless at close quarters, and reached for their short swords. But without shield or armor, every horse archer was prey to the crushing Roman onslaught and death-dealing legionary swords. As horsemen at the front were taking the brunt of the Roman charge, those behind began to panic and attempted to turn back. Riders who did manage to turn crashed into cavalry coming up behind them, spilling many of their comrades from their saddles, then overrunning them. In their panic, Parthian cavalry killed and maimed as many of their own men as did the Roman legionaries.

In minutes, the hillside was a scene of slaughter and mayhem. Most of the heavy cataphracts coming up behind couldn't get to the Romans for the sea of horse archers being pushed back down on the hill toward them, and even when they did, it was in a close-quarters melee in which many noblemen were soon unhorsed. Blind with terror as the unstoppable Roman legions came slicing down the hill, surviving Parthian horsemen galloped off down the valley. In their desire to escape, they rode away from the camp of their ally Labienus, not toward him, and into Cilicia.

Now General Ventidius ordered his entire force forward. He personally led the cavalry in chasing isolated Parthians toward Labienus's camp. His troopers wanted to give chase as far as it took to kill every Parthian, but Ventidius called a halt outside the enemy's infantry camp. The Roman general could see Quintus Labienus on the camp wall with his men. And it was the traitor Labienus whom Ventidius wanted. As his cavalry mopped up on the battlefield, the general waited outside Labienus's camp with his legions in battle order, inviting him to come out and fight.

During the afternoon Labienus was seen to form his greatly outnumbered troops in battle order inside his camp. But the gates never opened. Unlike his father, who had nerves of steel and courage to spare, young Labienus's nerve failed him, and he didn't venture out to fight. Night fell, with the young man cringing in his camp. Setting up pickets around the camp, Ventidius marched his victorious army back up to their own hilltop camp.

During the night, deserters slipped over the walls of Labienus's camp and came up the hill to Ventidius's entrenchments. When they were brought to General Ventidius at his *praetorium*, his headquarters tent, they revealed that morale in Labienus's camp had sunk to rock bottom and that Labienus himself was planning to break his troops out of his camp in groups in the darkness of the early morning. The deserters knew where and when most of these breakouts were to occur, and based on this information Ventidius sent detachments of legionaries to set up ambushes for Labienus's men.

The information proved correct. And in the early hours of the next day the vast majority of Labienus's Roman troops ran straight into the waiting ambushers and were killed or captured. Labienus's own escape plan had not been made known, and he was able to slip by the waiting troops and disappear into the wilds of Cilicia wearing local peasant clothing.

The next day, after conducting an assembly at which numerous legionaries were presented with bravery decorations, as was the Roman custom following a victory, General Ventidius ordered his cavalry commander, General Silo, to take most of his cavalry east. Silo was to ride as far as the Cilician Gates, the narrow pass in the Taurus Mountains through which ran a military highway built on Julius Caesar's orders and that led all the way to Antioch in Syria. While Silo set off to secure the pass, Ventidius marched the legions down to the city of Tarsus, where he arrested Labienus's lackeys and took over administration of the province.

A price was put on Labienus's head, and this naturally attracted bounty hunters. The governor of the island of Cyprus at this time, appointed by Mark Antony, was Demetrius, one of Julius Caesar's former freedmen. Later that same year, learning from informants where Labienus was hiding in Cilicia, Demetrius crossed to the mainland, tracked Labienus down, and arrested him. We hear no more of young Quintus Labienus, briefly lord of the Roman East. Undoubtedly he was executed.

But well before Labienus was captured, General Ventidius received a desperate dispatch from his cavalry general. Silo was surrounded by Parthians at the Cilician Gates. Ventidius promptly dropped everything and marched with the legions to relieve Silo. The Cilician Gates pass had acquired its name from the wooden gates that had once blocked the way here. The gates were gone, but a sizable garrison of Parthian cavalry under Prince Pacorus's deputy Pharnapates was now in place here. That garrison, bolstered by cavalrymen who had escaped from the Battle of Mount Amanus, had fallen on Silo's unwary mounted column as it approached. Even though they outnumbered the Parthians, the Roman cavalrymen were no match for them and were soon in dire straits. Surrounded, their only hope was to hold out until General Ventidius arrived.

Fortunately for Silo, the arrival of Ventidius and the legions took his Parthian attackers completely by surprise. Coming up behind them, Ventidius's legions slaughtered a large number of the Parthians, including Pharnapates, their commander. This battle, the Battle of the Cilician Gates, secured the pass. When news of Ventidius's victories in Cilicia reached

Pacorus in Syria, where he had set himself up as regent, the Parthian prince collected his remaining troops and withdrew across the Euphrates into Parthia to regroup.

In the spring, the 3rd Gallica marched into Syria with General Ventidius and the rest of his legions. But to their surprise they weren't welcomed wholeheartedly by the people of Syria. Prince Pacorus, it turned out, had made himself very popular during his time in Syria because of his mildness and his justice. The Syrians, said Cassius Dio, came to hold Pacorus in as much affection as the greatest kings who had ever ruled them. Certainly no Roman governor had engendered as much affection in the twenty-five years since Pompey the Great had made Syria a province of Rome.

It soon became apparent to General Ventidius that if Pacorus led another Parthian army across the Euphrates, many in Syria would throw their support behind him. Ventidius set his mind to ridding Rome of the threat posed by the dashing prince.

The 3rd Gallica Legion was going against the Parthians again. It was now 38 B.C., and a year had passed since the legions had defeated Labienus and Pharnapates in Cilicia. And now wily old General Ventidius had lured Prince Pacorus into a trap.

Following his 39 B.C. victories, Ventidius had raised two new legions in Syria on Antony's authority, partly from Labienus's former men but mostly from new Syrian levies. As the winter of 39–38 B.C. had arrived, he sent all eight of his legions into winter camp around Syria and Cilicia. Early in 38 B.C., Ventidius had learned that Pacorus was assembling another Parthian army east of the Euphrates to again invade Syria. Having ascertained from spies that a Syrian noble named Channaeus was in contact with Pacorus, Ventidius wined and dined Channaeus. During their intimate conversations Ventidius seemingly let it slip that he was afraid that Pacorus would cross the Euphrates at a point in southern Syria where it was flat and suited to cavalry, rather than at nearby Zeugma once again—where the hilly terrain was suited to Roman infantry. That information had been duly passed to Pacorus, who, in the spring, took the bait and led his army many miles south, crossing the Euphrates into Syria just where General Ventidius wanted him to cross.

Ventidius had meanwhile summoned his legions. By invading in the south, Pacorus had given Ventidius valuable weeks in which to assemble his forces. Once Pacorus crossed the river, he pushed north without encountering resistance. Weeks into the invasion, entering the Cyrrhestica district of Syria, his scouts reported General Ventidius's legions camped ahead, on the slopes of Mount Gindarus. Determined to destroy Ventidius, Pacorus marched to the mountain.

Ventidius, at assembly that morning, told his legionaries that Pacorus and his cavalry had fallen into his trap. Today, he said, Mars, god of war, would smile on them. The usual prebattle animal religious sacrifice had produced auspicious omens. Today the legions would destroy the Parthians. It was the will of the gods, for this was exactly the same day on which, fifteen years before, Marcus Crassus had died at the hands of the Parthians at Carrhae. Feeling that the foolish Parthians, lured into Ventidius's trap, had no chance of victory, and that, as the Romans said, "Fools must be taught by the result," the legions confidently formed in battle order on the slopes outside their camp.

The Parthians were full of bravado and rushed to the attack. Whether this charge was spontaneous or on Pacorus's rash order we are not to know. Once again, Ventidius had claimed the high ground. Up the slope charged the Parthian horse archers. And once again, at the crucial moment General Ventidius ordered his legions to charge. Down the slope rushed the men of the 3rd Gallica and the other legions.

It was a repeat of the slaughter at the Battle of Mount Amanus. Horse archers, caught in close-quarters combat with the legionaries, were slaughtered. Others, driven back down the slope and panicking, crashed into companions in their desperation to escape, and fell or fled. Only the cataphract heavy cavalry, led by Pacorus himself, held their ground at the bottom of the hill. The legions swept down around them like a river at the flood. Vastly outnumbered by twenty or thirty to one, the nobles of the heavy cavalry were surrounded. But instead of sending his infantry against the well-armored Parthians, General Ventidius held the legionaries back and sent in his slingers.

Roman forces in the East used slingers from Crete and parts of Greece to great effect. These slingers, trained since childhood to protect sheep and goat herds from predators by using their slings, were deadly accurate with stones and lead bullets over remarkable distances, often up to several hundred yards. Their slingshot in fact had a greater effective range than Parthian arrows. But that was not a factor, now that the enemy horse archers had been put to flight. On high ground, Ventidius's slingers were able to stand off and rain missiles down on the Parthians and their horses without any fear of return fire. The air was filled with clouds of projectiles, which came at the Parthians with a speed approaching that of modern-day rifle bullets—thousands of them.

The men of the 3rd Gallica and the other waiting legionaries watched with fascination. They heard the sound of slingshots in the air, like the hum of swarms of bees. They heard the rattle and clatter as the projectiles hit Parthian armor, heard cavalrymen cry out in pain and horses whinny in panic. And they watched the antics of the targets trying to avoid being hit. Laughter rolled through the Roman ranks. To the legionaries, this was as entertaining as watching a gladiatorial contest, but much more satisfying. Not only was this barrage disconcerting to the haughty Parthians, the slingshot also could take out an eye, human or equine, or cause bloody facial wounds. Horses reared and bucked. Riders swayed and ducked. And then suddenly Roman trumpets were sounding, the barrage lifted, and with a cheer the legions were charging in for the kill.

Made obvious by his standard, his large entourage, and his expensive armor, Prince Pacorus attracted the focus of the attack. Dragged from his horse, he went down under a crush of blows. His bodyguards fought desperately to save him, but when it was clear their prince was dead, they fought to prevent his body from falling into Roman hands. The legionaries pressed in. And then a cheer rang out from the legions as the last Parthian bodyguard also fell dead over his master's corpse. With the flash of a sword, Pacorus's head was severed. A centurion held the prince's bloodied head aloft, bringing another triumphant, bloodthirsty roar from the men of the 3rd Gallica and their fellow legionaries.

Only now, when their commander was dead, did some of the Parthian nobles attempt to fight their way out of the encirclement. A few managed to bulldoze their way through atop ironclad steeds. Some turned south, following the retreating horse archers who were fleeing back toward the Euphrates crossing. Others galloped north; they would ride all the way to the mountainous, landlocked kingdom of Commagene. There they would seek asylum from its king, elderly Antiochus I, who was related by marriage to Parthia's king—his daughter was Orodes's wife, and their children his grandchildren.

Ventidius had anticipated that some Parthians would attempt to escape back the way they had come. He had regretted that so many had managed to get away after Mount Amanus, and this time he was prepared. To the south, Roman cavalry and infantry lay in wait, knowing what route enemy escapees could be expected to take. Cutting the fleeing Parthians off from the crossing across the Euphrates, they surprised and destroyed them.

Following a victory assembly, Ventidius dispatched the head of Prince Pacorus on a tour of Syria, to prove to Syrian leaders who had wavered in their loyalty to Rome that the Parthian royal was dead. The grim message had the desired effect. Syrian nobles rushed to congratulate the Roman general and vow their undying loyalty to Mark Antony and the Senate and people of Rome. It would be hundreds of years before a Syrian noble again challenged Roman authority in the province. The men of Ventidius's legions, meanwhile, shared the rich booty from Pacorus's baggage train, stripped the dead Parthians naked to sell their equipment to the traders who followed the legions wherever they went, and enjoyed the praise and awards lavished on them by their general.

Just a few weeks later, Ventidius received orders from Mark Antony in Athens, to send troops to reinforce King Herod in Judea. For two years Herod had battled the high priest Antigonus. Herod had gained control of Galilee with a sizable force of Galileean volunteers, but Antigonus had shut himself up inside Jerusalem with a large number of armed Jews. Now, too, General Ventidius learned that King Antiochus of Commagene was sheltering Parthian nobles who had escaped after the Battle of Mount Gindarus.

So Ventidius ordered the legions to prepare to march once more. The two newly recruited legions and a thousand cavalry were sent south to support Herod. The remainder of the Roman army—Ventidius's six original legions and most of the cavalry and auxiliaries—was heading north, in pursuit of the escapees, and invading Commagene. Ventidius was going to ram home the point that Roman authority was once more stamped on the region.

V

PUTTING KING HEROD ON HIS THRONE

C lad in military uniform and armored cuirass, and smiling, Mark Antony walked into General Ventidius's tent outside the city of Samosota. It had taken Ventidius's spectacular defeat of Prince Pacorus to bring Antony all the way from Athens.

Antony had been living in Greece for the past year. There, his new wife, Octavia, had borne him a daughter and swiftly become pregnant by him again. In Athens, Antony, dressed in the Greek fashion, had been feted by the Athenians and had enjoyed the city's theater and music. He had wined and dined and left the business of politics and soldiering to underlings. He had always felt comfortable in Athens, more comfortable than anywhere else. But his worry-free life had been shaken. Not by his rival Octavian or the ambitious Sextus Pompey. Nor by the Parthians— but by the Roman general who had ended their brief reign over Syria; his subordinate. All everyone in Athens had wanted to talk about was Publius Ventidius. First it was how Ventidius had whipped young Labienus. Then it was how Ventidius had terminated Pacorus's invasion, and his life, in yet another spectacular victory. To Antony's face, people had praised him, for Ventidius had been acting in his name. But Antony knew what they were really thinking—there was Antony living an idle life in Athens, while other men did his work and won the glory. Jealous of Ventidius's sudden fame, Antony packed up and left Athens. He had come to the siege of Samosota, capital of Commagene, to take personal charge of the Roman offensive.

Samosota, today the location of the Turkish village of Samsat, was then a rich, fortified city standing beside the Euphrates River, guarding an important crossing used by traders on the east-west trade route. Here, King Antiochus of Commagene was holed up with his army and Parthian nobles who had escaped from Mount Gindarus. And here General Ventidius's legions had been entrenched for months, besieging the stubborn king.

General Ventidius warmly welcomed his commander in chief and briefed him on the state of the siege. Antony continued to smile and took it all in. Then he informed Ventidius that he had done enough, had served Rome above and beyond the call of duty. With indications that Ventidius was not a well man, Antony removed him from his command. The Senate had voted Triumphs to both Antony and Ventidius for smashing the Parthians. Antony told him to go home, to take his Triumph, and retire.

So Antony's best general departed the scene and left the East. Later in the year he would celebrate his Triumph, parading through Rome in a golden *quadriga*, a chariot drawn by four white horses, passing along a Triumphal route lined by hundreds of thousands of cheering Romans to the Capitol. There, after a prisoner—the most senior Parthian noble captured in his eastern campaign—had been garroted, Ventidius would carry out religious rites at the Temple of Jupiter Optimus Maximus (Jupiter Best and Greatest), then host a feast for thousands of guests. Plutarch would remark that Ventidius's Triumph was the only one in Roman history up to that time celebrated by a Roman general for a victory over the Parthians. Following the Triumph, without another appointment from his patron Antony, he went into quiet retirement. Within a year he would be dead, from natural causes.

Meanwhile, at Samosota, there had been an offer on the table to Ventidius from King Antiochus—24 million sesterces in gold if the Romans would go away. Ventidius had deferred to his master, but now Antony disdainfully dismissed the offer and continued the siege. But even though they were surrounded on three sides by Roman trenches and artillery mounds, with the river on the other, the Commagenians were in a strong position behind the city's high stone walls. They had food stockpiled, they could draw water from the Euphrates. Antiochus was prepared to sit it out. Antony quickly grew impatient with the standoff. He was receiving letters from Cleopatra in Egypt, urging him to return to her now that he was in the East. So he sent to potentates throughout the region to provide him with reinforcements to help complete the siege.

King Herod was one of those to answer Antony's call. The two legions sent by Ventidius had not been enough to take Jerusalem. They sat at Emmaus, just to the north of the Jewish capital, fighting off guerrilla attacks by Antigonus's men. As the two legions were under Antony's orders to stay where they were, Herod left part of his own force there under the command of his younger brother Joseph, and marched with several thousand infantry and cavalry to aid his friend Antony. When he arrived at Antioch, the Syrian capital, he found a number of worried local nobles congregated there. They wanted to go to Antony's aid, they said, but they were frightened by reports of a mounted Parthian expeditionary force lying in wait in the hills south of Samosota and butchering all the supply trains that had been trying to reach Antony's army from Syria. The thirty-five-year-old Herod shrugged off their concerns and said he would fight his way through to Antony no matter what. This mission, the Jewish historian Josephus would point out, would allow Herod to display his courage and would put Antony in his debt. Emboldened by Herod, the other nobles joined his column with their troops.

As he entered Commagene, Herod deliberately put the baggage train at the front of the column. Two days' march south of Samosota, the road taken by the column coursed through a narrow pass in tree-lined hills, with the plain within sight ahead. Suddenly a force of five hundred Parthian cavalry drove from the trees and fell on the front of the column. As Herod had hoped, the attackers had been attracted by the spoils offered by the baggage train. Herod himself, riding near the rear of the column, had been expecting this ambush. Now he led a counterattack from the rear. Herod's terrified advance guard was fleeing in all directions, and the Parthians were into the baggage train when his main force came up, with the king himself riding hard at the forefront. Taking the Parthians by surprise, Herod and his troops from the rear killed the enemy in their hundreds. Seeing this, the men of the advance guard re-formed and joined the fight. Some riders escaped, but the Parthian force was destroyed as a fighting unit. Because of Herod, the road to Samosota would now remain open to reinforcements and supplies coming up to Antony from the south.

At Samosota, Antony, hearing that Herod had fought his way through the hills after a march of 340 miles and was approaching, sent a Roman honor guard in full decorations to escort him in. As the two men came together, Antony held out his right hand. In those times the friendly handshake we know today took a different form. Then, when you clasped right hands, you gripped the other man by the wrist, with one hand having the upper position, the other the lower. The upper was the most honored, and as Antony and Herod grasped each other's wrists Antony voluntarily took the lower position to honor his friend. Antony then pulled Herod to him and embraced him like a brother.

The siege dragged on through the summer. In reality the addition of Herod's men and the other reinforcements from Syria made no great difference to the ability of the attacking force to take the city. Inside Samosota, King Antiochus knew that Antony had received reinforcements. But he was also hearing rumors that Cleopatra was urging Antony to join her in Egypt. So he sent out envoys with another peace deal: he would hand over Parthian fugitives and pay Antony in gold if Antony gave up the siege.

This time the king's financial offer was little more than 7 million sesterces, more than three times less than the offer he had made to General Ventidius. But Antony was increasingly impatient to get away to Egypt and Cleopatra. And, says Cassius Dio, Antony was also aware his legionaries were unhappy with him for sending away General Ventidius. Not only had Ventidius proven himself a very able tactician; but also legionaries were highly superstitious, and now Antony had deprived them of a general who had been lucky for them. Legionaries, like all Romans, saw ill omens in the flight patterns of birds, in the weather and other natural phenomena, in unusual events. It was commonly said among the legions that Cassius had been doomed to die at the First Battle of Philippi because, when he had been blessing his legions' standards prior to the battle, in the Lustration Exercise, his sacred garland had been accidentally placed back to front on his head, and a boy carrying a statue of Victory in the procession had stumbled and dropped it. Legions fearing that luck had deserted them soon lost heart, even mutinied. Three times in the past, when Caesar was alive, legions under Antony had mutinied, and each time it had taken Caesar to right the situation. Mutiny was not what Antony wanted or needed now. He accepted Antiochus's offer. The king opened the city gates, handed over the gold and two senior Parthian nobles as hostages, and agreed to refrain from giving further moral or physical support to the Parthian Empire in the future.

While this meant an end to the siege, it also meant an end to legionary hopes of booty, for the Roman rules of war dictated that if the legions took a city by storm, the booty was divided among them. But if a city surrendered, its fate was in the hands of the commanding general. And in this instance Antony took Antiochus's money, shared his gold with Herod and other senior supporters, left Samosota untouched and Antiochus on his throne as a new Roman ally, and ordered his troops out of Commagene.

As Antony himself hurried away to sail from Syria to Alexandria, he appointed Major General Gaius Sossius governor of both Syria and Cilicia. Sossius had orders to take his army to Judea, to remove Antigonus and install Herod as king of Judea, as the Senate had ordained two years earlier. To achieve that objective, an advance guard of two legions was to hurry south with Herod. General Sossius was to follow as quickly as possible with the remaining four legions and the heavy equipment. Sossius also had Antony's authority to raise more troops in Syria and Cilicia and add them to his force.

Herod and the advance force left at once. As General Sossius marched from Commagene with the main legion column, he was soon aware of grumbling in the ranks. Accustomed to loading themselves down with booty after the defeat of the Parthians, the men of the legions were not happy with the unprofitable outcome of the siege of Samosota. So General Sossius, an astute commander, let his men know that at Jerusalem there awaited a prize far richer than Samosota. There stood a heathen temple filled with more gold and silver than they could ever dream of. With that incentive, spirits in the ranks began to pick up, as did the pace of the march south.

Ahead of the main force, Herod reached Daphne outside Antioch in Syria to learn to his horror that his brother Joseph was dead. Joseph had led five cohorts from one of the new Syrian legions to Jericho to cut wheat to supply their army. There, Joseph had been ambushed by Antigonus's troops. Joseph was killed and the five raw legionary cohorts wiped out. The remaining Roman troops had withdrawn down to Samaria and the coast, under attack and losing another cohort, taking refuge in a fortress at the town of Gitta. Hearing of these reverses for Herod and the Romans, Antigonus's supporters had risen up throughout Galilee and killed Herod's officials. Now Herod had to reclaim all of Galilee and Samaria before he could even think about Jerusalem. Rushing into Galilee with his two Roman legions, he began the task by retaking one city after another.

Once Sossius also reached Syria, he bolstered his force with the addition of three more legions. It seems that these new legions were raised by Sossius in the provinces of the East. They joined his army before the end of the year. Gradually Herod's Jewish forces and Sossius's Roman units reoccupied Galilee and Samaria, taking some towns by storm while others quickly submitted. Sossius then climbed up into the hills and took Jericho. With winter coming on, the legions went into camp.

In the spring of 37 B.C., General Sossius led his combined eleven legions to Jerusalem in company with Herod and his Galileean troops. Surrounding the city with three trench lines, the army of sixty thousand men launched an assault against Jerusalem's north wall, near the Temple, the same location used by Pompey the Great when he had successfully besieged Jerusalem twenty-seven years earlier. Here the men of the 3rd Gallica and the ten other legions undertook a grueling assault. The first of Jerusalem's three stone walls was overrun within forty days, the second just fifteen days later. But the last wall was stubbornly defended by Jewish fighters who used artillery from the walls, dug mines under Roman earthworks to collapse them, and launched raids to burn Roman artillery and siege equipment outside the wall. Five months into the assault, twenty chosen men from Herod's forces and a similar number of centurion volunteers from Sossius's legions went over the last wall at night and opened the way for the rest of the besieging army.

Once inside the city, the legionaries ran amok, "as if they were an army of madmen," says Josephus. They killed men, women, and children in the narrow streets and alleyways as they plundered the houses and drove toward the Temple with all its fabled riches. Herod himself entered the city, and begged General Sossius to spare his people and to keep the Roman troops out of the sacred Jewish Temple.

"Will you Romans empty the city of both money and men?" Josephus says Herod angrily demanded. "Leaving me king of a desert? It wouldn't be enough for me to be king of the whole world if the price were the murder of my citizens."

Sossius shrugged. "This plunder is just. I allow my soldiers to do it because it's their right, after they've endured the long siege and conquered the city by storm."

"Then I will pay every one of your soldiers personally," Herod retorted, "if you stop the looting now."

Sossius took Herod at his word, and issued orders for his centurions to rein in the rampaging legionaries and to keep them out of the inner Temple. The killing stopped. The city fell to the Romans. And the Temple's inner sanctum was not violated. Herod kept his word. The legionaries of the 3rd Gallica Legion, along with the men of the other legions, all received a handsome bonus in gold from Herod's own treasury. Centurions each received proportionately more, the tribunes more again, and the generals even more, with General Sossius receiving a bounty fit for a king.

As for Antigonus, who had been ruling Judea since the Parthians installed him as high priest three years before, he came out of the Jerusalem citadel, prostrated himself in front of General Sossius, and begged for mercy. Sossius laughed, calling Antigonus a girl, and ordered him lashed to a cross and whipped, before, on Antony's orders, he was sent to Antioch.

Antony had plans to keep Antigonus alive long enough to be dragged through the streets of Rome in the Triumph he'd been voted by the Senate, and then garroted. But with the likelihood of his returning to Rome in the near future diminished by changing events, and concerned that while Antigonus remained alive he would be a focus of opposition to Herod, Antony subsequently ordered the Jewish leader beheaded.

At summer's end, with Herod now installed at Jerusalem as king of Judea, the men of the 3rd Gallica Legion marched back to winter quarters in Syria. As they marched, orders circulated that over the winter they were to prepare their equipment for a major new campaign the following spring, and a rumor swept through the legion that Mark Antony planned to invade Parthia in the new year. After what they had achieved, that did not seem so daunting. With their track record of successive victories in Cilicia, Syria, Commagene, Galilee, Samaria, and now having taken Jerusalem, and having placed King Herod securely on his throne, the men of the Gallica must have felt invincible. And they'd never had it so good. "They all went away full of money," Josephus was to remark.

But it was not the last the 3rd Gallica Legion would have to do with Judea. The legion's future and Judea's future were inextricably linked.

VI

MARK ANTONY'S
MISTAKE

L ooking back, the men of the 3rd Gallica Legion could see the Roman army trailing away to the horizon across the flat, barren, nearly treeless landscape. It was the summer of 36 B.C., and Mark Antony was invading the Parthian neighbor and ally Media. And he was doing it with 113,000 men. It was one of the largest Roman armies ever to take the field.

Much had transpired over the past twelve months. While his legions had been taking Jerusalem and cementing Herod on his throne, Antony had sailed to Italy with a fleet of three hundred warships and a combative attitude. Antony had taken offense at his fellow triumvir Octavian because of adverse stories reaching him from Rome, and Cleopatra, wanting to reignite conflict between the two, had quickly urged Antony to confront Octavian on his doorstep. The other woman in Antony's life, Octavia, Antony's wife and Octavian's sister, had stepped in to resolve differences between the two. She had joined Antony as his fleet coasted past Greece, and at the port city of Taranto, in the boot of Italy, she had gone ashore and met with her brother. Declaring that if a war broke out between the two she would be the loser no matter who won—for either the husband she loved or her brother she loved would perish—Octavia succeeded in brokering a peace conference at Taranto.

There Antony and Octavian had sealed a treaty renewing their triumval power-sharing agreement for another five years. Both men had military plans they wanted to put into effect. Antony wanted to invade Parthia, so Octavian promised him two legions for the operation. Octavia later also extracted a thousand men of Octavian's Praetorian Guard for Antony.

Octavian, meanwhile, wanted to eject Sextus Pompey from Sicily, so Antony provided 120 of his warships for that operation.

Antony then sent Octavia back to his mansion at Rome. Years before, he had taken Pompey the Great's house in the Keels district for himself; there Octavia not only raised the children she had by Antony, she also took in Antony's children by Fulvia and raised them as her own. Antony himself sailed back to Syria to launch his Parthian operation. And as he did, he sent a senior officer to Cleopatra in Egypt with instructions to bring her to him in Syria. Plutarch was to write that better thoughts had seemed to consign Antony's passion for Cleopatra to oblivion in recent times, and it certainly seems that while he was under Octavia's influence his actions were reasonable, considered, and realistic. But now that he was returning to the East, the old passions—for Cleopatra and for glory—erupted.

Cleopatra quickly came up to Syria, bringing funds, equipment, and munitions for Antony's massive Parthian operation, and bringing the twins, a boy and a girl, whom she had borne him. And in return Antony lavished gifts on her, gifts that astonished both his friends and his enemies: he bestowed parts of Syria and most of Cilicia on her, and all of Cyprus. He also gave her part of Nabatea, an Arab kingdom to the south of Judea, and a fertile part of Herod's Judea, too.

The Parthian operation had been made all the more feasible by the recent death of Parthia's king, old Orodes II. The Parthian ruler had taken the death at the hands of the Romans of his favorite son Pacorus badly, and had wasted away. Cassius Dio says that Orodes died of natural causes, and before he died he made his eldest remaining son, Phraates, his successor. Plutarch has it that Phraates murdered his ailing father and took the throne for himself. Either way, Phraates was the new king of Parthia. But the vicious Phraates soon alienated many of his own nobles, and some fled to Syria, where Antony granted them asylum.

With Parthia made unstable by these events, and with the reputation of Rome's force of arms now sky high in the East, Antony had reckoned this the ideal time to press forward with his invasion. Pretending he only wanted peace, Antony had sent one of the Parthian defectors back to King Phraates and negotiated the return of the standards wrested from Crassus's legions in 53 B.C. at Carrhae. King Phraates had also agreed to the return of Roman legionaries captured back then—these men had been toiling as slaves on farms in the easternmost regions of Parthia for the past sixteen years.

All this was meant to put the Parthians off their guard. But after Antony marched from Antioch with his invasion force, accompanied by

Cleopatra, he reached the Euphrates to find Parthian garrisons posted along the opposite bank. Phraates hadn't been fooled—he was expecting Antony. Determined not to lose face, and urged on by Cleopatra and his new ally King Artavasdes II, ruler of Armenia for the past sixteen years, Antony changed his plan. Now he would invade the Parthian ally Media, farther north. So, sending Cleopatra back to Egypt while he went to war, Antony gave the army new marching orders—north, to Armenia, and then east into Media, a kingdom covering what today is Kurdistan, Ajerbaijan, and Kermanshah, above Iraq and Iran.

Cleopatra undertook the first part of her journey back to Alexandria overland, deliberately stopping at Jerusalem to visit King Herod. There, according to several classical authors, including Josephus, she tried to seduce Herod, hoping he would gift her more of his territory, but Herod was too smart for her and resisted her advances.

The Roman invasion force now traipsing over the wastes of barren western Media included Antony's eleven legions. They had a total of fifty-seven thousand legionaries between them; all but the newest legions were understrength, due to battle casualties and sickness over the past few years. Three thousand Praetorian Guards also marched with Antony. In addition to his original Praetorian cohort of a thousand bodyguards, known as the Brindisi Cohort because he had recruited these men from his legions at Brindisi in 44 B.C., he had the Praetorian cohort that Octavia had acquired for him from Octavian and one other. He also had ten thousand Gallic and Spanish cavalry. Added to that, King Artavasdes was leading seven thousand Armenian infantry and six thousand cavalry. Artavasdes's cavalrymen were horse archers and heavy cavalry in the Parthian style. In fact, the Armenian cavalry had been trained by Parthian officers, for until recently, Artavasdes had been a Parthian ally—his sister was the widow of Prince Pacorus. Only since the death of Pacorus, the defeat of Parthian forces by Rome's General Ventidius, and the ascent of Phraates to the Parthian throne had the Armenian king thrown his loyalty behind Mark Antony and Rome.

Other eastern potentates allied to Rome, such as Polemon, new king of Pontus, had contributed a further thirty thousand infantry and cavalry from their own nations. Some, like Artavasdes and Polemon, anxious to impress Antony with their loyalty, were personally leading their national contingents.

Antony didn't have his two most successful generals with him—Ventidius was by now dead, and Sossius, conqueror of Jerusalem, had returned to Rome to take up a consulship. But Antony still had a number of excellent

officers on his staff. One was Major General Publius Canidius Crassus—
Canidius to Roman writers. The previous year, General Canidius had led
a Roman military expedition of several legions newly raised in Asia plus
allied support units that marched all the way from Armenia around the
Caspian Sea to the Caucasus. He had successfully beaten off the forces of
several local potentates along the way. Canidius had then become
Antony's ambassador to Armenia. Gnaeus Domitius Ahenobarbus, former
admiral to Pompey the Great, later a pirate, and more recently governor
of Bithynia, was here with Antony. So, too, was the efficient young Brigadier General Marcus Titius, who was serving as the army's quartermaster.

The men of the 3rd Gallica Legion, marching in the massive army's
vanguard, would have felt confident of success. The very size of the invasion force was enough to excite feelings of pride and invincibility. Plutarch says that news of Antony's huge army driving east into Media
reached all the way to India, scaring millions of people in between and
raising memories of Alexander the Great's past conquests.

The army had finally come together in Armenia late in the summer,
and then Antony had ordered commencement of the invasion. Plutarch
was to criticize Antony for pushing on with his invasion so late in the
campaigning season. He says the legions had already marched a thousand
miles from their bases in Syria, and should have gone into camp for the
winter, resting before launching their eastern advance at the beginning of
the following spring. According to Plutarch, Antony only wanted to get
the operation over and done with so he could reunite with Cleopatra in
Syria for the winter. But Antony was also very much aware that if he
launched his invasion now he would catch the Medes and their Parthian
allies by surprise. If he set up camp in Armenia and waited until the following February, news of his massive army sitting in Armenia would reach
the other side, and come the spring the enemy would be ready and waiting.

The men of the 3rd Gallica would certainly have been of that view.
And now, two years since General Ventidius had departed, and with Mark
Antony leading them personally, their confidence in Antony had multiplied. After all, he came from the best of families, and was related on his
mother's side to the Caesars. What was more, the legionaries would have
reminded each other, Antony was reputedly descended from the legendary
warrior and bringer of luck Hercules, son of Jove, king of the gods. A warrior Antony was. Strong and athletic, he looked the part, and when he
addressed his men at assemblies, he sounded the part. There was no rhetoric of philosophy from him, just plain soldier's talk, like General Ventidius. And Antony had developed the common touch. There was a time,

thirteen years back, when Antony had not even wanted to receive deputations from the soldiers under him. Now, older, wiser, he walked among
his soldiers in camp and talked to anyone and everyone no matter what
their rank. Antony would act rashly and impetuously when it came to
major decisions in his life; that habit he would not change. But in recent
times someone he respected must have advised him to win his soldiers'
hearts by being seen to be one of them. Perhaps it had been Ventidius, the
former commoner, before he went home to Rome. And Antony had followed that advice. Now his soldiers felt that while he led them they could
not lose.

They were marching into Atropatene, a western province of Media.
Catching the people of the region completely unawares, they met no
opposition. In the words of Plutarch, the legions laid waste the province.
They emptied every town and village of its food and valuables, and filled
the army's baggage train to overflowing with plunder. That baggage train
consisted of three hundred lumbering wagons and some eleven thousand
pack animals. There was one pack animal for every ten-man squad in the
legions, to carry each squad's tent, grinding stone, and bread-making
equipment. Allied units would have used a similar number. In addition to
food, ammunition, and booty, wagons carried the army's artillery and siege
equipment, including, on this operation, a specially built wheeled battering ram eighty feet long. The Romans called baggage trains *impedimenta*,
from which we get the term impediment, meaning something that slows
us down. While a legion at forced march pace could cover thirty miles a
day, baggage trains slowed an army to the pace of the slowest wagon, and
that could be just a few miles a day.

Unhappy at the slowness of his advance, the impatient Antony
decided to offload the wagons of the baggage train. The mules and packhorses would remain with the army, but the wagons would be left to follow at their own pace. Antony put Brigadier General Oppius Statianus in
charge of the wagon train, and as escort he detached one legion—probably the most recently recruited and inexperienced unit, one he could
spare—and a similar number of allied troops, another six thousand men,
under King Polemon of Pontus. Antony continued with the army at a
much more rapid pace. Statianus had orders to meet him at the city of
Praaspa, capital of Media Atropatene, guided by a native of the city of
Marde, today's Mardin in southeastern Turkey, who knew the area and
Parthian habits.

The king of Media, whose name, like that of the king of Armenia, was
Artavasdes, was by now fully aware of the Roman army's incursion into

his territory. He responded by locking his wives, children, and treasure away at Praaspa, his most formidable fortified city, with a sizable defense force, and by sending messengers galloping south to beg urgent military aid from Phraates, the new king of Parthia. Meanwhile, he took to the field with the Median army. That army consisted mostly of horse archers and heavy cavalry in the Parthian style. But for now, the Medians merely kept watch on the invaders, and noted that Antony had pulled ahead with his main column and left his wagons crawling along behind. In Parthia, King Phraates was quick to respond to his ally's request for help. He personally led an army of tens of thousands of Parthian cavalry that rode north and linked up with the Medians. At Carrhae sixteen years earlier the Parthians had been supported by a column of a thousand camels carrying food, water, and arrows, and a similar supply train would have followed Phraates north.

Without meeting any resistance, Antony arrived at Praaspa, in the northwest of today's Iran. The city gates were closed, and its high stone walls were lined with defenders. The Roman legions quickly dug entrenchments that surrounded the city and cut it off from the outside. Those entrenchments were typically dotted with forts, legion camps, and artillery mounds for their entire length. Antony also commenced work on a giant ramp of earth and stone against one of the city walls. Once that ramp was complete—it would take months for his troops to build it—the legions would be able to march up the ramp and go over the wall and enter the city. It was a slow but certain method, but given enough time it promised a positive result.

Meanwhile, King Phraates led the combined Parthian and Median cavalry armies in a sweep around behind Antony, to catch the wagon train by surprise as it trundled along in the open. The legion and allied troops of the escort attempted to put up a fight, but outnumbered by enemy cavalry four to one, they were quickly and bloodily overrun. The escorting legion was destroyed. General Statianus, the baggage column's commander, died trying to lead the defense. Many of the allied troops were also cut down. It was all over very quickly. Ten thousand soldiers of the escort were butchered. Several thousand more were taken prisoner. The only senior officer spared by the Parthians was King Polemon of Pontus—they would offer to free him on payment of a ransom.

The wagon train's Mardian guide managed to fight his way out of the massacre and ride to Antony at Praaspa with a few companions. Shocked by the news brought by the guide, Antony sent a cavalry force back with the Mardian to check out the state of the wagon train. Where the battle had taken place they found a sea of naked bodies. The Roman dead had been stripped of their clothing and equipment and left where they had fallen. Drilled with arrows, or displaying horrible wounds from lance and sword, the corpses lay bloating in the Median sun. The escort legion's sacred silver eagle and all of its cohort standards had been taken as trophies by the enemy. Nothing of value or use remained. The legions' artillery and siege equipment had been hacked to pieces and burned. The contents of the wagons, including supplies and valuables, had been looted.

When his officers returned with this glum confirmation of the disaster that had befallen Statianus and the wagon train, Antony knew that he was in trouble, on two scores. First, he no longer possessed the heavy equipment he needed to carry out an assault on Praaspa, and with the region's few small trees fit only for firewood, there was not the timber available to build new artillery and siege machines. Second, his troops were now dangerously low on rations.

This major reverse, so early in the campaign, sent a wave of gloom through the Roman army, and King Artavasdes of Armenia decided that it was pointless continuing with the campaign. When he couldn't convince Antony to withdraw the entire army, Artavasdes ordered his troops to pack up and follow him back home to Armenia. Despondently, the men of the 3rd Gallica and the other Roman legions watched the Armenians pull out and march back the way they had come. It was made all the harder to take by the fact that the Armenian king had been the chief promoter of the invasion. And while the reduction of the huge Roman army by thirteen thousand troops need not have a significant impact, the Armenian cavalry were horse archers and heavy cavalry in the Parthian style and would be sorely missed. Antony had planned to use them against the Parthian cavalry, fighting fire with fire. Now the legions had to douse that fire.

The Parthians deliberately let the Armenians withdraw unhindered, to encourage other allies to also desert Antony. As the Armenians went, the combined Parthian-Median army descended on Praaspa. While the main cavalry force stayed just beyond the horizon to the west, skirmishing parties set off to harry Roman detachments scouring the district for food. Others rode to the Roman entrenchments and called out insults to the besiegers.

Antony, worried about fast-diminishing supplies, and impatient to quickly draw the Parthians into a full-scale battle, ordered all ten remaining legions as well as the three Praetorian cohorts and all his cavalry to prepare to march. At dawn, leaving allied troops to man the entrenchments around Praaspa and to keep building the assault ramp, Antony led the Roman troops west, intent on sacking towns and villages in their path for supplies, and hoping to draw the enemy into a decisive full-scale battle. For a solid morning the legions marched, with their baggage animals in the middle of the column as usual. Then, in the afternoon, they pitched a marching camp. Soon, large groups of Parthian and Median cavalry appeared, and hovered close by.

Antony now ordered his standard raised from his *praetorium*, a signal to his troops to prepare for battle; a signal the other side also saw, and recognized. But at the same time, Antony ordered his men to dismantle their tents. The lead elements of the army began to set off toward the southwest, as if heading for Syria and home. The legions fell into place behind. But this time they marched in battle order, not in marching order—they wore their helmets, their shields were on their left arms, and in their right hands they carried several javelins, ready to let loose.

Most of the Parthian-Median army now moved into the path of the Roman column, in a vast crescent formation. This classic formation, used with infantry by generals including the famous Hannibal in the past, was designed to draw attackers into the center of the line, after which the wings would wrap around and complete an encirclement. We don't know the identity of the astute Parthian commander here—King Phraates never personally led his troops in battle and was hanging well back from the scene of the action with his bodyguard unit, letting others command the fighting men.

Antony, riding with his cavalry to the front of the Roman column, ordered his troopers to put themselves between the enemy and his infantry, and to slow their progress enough to allow all the legions to catch up with them. In this way Antony led his army close by the vast enemy half-moon formation. The horsemen stood watching the Romans with fascination. Plutarch says the Parthians greatly admired the legions as they marched close by them with complete discipline, "rank after rank passing on at equal distances and in perfect order and silence." All of a sudden, Antony gave an order. Trumpets sounded. The Roman cavalry wheeled to their right, and with loud cheers, charged the surprised Parthians. The thousands of Roman troopers closed the gap so quickly that the enemy archers didn't even have time to load and fire their bows. Desperately, the Parthians drew their swords, as, tightly packed and outnumbering the Roman cavalry, they held their ground.

In the meantime, the legions had drawn level with the scene of battle. On a trumpeted order, the legionaries also turned right. Now, in their prepared battle lines, they began to advance at the march toward the fighting cavalry. They had received specific instructions about what to do as they made this advance, and with each step they took they rapped their javelins against their shields. The noise the fifty-four thousand legionaries and Praetorians made as they clashed javelin on shield in perfect unison sounded like a succession of thunderclaps. The noise terrified the horses of both sides, but the Parthians, unable to hold their skittish mounts, pulled out of the contest. Even before the Roman infantry could join the fight, the Parthians were galloping away in disorder.

Antony, determined to gain a major victory and end Parthian-Median resistance, ordered most of his troops to give chase. While some men guarded the baggage animals, most of the legionaries followed the fleeing enemy for six miles. The Roman cavalry kept up the chase for twenty miles. But the opposition neither gave up nor attempted to turn and fight. In the end, when Antony recalled his men, the engagement and subsequent chase had only resulted in the deaths of eighty Parthians and the capture of thirty more. As his troops straggled back, Antony ordered them to return to the site of their marching camp for the night.

That night in camp, complaints were beginning to be heard in the legionary ranks. This engagement had been a victory, sure enough, but to what advantage? Yet, when the Parthians had won a victory at the wagon train, it had been total. For now, these complaints were isolated; most men argued that the legions were intact and undefeated.

The next morning the Romans struck camp again. With the baggage animals reassembled and loaded, Antony led the column back toward Praaspa to resume the siege. They were soon being shadowed by parties of Parthian horsemen. The nearer the legions came to Praaspa the larger those parties became, and before long the enemy cavalrymen were dashing in and harassing the marching troops with barrages of arrows. Roman cavalry would drive the attackers off, only for a fresh attack to be launched somewhere else along the line. These mosquito bites caused the Roman troops pain, irritation, and annoyance all the remainder of the way back to the encircled city.

Antony was already in a foul mood after the failure of his latest operation to either secure supplies or inflict a major defeat on the enemy. Now, as his legions filed back into the Praaspa encirclement camps, he learned that the allied troops he'd left at the encirclement had allowed themselves to be surprised by Median raiders from inside the city. The defenders of the assault mound had deserted it, allowing the Medes to cause great damage to the earthworks. Antony ordered the decimation of allied troops involved.

This ancient form of Roman military punishment, which Antony had employed against his own troops twice before, in Italy in 49 B.C. and 44 B.C., had three components. Decimation literally means to reduce by one tenth. All the troops who had deserted the mound were lined up, and they were required to draw lots. One man in ten drew a short straw. The other nine were given wooden cudgels and ordered to beat their unlucky comrade to death. The survivors then had their wheat ration replaced by barley, which was considered greatly inferior to wheat. Decimation could also see the survivors made to sleep outside the walls of their camp, but Antony did not apply that here.

Even as Roman foraging parties were subjected to constant attack, work resumed on building the assault mound. But Antony was beginning to have second thoughts about this entire campaign. It was now late September. The autumnal equinox had just passed, and in these parts the fall brought increasingly cold weather. In winter, snow many feet deep would accumulate here. Antony could not afford to be trapped outside Praaspa.

King Phraates, meanwhile, was having similar concerns. Food was scarce for both sides now. There was also a strong possibility that as the weather closed in, Phraates's soldiers would desert and go home rather than spend the winter in the field. Phraates knew that he either had to beat Antony or make him retreat, and soon. To achieve that, Phraates decided to use psychological warfare. Latin-speakers among his men were included in the skirmishing parties that usually harried Antony's foragers. These men had orders to permit some Romans to carry off supplies if they found them, and to call out to them that they were brave men, that their king considered them the bravest soldiers in the world. Once the Parthians had Roman confidence, they were to ride closer, and then curse Antony for his obstinacy, and declare that their king only wanted peace. Reports of these encounters began to filter back to Antony. Phraates, said his messengers, was ready to parley to save Roman lives, yet Antony allowed his men to sit in their trenches awaiting the two fiercest enemies of all: winter and famine.

Antony saw a possibility of extricating himself from the deepening quagmire without losing face. First, to appear determined to stay, he sent envoys to King Phraates to negotiate the return of the legionary standards captured by the Parthians at the wagon fight, along with the return of King Polemon and the other prisoners. The alternative, the envoys were to tell King Phraates, was unrelenting Roman operations in Media.

Cassius Dio says that when Antony's envoys were escorted into the king's pavilion they found Phraates sitting on a golden throne and twanging the string of his bow. Dio says the young king then lectured the Roman envoys at length about Antony's folly. Once they were finally permitted to present Antony's demands, the Parthian monarch informed the envoys that Antony should not worry about the standards or the prisoners; they were not open to negotiation. But, he said, if Antony wanted to retreat, he could do so at any time in peace and safety. This was the message the envoys took back to Antony.

With the air becoming colder with each passing day and rations running low, Antony decided not to waste any more time with sophistry. Despondent now, he ordered his entire force to prepare to march. It took several days for the camps to be dismantled and the baggage animals loaded up. Normally he would have addressed the troops prior to the march, but Antony was so dejected, his ego was so dented by this graphic admission of failure, he couldn't face his men. Instead, out of shame and sadness, says Plutarch, Antony sent General Ahenobarbus around the camps on the siege perimeter to inform the troops that they were going to march out of Media.

In the ranks, some men of the 3rd Gallica and the other legions resented the fact that Ahenobarbus had been sent to speak to them in Antony's stead. "It undervalues us!" Plutarch says these legionaries declared as they stood at assembly and Ahenobarbus mounted the tribunal. They wanted Antony himself to address them. But others, the majority of the men in the ranks, pitied Antony. Some even argued that they owed him even more respect and obedience because he had made such a difficult but sensible decision in ordering the withdrawal.

Pleased to be pulling out of this inhospitable place, and encouraged by the Parthian king's offer of safe passage, the legionaries packed away their pride with their tents and camp equipment and prepared to commence the retreat.

VII

THE BLOODY RETREAT

O utside, a centurion and a team of legionaries waited to haul down the commander in chief's *praetorium* tent. It hadn't taken long to empty the pavilion of its contents and load them onto pack animals. Most of Antony's expensive furniture had been lost when the wagon train had been taken by the Parthians. Since then, Antony had been using a folding cot, stools, and gold-inlaid folding tables, and a quantity of gold dining plate and jewel-encrusted gold goblets, all of which could be carried on pack mules. His tent, in sections, would be divided among several animals.

Antony, dressed in uniform, gold-decorated armor and scarlet *paludamentum*, the cloak of a republican Roman commander in chief, was preparing to lead the army in retreat. Now, the Mardian guide who had survived the wagon battle was escorted to him, at the guide's request. The Mardian asked if the general was planning to take the same level, almost treeless route out of Media by which he had come. According to Plutarch, when Antony said that was the case, the guide earnestly shook his head.

"General, keep the mountains close on your right hand," he urged.

"Why?" responded Antony.

It would be fatal, said the Mardian, to expose his men to the Parthian cavalry in the open country. "Phraates with his promises has persuaded you to give up the siege deliberately, so that he can easily cut you off in your retreat. With your permission, I will guide the army by a nearer, safer route, one on which you will also find more provisions." This route, he said, was both shorter and more inhabited.

Antony didn't want to be seen to be mistrusting the Parthians after Phraates had promised him safe passage. But he would have remembered a famous incident in 54 B.C., when he was on Caesar's staff during the conquest of Gaul. A Roman force that included the 14th Legion had been camped in Belgium for the winter. Surrounded by an enemy army, the

Roman general in charge had taken the enemy's word of safe passage if he withdrew. The Roman force had subsequently been ambushed as it pulled out, and wiped out.

Antony was attracted to the idea of a shorter and more inhabited route. But what if the guide was a traitor? "What assurance can you give me that you are being truthful?" he demanded.

The Mardian answered by offering to ride with his arms bound until the Roman army succeeded in reaching the safety of Armenia. Antony took him up on his offer, ordering the guide bound and put under guard.

They were into the third day of the march. Following the route designated by the bound Mardian guide, who rode at the head of the column with Antony, the Roman army had gone unmolested, without a sign of the Parthians. Antony was so impressed that he now ordered the Mardian freed of his leather bonds. And he allowed the legions to march in loose order instead of keeping precisely to their ranks and files—which took some concentration and effort—permitting various units to mix and talk among themselves as they marched. Antony himself, says Plutarch, now ceased to worry about the threat posed by the Parthians, being convinced that King Phraates had kept his word.

But as the third morning of the retreat passed and the column's lead elements reached a river, the guide became worried. He pointed to where the bank of the river had been cut away, so that the waters overflowed onto the road they were taking. That, he told Antony, had been done deliberately, to slow the Roman progress. "The enemy are close by, General," the guide cautioned Antony.

Trusting the Mardian's warning, Antony commanded battle order to be assumed and instructed his slingers and dartmen—allied troops equipped with short throwing javelins called darts—to assemble at various places along the column, ready for immediate action. No sooner had this been done than Parthian horse archers came charging from the undergrowth. The slingers and dartmen took a number of casualties from Parthian arrows, but their own missiles wounded many of the attackers. The Parthians withdrew, only to regroup and launch a new assault. This time they were met by a squadron of Gallic cavalry, which quickly drove them off. The Parthians were not seen for the remainder of the day. But it was clear that the enemy had no intention of allowing the Romans to escape unmolested.

During the afternoon, the men of the 3rd Gallica joined other legions in building a marching camp. That night, as they sat around their campfires, eating bread soaked with olive oil, their standard ration, they reminded each other that Parthians famously would not fight by night. At least, the legionaries told each other, they would get a good night's sleep.

The next day, with no sign of the Parthians and with their water containers filled from the river, the legions forded the waterway and continued southwest toward the Araxes River, today's Aras, which constituted the border between Armenia and Media. Expecting more Parthian attacks, Antony now formed the marching column into a hollow square or box formation, with legions and allied infantry on all sides of the box. Because they had proven so effective in repelling the enemy, he placed his slingers and dartmen as rear guard and also on the outside of the two flanks. Some of the cavalry scouted ahead, but most moved inside the square with the baggage animals, under orders to break out and chase off any party of Parthian horsemen who attacked the column, although they were instructed not to chase far, to prevent them from being lured into a trap. Antony himself marched at the head of the square, with the 3rd Gallica Legion.

For four days the army of ninety thousand men made its way south in this vast, unwieldy but effective box formation, with the weather growing colder each day and the legionaries wrapping their blood-red cloaks around them on the march. Each day they were hounded by parties of Parthian cavalry that darted in, let fly a cloud of arrows, then galloped away again followed by a barrage of missiles and squadrons of pursuing Roman cavalry. Antony and his men did not know it, but the Parthian cavalrymen, growing tired of achieving nothing with these hit-and-run tactics, were complaining to their officers that winter was closing in, and pressed for the order to give up the pursuit and return home.

In the Roman ranks, Brigadier General Flavius Gallus, a divisional commander, had taken enough of this unending harassment. Unaware that the Parthians were losing heart, on the fifth day since leaving the river General Gallus approached Antony with a proposal. "Give me some light infantry out of the rear and some cavalry out of the advance guard, Commander, and I'll do the enemy considerable damage."

Knowing young Gallus to be brave and energetic, and being himself equally as anxious to get the Parthians off their backs, Antony agreed. So General Gallus selected a detachment of light infantry and several squadrons of cavalry totaling some three thousand men. The next time the Parthians attacked the rear of the column, Gallus led his force out in a counterattack that drove the enemy back. But instead of retreating to the main column as it marched on, Gallus held his ground and continued to attack the surprised enemy. At first this bold strategy warmed the hearts of the Roman officers commanding in the rear of the box formation, but as the army continued on, the distance between them and Gallus's force increased, until the latter were out of sight.

Major General Canidius and other worried officers in charge at the rear now sent messengers galloping to Gallus to urge him to rejoin the main force. But Gallus was enjoying himself, and ignored them. Brigadier General Marcus Titius, the quartermaster, then personally rode back to Gallus and tried to convince him to withdraw at once. According to Plutarch, Titius declared, "You are leading many brave men to destruction, Gallus!"

But Gallus countered that he was acting on Mark Antony's authority and would not retreat.

Furious, the short-tempered Titius grabbed the standard of a cavalry unit from its startled mounted standard-bearer and turned it around, and then did the same with another, yelling to the men around him that this was now the direction they should be heading—back to the main column.

"Stand firm!" Gallus ordered his men. They all obeyed.

As the frustrated Titius returned to the column alone, Gallus led a fresh charge at the nearby enemy, who withdrew. As Gallus and his men enthusiastically gave chase, a large Parthian force appeared from nowhere and galloped in behind him, sealing his detachment off from the main Roman army. Soon completely surrounded, and with his cavalry close to wiped out, Gallus now realized his folly. As his trapped survivors fought for their lives, he sent a messenger, who managed to gallop off as the Parthians withdrew from one of their attacking runs, and that messenger reached General Canidius with a plea for help.

Annoyed that only now did Gallus acknowledge his error, Canidius dispatched two or three legion cohorts and some troops of cavalry to relieve him. When these cohorts reached the embattled force in the rear they were overwhelmed by Parthian cavalry. Some of these men fled back to the main column. So Canidius sent several more cohorts and a few more troopers, and these, too, were chewed up like mincemeat. Again survivors came panting back, reporting the bloodshed they had escaped. Failing to learn from his mistakes, Canidius sent yet another relatively small force back, with the same inevitable bloody result. All the time, more and more Parthians were arriving, attracted like vultures to carrion, seeing now an opportunity to destroy the Roman army piecemeal.

Only now did Mark Antony learn of the carnage in his rear. Immediately, he ordered the column to make camp for the night and instructed the 3rd Gallica Legion to turn around and march with him to the rear.

With Antony at their head, the legion passed through the box and to the scene of heavy fighting around Gallus. The 3rd Gallica, in perfect formation, spread the Parthians in their path, marched through the body-strewn position being held by their previously surrounded comrades, and with flailing swords resolutely pushed the enemy back, saving the day.

Behind Antony and the 3rd Gallica came baggage animals that had been stripped of their loads. Using these beasts and the horses of dead cavalrymen, five thousand Roman wounded from Gallus's fight were carried away to the camp being built to the southwest. General Gallus himself was among the seriously wounded. The few unharmed survivors also scurried back, while the 3rd Gallica continued to protect the rear. Then the men of the Gallica also rejoined the column at the campsite, marching in perfect order. They had to leave three thousand dead Romans, victims of Gallus's folly, strewn on the field.

Once the army's tents were up, Antony went around all the wounded as they lay on their bedrolls. At every tent where wounded men lay, Antony stooped to talk with his soldiers. Men with terrible wounds, many of them mere boys, grasped his hand. Plutarch says they had looks of joy on their faces because Mark Antony had come to see them.

"Go see to yourself, General," said one legionary after another, Plutarch writes. "Don't worry about us."

"If you do well, General," said one wounded soldier, "then we will be safe."

Before long there were tears in Antony's eyes. He ordered that nothing was to be spared to make the wounded as comfortable as possible, as he realized that his men had become devoted to him, despite the fact that the army was in retreat. General Gallus, the cause of all this new misery, had four Parthian arrows through his body. Gallus didn't last the night. During that night, the sentries on the camp walls saw Parthians lingering close to the camp, defying the stories that the Parthians were afraid of the darkness.

By dawn, fresh columns of Parthian cavalry had arrived on the scene. King Phraates, although he himself still remained some distance from the action, sent every man at his disposal, including his elite personal bodyguard, unit to finish off the Romans. In excess of forty thousand enemy cavalry were now outside Antony's camp—more than four times the number who had destroyed Crassus's army a little farther south in 53 B.C. No longer were the Parthian horse soldiers talking about going home. The heavy Roman casualties of the previous day had convinced them that Antony's army was on the ropes. They were certain that Antony would now have to abandon his thousands of baggage animals to enable him to march light and fast for the Aras. And they slavered at the prospect of the plunder—not only the animals but also all that they would be carrying.

With the dawn, Antony called for an assembly. He considered wearing a black cloak, as if in mourning for the Romans who lay dead out in the Median countryside thanks to Gallus's impetuosity. But his staff talked him out of it as being too theatrical. Instead, he climbed onto the tribunal in his scarlet commander in chief's cloak. He began by praising the men of the 3rd Gallica for the courage and resolution that had saved him and the army the previous day.

"We promise you, we will be successful against the Parthians, General," called a legionary of the 3rd Gallica, and his comrades roared their agreement.

Nodding his approval, Antony turned to the surviving legionaries of the cohorts sent to Gallus by General Canidius, and condemned them for fleeing back to the main column and not standing and fighting, despite the odds they had faced. Feeling ashamed of themselves, these men called on Antony to decimate them, or punish them any other way he saw fit, but to then forgive them and forget their brief failure. In response to this, Antony raised his hands to the sky and prayed to the gods.

"If you have any judgment in store," he cried to the heavens, "to balance the many favors you have done me, rain that judgment down on my head alone, and grant my soldiers victory."

The assembled legionaries chorused their support for their general. Without ordering any punishment of the previous day's wrongdoers, Antony ordered his men to prepare to resume the march to the Aras, and left the tribunal. Industriously his troops dismantled the camp and loaded up the baggage animals, with every man determined to prove that he was worthy of Mark Antony's fondest hopes and praise.

In good order, the army marched from the dismantled camp and headed southwest, through hilly country. Seeing the Romans on the move, the tens of thousands of Parthian cavalrymen converged on the site of the abandoned camp, only to be disappointed. The Romans had taken all the baggage animals with them. They had left behind some tents, grinding stones, and other camp implements; for the thousands of Roman wounded were now being carried on the backs of baggage animals and the mounts of dead cavalrymen. But these were not the spoils the Parthians had been hoping for. Angrily, they gave chase. But when they came up on the Roman column they were met by a shower of missiles. The Romans were obviously far from dispirited.

Shadowing the column for a time, the Parthians saw that the Roman army's path would take it down a steep hill from the plateau to lower ground. When the Roman army broke step and slowed to go down the hillside, the Parthians struck, charging into the rear of the column in vast numbers. The slingers and dartmen of the rear guard took the brunt of the downhill drive and received the clouds of Parthian arrows. Unable to hold their ground, these lightly armed allied troops fell back to the legions. The Parthians pressed home their attack.

Now, with their light infantry made ineffective, the Roman legionaries used a tactic new to the Parthians. Cassius Dio gave no credit to Mark Antony or his officers for this tactic. He says it was the legionaries themselves who conceived it. As the slingers and dartmen slipped through the gaps in the legionary line to reach the comparative safety inside the box, centurions barked commands, and the legionaries of the rear line turned to face the Parthian attack. Every man of the very last rank then dropped onto his left knee and placed his shield upright in front of him, with the bottom edge on the ground. The men of the next rank closed up and held their shields over the men of the first rank. The legionaries of the next rank raised their shields even higher, and locked them with those of the men in front of them. And so it went, back through the ranks. Plutarch likened the effect to the interlocked tiling of a house's roof, or the banked rows of seats in a theater.

This was a variation on the legion formation called the *testudo*, or tortoise, which was normally used in assaults on fortified positions, with men hacking at gates and walls from beneath the shelter of the shields of their comrades. Cassius Dio, himself a Roman lieutenant general with considerable experience leading legions, was to say that the testudo was so strong that men could walk on it. He had even known horses and vehicles to be driven over a testudo of shields being held aloft by legionaries. As a defense against archers, he says, an entire Roman army column could be covered by a testudo. In that event, legionaries would form a rectangle and create the outer rim, with auxiliaries, cavalry, and the baggage train in the middle. He says that Roman cavalry horses were trained to lie down on command, and that auxiliaries would raise their flat shields in the middle of a testudo to also cover themselves, the horses, and the baggage train, so the entire column was covered by one complete tortoiseshell.

Now, says Plutarch, Parthian arrows simply glanced off the firm shell of interlocked shields that confronted them. But the Parthians, seeing ranks of Roman legionaries on their knees, thought the Romans were either exhausted or wounded. Laying aside their bows, Dio says, the horse archers drew their short swords, jumped down from their horses, and attacked the shield line on foot. To the astonishment of the overeager Parthians, the legionaries of the front rank suddenly rose to their feet as one, and with a great cry launched themselves at the dismounted archers. Without armor or shields, the Parthians at the forefront of the attack were cut down in droves. Those behind them fled in terror. The Parthian attack was broken up with heavy casualties.

As the march continued over the next few days, Parthians still harried the rear and flanks of the column, but they had lost their enthusiasm for the fight. Now the Parthians were not the Romans' main enemies. Hunger and exhaustion were weakening Antony's troops; each day the distance they covered was less than that of the day before. Men began to dream about food. To Roman legionaries, meat was considered merely a supplement, and no one considered butchering mules or horses for food. The staple diet of the legionary was bread, and each ten-man squad of a legion ground its own wheat to make flour, then baked bread at its tent—there was no mess hall in a Roman camp.

The wheat ration had by this time in the retreat become so small that men began to fight over it, accusing each other of stealing their ration or of having more than they were entitled to. Many squads had left their grinding stones behind so wounded could be carried on their mules, and squads with stones began charging for their use, or charging to make bread for other squads. Meanwhile, some men hoarded their rations, to sell at inflated prices. Plutarch says that a quart of wheat was now selling in camp for 50 sesterces, or almost three weeks' wages for a legionary, while loaves made from barley, considered inferior to corn bread, were selling for their weight in silver.

Hungry men will eat anything, and Antony's legionaries began digging up native vegetables and roots and trying to eat them. Most of these were inedible. Some were fatal. One particular herb affected the mind, emptying the head of memory and reason. As they camped beside a river, the men of the 3rd Gallica saw comrades who had eaten this herb mindlessly moving and stacking large stones, acting as if the task was of the greatest importance. The army's medical attendants had only one antidote for poison: wine. But this failed to help these particular men, who vomited bile, then died horribly within a few days of eating the unidentified deadly herb.

Roman foraging parties were now approached by enemy horsemen who told them the Parthians were going back south, to their homes and families. The Parthians said that a few Median troops would follow the retreating column for another two or three days to protect some villages ahead, but after that the Romans could expect an unhindered passage to Armenia. Based on this information, and hearing from his guide that the mountain route offered few chances of obtaining water, Antony was thinking seriously about leaving the mountains and going down to the plains, which offered a quicker, more direct route out of Media. Then, in the early evening, Mithradates, a Parthian nobleman, arrived at the Roman camp. The cousin of a Parthian defector who had previously been granted asylum in Syria by Antony, Mithradates claimed, through an interpreter who spoke Syriac, an Aramaic dialect used widely in the East, that King Phraates wanted Antony to take the plains route.

"It is there," Plutarch records Mithradates saying, pointing to hills lining the distant plain as he spoke, "that the entire Parthian army lies in wait for you." If Antony did leave the mountains, he said, the Parthian cavalry would sweep down and catch his army in the open. "If you cross the plains," he told the interpreter, "Antony must expect the same fate as Crassus."

This reference to Crassus would have sent a chill down Antony's spine once the message was relayed to him. Calling a council of war of his senior officers, he sent for the Mardian guide. The Mardian expressed the same opinion as the Parthian informant: stick to the mountains. He agreed that there was no water immediately ahead, but they would reach a river within a day's march. Antony's officers agreed that the mountain route was the safer course, so Antony, remembering that Julius Caesar had been fond of night marches to fool the enemy, ordered the army to pack up and march at once. Every man was instructed to take as much water as he could carry for his own use.

Through the night the Roman army stumbled, exhausted, and guided only by moonlight. Many soldiers had no water containers, so some had fashioned gourds from skins. Others carried their upturned helmets slopping with water as they marched. Struggling through the night, the Romans could hear, and sometimes see, Parthian cavalry following them. Driven on by Antony, his troops covered thirty miles that night. As dawn was breaking, a large force of enemy horse archers launched an assault on the rear of the column. Clearly the Parthians had not gone home, and Mithradates's warning had been valid.

Roman troops in the rear, cross-eyed from lack of sleep and dejected because the Parthians wouldn't relent, put up a weary defense. Meanwhile, the advance guard reached the river that had been the goal of their forced march. The water was cool and clear, but still and brackish. The first men to drink from it were immediately struck by pains in the bowels, and their thirst raged even more intensely. Despite this, more men pushed aside those who tried to keep them back from the river, drank the tainted water, and also became ill. Antony dashed from place to place along the river-bank, urging his men not to drink from the river. He told them that according to the Mardian guide, there was another river not far ahead. It was reached over stony ground that would make it difficult for the Parthian horses to continue the pursuit. In the end most of his men lis-tened and the river was boycotted as tents were erected to create shade for the wounded and the weary.

The tents had been up only a short while when Mithradates the informer came to Antony again and urged him not to stay here. Press on at once to the next river, he said, because King Phraates had promised his unhappy troops that he would not make them pursue the Romans beyond that river. In thanks for this advice, Antony gave Mithradates all the golden tableware he could hide under his clothes. As the Parthian slipped away, Antony ordered his weary troops to pick themselves up and march to the next river. This, he promised the men of the 3rd Gallica and his other legions, would be the last challenge.

The exhausted army covered only a few miles more before Antony saw that his men were dead on their feet. He called a halt. A new camp was erected and the army settled down for the night. Antony himself had just dropped off to sleep when there was a commotion next to his bedchamber that awoke him with a jerk. Thinking that the Parthians must be in the camp, Antony jumped up as Rhamnus, the powerful freedman in charge of his guard, barred the tent entrance. Antony made Rhamnus promise to run him through with his sword and then chop off his head and hide it rather than let him fall into Parthian hands—alive or dead. But it turned out that a party of his own soldiers had lost their heads and run amok, breaking into Antony's pavilion and hacking up his gold-inlaid tables and jewel-encrusted gold goblets for the spoils. With these men soon subdued by Antony's guards and dragged off to face a court-martial in front of their tribunes, the camp, previously in tumult, returned to a peaceful state.

At dawn, as the army began the march once more, and as the Romans came out of the rocky country, the Parthian cavalry reappeared and threw itself on the column's rear one more time. Once again, the Roman rear guard formed a testudo that entirely frustrated the Parthians, who didn't attempt to attack on foot this time. This permitted the Roman vanguard to reach the river that had been beckoning for days. Here, Antony lined up his cavalry along the riverbank, facing the enemy, while, at a fording place, the Roman wounded were carried across and landed on the far side, where a camp was established. The river water was clear and clean, and the Romans and their allies gratefully drank their fill without adverse affect.

Parthian cavalry shadowed the rear guard, and as the last legionaries were preparing to cross the river under the protection of their cavalry, Latin-speakers among the Parthians called out to them that they were now truly going home and the valorous Romans could depart without further fear. Long after the Parthian horsemen had melted away, the Roman troops were edgy and on their guard, for they had heard this sort of story from the lying Parthians many times before.

But when they set off for the Aras again the next day, there was no sign of the enemy. For six more days they marched, unmolested, until at last they reached their destination, and crossed the Aras River into Armenia. Once on Armenian soil, the men of the 3rd Gallica and the other legions dropped to their knees and gratefully kissed the ground.

The retreat from Praaspa had been twenty-seven days of pure hell, during which they had fought eighteen running battles with the Parthians and survived lack of food, deadly plants, and poisoned water. The 3rd's young men from Gaul looked at each other and shook their heads. When they had started out on this campaign back in the summer they had been clean-shaven, fit, and healthy, and their equipment had gleamed. Now each man had a shaggy beard, his cheeks were sunken, and his eyes were red. Every man had lost many pounds in weight. His torn tunic and cloak were filthy with dirt, sweat, and blood. His belts and scabbards, once shining at assembly, were grimy, and his shield was battered and holed by arrows. The legions had lost plenty of personal property, from the wagon train and on the march. And they had come out of Media without a sesterce's worth of booty. Yet, for all that, unlike Crassus's army back in 53 B.C., they were alive and had not disgraced themselves. Shedding tears of joy, they embraced each other. Plutarch was to liken the feelings of the Roman troops on the crossing of the Aras to that of men sighting land after surviving a storm at sea.

The Parthian storm had passed, yet a new storm was about to batter Mark Antony's army, for once they were in Armenia, foraging parties returned laden with food from plentiful Armenian towns, and men who had existed for weeks on just a crust of bread each day gorged themselves with food and drank until they could eat or drink no more. Dysentery and other afflictions, including edema, a symptom of starvation, were rife in the Roman camp. First to succumb were the thousands of wounded, who were too weak to stave off illness. Within days, men were dying in their hundreds. When Antony called an assembly, his tribunes reported that twenty thousand infantry and four thousand cavalry had died in the campaign, from wounds or from illness.

Despite these appalling casualty figures, Antony was determined to claim that his campaign against the Parthians had been a victory. He sent messengers to Octavian in Rome and Cleopatra in Alexandria with the story that he had subjected both Armenia and Media. Octavian would soon know differently, as did Antony's senior supporters at Rome, including Generals Sossius and Pollio, for stories of the disastrous Parthian campaign reached Italy from Syria the following spring with the first cargo vessels of the sailing season. Octavian, to preserve his treaty with Antony, and urged by his sister Octavia to preserve Antony's reputation, would suppress these stories at Rome.

Meanwhile, as some of the allied kings led their contingents back to their own countries, Antony led the legions south through icy passes, determined to quickly return to Syria, where he had agreed that Cleopatra should join him for the winter. Now, too, the snows came, and the army struggled on in their military sandals and with bare legs, battling freezing cold and illness. Over these harrowing weeks, Antony lost another eight thousand men to sickness and the elements. The losses from his grand Parthian campaign came to total thirty-two thousand soldiers—legionaries, allied troops, and cavalry. The operation had proven a costly mistake. And a humiliating one, for, while Antony was in retreat in the East, in the West, Octavian and his best friend and best general, Marcus Agrippa, had defeated Sextus Pompey in a series of naval battles and land actions in Sicily. Octavian had subsequently brought Sicily and Sardinia into his realm of control, and had consolidated young Pompey's legions and those of Marcus Lepidus into his own army. Sextus, meanwhile, was fleeing east, hoping to find sanctuary with Antony. Octavian, at just twenty-eight years of age, was more powerful than he had ever been. And Antony was reeling from a reverse that had cost him thirty-two thousand men and considerable prestige.

On reaching Syria, Antony camped his troops on the coast between Beirut and Sidon as he waited impatiently for Cleopatra to arrive, and drank heavily. When Cleopatra joined him she brought clothing for his troops, and money—although not enough money to meet his needs. Borrowing from friends and allies, Antony added to Cleopatra's funds and handed out a bonus of 400 sesterces to every surviving soldier of his legions, to make up for the lack of booty from the campaign.

To the men of the 3rd Gallica Legion, this bonus went some way toward compensating for the disastrous summer and fall, as did the promise from Antony that he was not yet finished with Parthia—he would need the 3rd Gallica again before long, he assured them. Antony's ego was such that he would not let the sickly stripling Octavian outdo him.

And as the 3rd Gallica Legion wintered in Syria, its men found that their unit's reputation as the legion that had saved Mark Antony and his army from the Parthians was spreading far and wide.

VIII

THE SUN-
WORSHIPPING 3RD

T he 3rd Gallica was on the road north once more, swinging up the highway in marching order at the head of another massive Roman army, and in good spirits. It was 34 B.C., and Mark Antony was marching into Armenia.

The men of the Gallica and Antony's other legions had been given twelve months to recover from the rigors of the failed Median operation. Over those twelve months, too, Antony had rebuilt his army. The previous year, young Sextus Pompey had landed in Asia after fleeing his defeats at the hands of Octavian in Sicily. When Sextus had found Antony's governors far from welcoming, he had raised three legions from retired legionaries who had been settled in Asia by his father, Pompey the Great, some years before. He had also sent envoys to the king of Parthia, offering to serve as a general in his army. He then started hostilities against Antony's officials. Intercepting the envoys, Antony had learned of Sextus's offer to the Parthians. His generals had hounded Sextus until, lacking cavalry and with his mature troops losing heart, he had surrenderedto General Marcus Titius, throwing himself on Antony's mercy. The no-nonsense Titius had promptly cut off Sextus's head, ending the Pompey dynasty once and for all. After that, Antony had incorporated Sextus's three legions into his army, and by recruiting more new units in eastern provinces he brought the number of legions now marching for him up to sixteen.

The men of the 3rd Gallica had high hopes for this campaign. In the new year their sixteen-year enlistment would be up, and all the men of the legion who chose to do so would retire. This last operation was their opportunity to top up their by now substantial savings, to guarantee a comfortable retirement on plots of land they expected their general to provide for them, as had become the custom for retiring legionaries.

Once again, the 3rd Gallica was marching toward Media. But this time the Medes were to be their allies. In the ever-changing politics of the East, King Artavasdes of Media had the previous year fallen out with mean young King Phraates of Parthia. The Median king had subsequently sent envoys to Mark Antony proposing an alliance and a joint war against Parthia. To show his good faith, he had released King Polemon of Pontus, whom he had been holding for ransom since his capture at the destruction of Antony's wagon train, and sent him to Antony. Anxious to redeem his reputation after his last campaign, Antony had quickly agreed to the Median alliance. With massive contributions to his war chest by Cleopatra, he had made preparations for the new operation over the winter of 35–34 B.C. And now here he was, making his latest bid for military glory. Antony had agreed to meet the king of Media at the Aras River, and from there their two armies would march southeast together to invade Parthia, where King Phraates was experiencing considerable internal troubles.

Enjoying good spring weather, Antony's revitalized Roman army entered Armenia. Antony sent envoys to King Artavasdes of Armenia with messages of friendship, inviting him to a meeting and offering him a variety of incentives. According to Plutarch, legionaries who had survived the previous year's disastrous campaign blamed the Armenian king's withdrawal from Antony's force for the campaign's failure. So they were delighted when, after Artavasdes arrived at Antony's camp, Antony accused him of betrayal, arrested him, and clapped him in irons. He now divided up Artavasdes's kingdom, giving the western part, Lesser Armenia, to King Polemon of Pontus. Antony led his army on, and at the Aras River he kept his rendezvous with the king of Media and his army. But Antony suddenly lost interest in the Parthians. Possibly he didn't trust his new Median allies. But most of all, Octavian was playing on his mind.

Before Antony had set out on this latest campaign, messages had reached him to say that his wife, Octavia, had arrived at Athens, bringing two thousand of Octavian's Praetorians as a gift for Antony, and that Octavia wanted to talk to him. When Antony thought of going to Greece to see Octavia, Cleopatra, jealous of Octavia and of her influence over Antony, had used her best acting skills to pretend illness and keep Antony by her side. And once he set out on this latest operation, again she had accompanied Antony to the brink of hostile territory. By now, Antony was worried by Octavian's consolidation of power at Rome. Octavian had sent him a message refusing to share any of the spoils from his victory over Sextus Pompey unless Antony shared Armenia with him. And he had told him that he would not provide land in Italy for the men of Antony's veteran legions who would be retiring the following year, including the men of the 3rd Gallica, even though he would be giving land to his own men in Italy. Now that Antony was master of Armenia, Media, and Parthia, as he claimed, said Octavian facetiously, Antony could settle his retiring troops there.

Antony decided to pull out of the invasion of Parthia. To conciliate King Artavasdes of Media and cement an alliance between them, Antony agreed to betroth his son by Cleopatra, Alexander, to the daughter of the Median king. Both were still only children, but Roman marriage laws allowed women to marry at twelve, and men at fifteen.

Antony then returned to Alexandria with Cleopatra, taking the chained Armenian king, Artavasdes, with him. There he conducted a pseudo-Triumph through the streets of the Egyptian capital, celebrating himself as conqueror of Armenia and Media. At the end of the parade, the Egyptians executed King Artavasdes. Several days later, in a fabulous ceremony in Alexandria, Antony gave Cleopatra the title Queen of Kings, and to her son by Julius Caesar, Caesarion, the title King of Kings. And he bestowed various eastern territories on the two sons and a daughter whom Antony had fathered to Cleopatra. This entire episode upset many at Rome and lost Antony numerous friends. His legions, meanwhile, were not happy either—the summer had been unprofitable for them.

In the spring of 33 B.C., the surviving men of the 3rd Gallica Legion received their discharges and went into honorable retirement. Antony gave them plots of land in the Roman East, although exactly where we don't know. Of fifty acres each, these little farms would be the new homes of the soldiers from Gaul who had fought so resolutely for Caesar and Antony for the past sixteen years and gained for themselves an enviable reputation.

To replace the retiring Gallicans, Antony conscripted a new levy in Syria that spring. Some of the legion's centurions would stay on, and one or two men from the old enlistment would volunteer to sign on for another enlistment with the legion, preferring the dangers of military life to the unexciting farming life. But the majority of the legion's six thousand men were new Syrian recruits. All had one thing in common: they were worshippers of the Syrian sun god Baal. The Romans tolerated foreign gods, and absorbed them into the Roman pantheon. Baal, an ancient Egyptian deity, was identified by the Greeks with Zeus, king of the gods, and the followers of Baal considered him King of the Heavens. Baal, also called El Gebal, was worshipped throughout Syria, although his cult was centered on Emesa, the later Homs, in central Syria, 120 miles north of

Damascus. There, a line of priest-kings ruled the Emesa city-state within the confines of the Roman province of Syria.

A bull calf was sacred to the followers of Baal, so that the 3rd Gallica legion's bull symbol was more than appropriate, and was retained by the legion. Even its Gallica title was retained, despite the now very Syrian complexion of the legion. Legion battle honors had begun to play an important role in a unit's esprit de corps. And the 3rd Gallica's battle honors over the past sixteen years were worthy of celebration and emulation.

More than twenty legions in Antony's and Octavian's armies came up for discharge in this year of 33 B.C.—all were units raised by Julius Caesar in 49 B.C. in the early days of the civil war. But only after Antony had paid off his retiring legionaries and sent them marching to their retirement plots, and had contracted brand-new enlistments in their place, did he learn that Octavian had held off letting his men retire. Antony had seen what happened when Caesar kept men in service long after they were due for discharge—several times during the civil war his legions had mutinied. He would have been hoping that Octavian would bring himself similar troubles. But with the five-year treaty between Antony and Octavian soon to run out, most troubling of all to Antony was the indication that Octavian was keeping his veteran troops in uniform for a specific reason, to send them against a specific opponent. And Antony could only think of one such opponent: himself.

Two years had passed. For the Syria-born Romans of the 3rd Gallica legion, life had changed dramatically. It was the summer of 31 B.C. Mark Antony and Cleopatra had fought a naval battle against the fleet of Octavian at Actium, on the southwestern coast of Greece, and, losing most of their ships, had broken out and retreated to Egypt. The majority of Antony's legions had been in his camp onshore with General Canidius. Soon surrounded by Octavian's legions after Antony had deserted them, they sat for days behind their camp walls. After a week of this standoff, General Canidius fled. The officers of the 3rd Gallica and the other eleven legions in the camp then commenced negotiations with Octavian, and soon went over to him. While Octavian abolished and combined some of Antony's older units, he retained legions such as the 3rd Gallica in his army because their men were provincials and had been serving for only several years and still had many years of their enlistment left to run.

The following summer, after the 3rd Gallica had marched to Egypt as part of Octavian's army, Antony and Cleopatra committed suicide at Alexandria once Antony's remaining troops were beaten or surrendered without a fight.

Antony, a swashbuckling, hard-drinking, hard-living soldier, yet a man who had been dominated by his mother, two wives, and his mistress Cleopatra, would go down in history as a famous lover and a famous loser. Pompey the Great had once described him as a "feckless nobody." Cicero had called him "odious." Caesar's staff officer Aulus Hirtius considered him "treacherous." On the other hand, to those who followed him, Antony was heroic, charismatic, and irrepressible. Mark Antony was a man of many talents, but at the same time he could be lazy, covetous, and rash. In politics he had made a loyal and earnest subordinate. Yet, having climbed to power as a favorite of Caesar, he mishandled that power and as a leader served himself and those who supported him badly. Plutarch was to say that Antony owed his military successes not to good generalship but to good generals—subordinates such as Ventidius, Canidius, Sossius, and Titius. In war he was fierce and fearless, and had a total belief in himself. Unlike many a general, he always led from the front, was always in the thick of the fighting. It was this latter quality that endeared him to his troops, which won him the loyalty and esteem of the 3rd Gallica and his other legions.

Octavian, who would before long become known as Augustus, was now sole ruler of the Roman Empire. The 3rd Gallica Legion had a new master and a new future, stationed at the old citadel of Apamea in Syria as one of twenty-eight legions in Augustus's new standing army. Because the Gallicans were worshippers of Baal, from now on the pay of the men of the 3rd Gallica would be minted at the nearby city-state of Emesa. There, the king of Emesa, who was also high priest of Baal, maintained his own separate army of several thousand infantry and cavalry.

They may have a new master and a new home, but the legion's soldiers would not forget Mark Antony, just as the Roman world would not forget the 3rd Gallica.

IX

RIOT DUTY
IN JERUSALEM

G arrison duty at Jerusalem was irksome for the men of the 3rd
Gallica Legion. It was almost as if they were prisoners in the Jewish city. The year was A.D. 58, and the men of this enlistment of
Mark Antony's famous legion had just two years to go before they could
take their retirement.

Like the men of the legion's 33 B.C. enlistment, these legionaries were
natives of Syria, Roman citizens, and worshippers of Baal. Unlike the 33 B.C.
recruits, these soldiers were serving twenty-year enlistments. Between 10 B.C.
and A.D. 6, the emperor Augustus had increased the enlistment periods of
all his legions as their discharges fell due, from sixteen to twenty years. So
in 1 B.C., when the 3rd Gallica underwent its latest discharge, the term for
new recruits in its mass reenlistment had been upped to twenty years, just
as the term for men of the elite Praetorian Guard would be increased from
twelve to sixteen years. This had not gone down well with the legions, and
in A.D. 14, on the death of Augustus, riots had broken out in legions in Pannonia and on the Rhine, as legionaries who were mostly draftees demanded
a return to the old sixteen-year enlistment term. Germanicus Caesar, commander on the Rhine, had granted this demand, but within a year his
uncle and adoptive father, the new emperor Tiberius, overturned his decision, and the legionary enlistment period was confirmed at twenty years.

Most of the current legionaries of the 3rd Gallica were men who had
been enlisted in A.D. 40. But some, in the senior cohorts, had joined the
legion back in A.D. 20 and had volunteered for a second enlistment in
A.D. 40 so that they would celebrate forty years in the ranks by the time
the A.D. 60 discharge arrived.

Augustus had remodeled his legions once he established his standing
army. Now each legion consisted of nine cohorts each of 480 men and the

1st Cohort, of 800 men, plus a legion cavalry squadron of 124 officers and men. Instead of being commanded by tribunes, a legion's commander was normally a *legatus*, a brigadier general. As its second in command, each legion had a senior tribune, a "tribune of the broad stripe," also known as a "military tribune," the equivalent of a full colonel today. The two legions stationed in Egypt and the legion stationed in Judea were commanded by their senior tribunes, not a general. This was because the Roman governor in Egypt was a prefect, and the Roman governor in Judea was now a procurator. Both were outranked by a brigadier general, and a subordinate could not very well give orders to a superior.

The third most senior officer in the legion after its senior tribune held the new imperial rank of camp prefect, the modern-day equivalent being a major. Promoted from centurion, he was quartermaster of the legion and also led large detachments as required. Five junior tribunes, "tribunes of the thin stripe," served with the legion as officer cadets. We can best equate their rank with that of lieutenant colonel. These were young men of eighteen and nineteen, members of the Equestrian Order, the sons of Roman nobility just starting on the military/civil service ladder. A new batch of junior tribunes arrived each spring to join the legion, for just one season.

Legionaries in A.D. 58 were equipped much as their Antonian-era forebears had been—the same red tunics and cloaks, and similar helmets, although helmet plumes were now worn only on parade. Their weapons had not changed, but now they wore segmented metal armor, which was heavier and more effective than their predecessors' chain mail jackets. They also wore a woolen scarf knotted around their necks to prevent their armor from chafing. The scarf had become so fashionable that auxiliaries also wore it, even though they wore only the lighter chain mail armor and had no practical use for a scarf.

The 3rd Gallica received its Judean posting in A.D. 44. In that year King Herod Agrippa I, grandson of King Herod, had died of a heart attack at Caesarea while hosting a series of games in honor of the emperor Claudius. He had reigned as king of Judea for just four years. Claudius's predecessor, Caligula, had granted Agrippa the Judean throne, which had been vacant since Herod's death. The Christian community in Judea had breathed a sigh of relief when Herod Agrippa died. A fiercely Orthodox Jew, he had persecuted the Christian Jews, executing the apostle James, son of Zebedee.

The Roman legion previously based in Judea, the 12th Fulminata, had been relocated to Raphanaea in southern Syria from A.D. 41, and Agrippa had used his own small local army to police Judea. On Agrippa's death, Judea had reverted to Roman provincial status, governed out of Caesarea by a procurator who, like prefects of Judea in the past, reported to the governor of Syria. This change also saw the return of a Roman garrison, now consisting of the 3rd Gallica Legion, auxiliary light infantry, and cavalry.

As a rule during this era all the cohorts of a Roman legion resided at the same base, wherever they were stationed. But when the 3rd Gallica had been transferred to Judea in A.D. 44, its cohorts had of necessity been spread around the bandit-ridden and troublesome province. Five cohorts, including the 1st, were based at Caesarea with the legion's tribune—the 1st Cohort always accompanied the legion's commander. These 2,700 legionaries were supported by the legion's own 124-man cavalry squadron plus auxiliary light infantry cohorts and a wing of auxiliary cavalry made up of five squadrons—480 troopers—of unknown nationality. Josephus, referring to the Caesarea garrison at this time, says that "the greater part of the Roman force had been raised in Syria," meaning the cohorts of the 3rd Gallica Legion outnumbered the cohorts of auxiliaries at Caesarea. There are indications that some or all of the auxiliary infantry then in Judea were "German" (from western Germany and/or Holland). The remaining five cohorts of the 3rd Gallica were spread around the province. One was based at Jerusalem. Another was at the fortress of Masada, on the western side of the Dead Sea. One was at Machaerus, east of the Dead Sea. There was one at the fortress at Cypros on a ridge overlooking Jericho and the Jordan River. And the last cohort was stationed at the coastal city of Ascalon in the south—where a squadron of auxiliary cavalry also was based.

In Jerusalem, the 3rd Gallica's duty cohort was quartered at the Palace of Herod in the southwest of the city and at the Antonia, a massive stone fortress on a corner beside the Temple Mount. King Herod, just as he had rebuilt the Jewish Temple after it had been severely damaged by the 3rd Gallica and the other legions in General Sossius's assault of 37 B.C., also had rebuilt an old fortress called the Baris, renaming it the Antonia, after his good friend Mark Antony. Called the legion's *praetorium* in Jerusalem, the Antonia Fortress housed the garrison commander as well as the soldiers of the watch. Herod's Antonia was a massive rectangular building with towers on each corner, three of them 80 feet high and one 110 feet high, as well as extensive quarters, courtyards, a judgment hall, and prison cells. Built on a rocky precipice, the Antonia was accessed via a high gate from which a broad flight of steps led down to the narrow street opposite the Temple Mount wall—today's Wailing Wall. The Antonia was like a modern-day downtown police headquarters. And it was to the Antonia that Jesus Christ had been taken by troops of the 12th Fulminata Legion garrison following his arrest, to be whipped.

A number of restrictions were put on the legionaries stationed in Judea, as each succeeding Roman emperor—Augustus, Tiberius, Caligula, and Claudius—had attempted to mollify the Jews. Honoring the decrees of Julius Caesar, they ruled that no Jew was to be conscripted into the Roman army. And because of Jewish religious sensitivities, the display of graven images of any living thing was barred at Jerusalem. The cohort standards of Roman legions were decorated with images of the emperor, of the legion's symbol—in the 3rd Gallica's case, the bull—and of the animal corresponding with the astrological sign relating to the month of its creation. Some legions also had additional animal motifs on their standards; the 5th Macedonica carried elephants on its standards in celebration of its defeat of war elephants at the civil war Battle of Thapsus in 46 B.C., and the 6th Ferrata and 6th Victrix both carried the she-wolf on their standards. And, of course, the legion standard was an eagle, now made of gold. In deference to the Jews, the Roman garrison at Jerusalem was prevented from displaying its standards on the walls of the Antonia, and the legion had to cover its standards while marching in the province, a restriction that would have annoyed the proud legionaries immensely.

Back in A.D. 26, when Pontius Pilate had taken up his appointment as Prefect of Judea, he had been so incensed by this concession to the Jews that he had smuggled the standards of the 12th Fulminata and the other garrison units up from Caesarea. Then, at dawn one day, he had displayed them from the walls of Herod's palace and the Antonia. This had caused a massive wave of civil disobedience by the Jews, and Pilate had been forced to back down. Later, when Prefect Pilate dedicated four undecorated golden shields in the Palace of Herod, the Jews had again protested, even though the shields contained nothing more offensive than an inscription about their dedication by Pilate. When the "very inflexible" Pilate—in the words of Jewish philosopher Philo of Alexandria, who may have met him—refused to remove the shields, the Jews complained to the emperor Tiberius at Rome. To keep the peace with the Jews, Tiberius instructed Pilate to relocate the shields to Caesarea.

Life in Jerusalem was boring for the Gallicans of the garrison. This boredom was alleviated a little each year when the Jewish Passover came and millions of Jewish pilgrims arrived in Jerusalem from throughout both the Roman Empire and the Parthian Empire to sacrifice at the Temple.

Pilgrims stayed with friends and relatives in the city or camped in the surrounding hills. The Roman procurator came up from Caesarea with several more cohorts of the legion to maintain order, and, joined by their comrades from Caesarea, the Jerusalem cohort of the 3rd Gallica stood guard around the Jewish Temple to make sure there was no trouble.

Even this duty became tedious. In A.D. 48, a bored legionary of the 3rd Gallica stationed at the colonnades outside the Temple had turned and bared his backside to pilgrims flowing up and down the Temple steps, at the same time, says the Jewish historian Josephus, "making a noise as indecent as his attitude." This caused a riot, and when more Roman troops were called out, hundreds of stampeding Jews trampled their fellow rioters in their desperation to escape the baton-wielding soldiers.

A few weeks after that episode, in the Beth-Horon Valley just northwest of Jerusalem, a rider of Rome's Cursus Publicus courier service had been waylaid and robbed, a capital offense under Roman law. Soldiers of the 3rd Gallica had combed the district, looking for suspects. While searching a house in the Beth-Horon Valley a soldier of the legion had come across a copy of the sacred Jewish law. Disdainfully, the sun-worshipping Gallican had torn the Jewish text in two and tossed the pieces into the fire. News of this had caused more rioting in Jerusalem. Under pressure from the Great Sanhedrin, the new Roman procurator, Paulus Ventidius Cumanus, had instigated an investigation. The 3rd Gallica's commander, its senior tribune, Colonel Celer, ordered the centurions of the legion to identify the culprit. This legionary was subsequently dragged through the streets of Jerusalem in chains. Outside the city, he was beheaded.

This outcome only partly satisfied the Jewish community. There was no love lost between the Jews and the Baal-worshipping 3rd Gallica soldiers. Josephus says the Jews now called the legionaries of the Judea garrison "barbarians." In return, says Josephus, the legionaries began to increasingly favor the Greek-speaking peoples of the province.

In A.D. 51, four of the five 3rd Gallica cohorts stationed in Caesarea had rounded up Jewish suspects in Samaria after bloody and widespread fighting between Jews and Samaritans. This fighting had been sparked by the murder of Jewish pilgrims in the village of Gema while on their way to spend the Passover at Jerusalem. The Samaritans had subsequently complained to the governor of Syria, Lieutenant General Ummidius Quadratus, that both Procurator Cumanus and Colonel Celer had accepted bribes from the Jews to favor them in the dispute. General Quadratus had sent all the parties involved, including the Jewish high priest, to Rome, for the case to be heard by the emperor Claudius. While Claudius found the two

Roman officers innocent of bribery, he found that they had been too slow to act following the murder of the Jewish pilgrims, forcing the Jews to take matters into their own hands, which had resulted in many deaths on both sides. Procurator Cumanus was sent into exile. Colonel Celer was returned to Jerusalem, handed over to the Jews to be dragged through the streets in chains, and then given to his own former legionaries of the 3rd Gallica for execution.

In A.D. 54 the garrison arrangements in Judea had changed. Armenia, a buffer state fought over interminably by Rome and Parthia, had recently undergone two invasions. The king of Iberia, today's Georgia, had invaded Armenia, murdered its royal family, and put his dashing son Rhadamistus on the Armenian throne. In response, the Parthians had swept into Armenia. Rhadamistus was driven back to Georgia, and King Vologases of Parthia had placed his brother Tiridates on the Armenian throne and took control of the Armenian army. Rome had a new emperor in A.D. 54, the seventeen-year-old Nero Caesar, grandson of Germanicus Caesar, great-great-grandson of Mark Antony. Guided by his astute senior advisers Lucius Annaeus Seneca, his former tutor and now his chief minister, and Sextus Afranius Burrus, his Praetorian Guard commander—in effect, his military chief of staff—Nero had sent Lieutenant General Gnaeus Domitius Corbulo to the East to throw the Parthians out of Armenia.

Corbulo had gained Triumphal Decorations and widespread fame in A.D. 48 for using the armies of the Rhine to destroy German transrhine raiders led by the German Gannascus, a former officer of auxiliaries in the Roman army who had deserted. Surviving busts of Corbulo show a handsome, impressive man. Cassius Dio says he came from an illustrious old Roman family, had great bodily strength, was gifted with shrewdness and courage, and was fair to both friends and enemies. Officially, General Corbulo was merely the new governor of Galatia and Cappadocia, provinces west of Armenia in what is today eastern Turkey. But to enable Corbulo to achieve his secret mission, Nero had entrusted him with extraordinary military powers that could be said to equate with those of a modern field marshal.

When, almost two thousand years later, in November 1943, Field Marshal Erwin Rommel arrived in France to inspect German defenses against a potential Allied landing, it was with what the Germans called a *Gummibefehl*, an "elastic directive," which gave him power over all existing commanders in the region. General Corbulo arrived in the East in A.D. 54 with similar power over Roman commanders, including Governor Quadratus of Syria. And just as Field Marshal Gerd von Rundstedt, the German commander in chief in France in 1943, rankled at Rommel's intrusion, so Quadratus was unhappy at Corbulo's appointment and did all he could to make life difficult for him. But Corbulo had too much to worry about to be sidetracked by petty jealousies.

When the field marshal arrived to take up his new appointment, he was appalled by the state of the 6th Ferrata and the 10th, the two Roman legions that marched up into Cappadocia from Syria to form the basis of his Armenian task force. These legions had been stationed in Syria for decades without seeing action. To the professional soldier, peace can sometimes be more difficult than war. Many of the bored legionaries of the two legions had become lazy and unfit. Some had even sold their helmets and armor.

Corbulo, the tough, no-nonsense general who had knocked the Rhine armies into shape a decade earlier, a commander who marched bareheaded at the head of his army in all weather, quickly discharged the old and the ill. He rearmed those without equipment. And he tightened discipline. In the past, commanders of the 6th and 10th had excused men who went absent without leave. Corbulo reintroduced the death sentence for first offenders. And he marched his troops into the mountains of Cappadocia and made them camp out under canvas with him through the bitter winter, with some suffering from frostbite. To provide a model for the other legions, Corbulo summoned six cohorts of the better-disciplined 3rd Gallica Legion from Judea.

Led by the 3rd Gallica's camp prefect, Capito, four of those six cohorts would have come from the Caesarea garrison, leaving the 1st Cohort there with its senior tribune, the commander of the legion, and its eagle standard, and the remaining three cohorts spread around the province. The three thousand men of the 3rd Gallica detached to Field Marshal Corbulo were no doubt thrilled to see some real action after a decade playing corner cop to the fractious Judeans. No one would have been keener for some real soldiering than a 3rd Gallica centurion named Arrius Varus. Described by Tacitus as "an energetic soldier," Centurion Varus led one of the 3rd Gallica cohorts that marched up through Syria behind a *vexilla* cloth detachment standard to join the task force in Cappadocia.

Once the Gallicans arrived at the task force's camp and began setting up their own tents, Centurion Varus, who was to play a leading role in the story of the 3rd Gallica Legion, was summoned to the *praetorium* of Field Marshal Corbulo and given a special mission. It's likely that Varus, currently a middle-ranking centurion, had previously served under Corbulo on the Rhine. Corbulo had already sent a message to King Vologases telling him to choose peace over war and to hand over senior hostages as a way of guaranteeing that the Parthians would not infringe on Roman territory. King Vologases, wanting to take advantage of the situation and mask his own preparations for war, decided to hand over some of his less loyal nobles as hostages. Centurion Varus's mission was to take the hostages to Rome. But when he and his small party of men arrived in Parthia, Varus found that Governor Quadratus of Syria also had sent a centurion, Insteius, to pick up the Parthian hostages. An argument broke out between the two centurions. It was settled by an agreement to let the hostages choose who they would go with—Corbulo's man or Quadratus's man. Because of Field Marshal Corbulo's reputation, the Parthians chose his man. So Centurion Varus conducted the Parthian nobles overland to Syria and then escorted them to Rome by sea.

Once he had arrived at Rome and handed over the hostages to Prefect Burrus, the Praetorian Guard commander, the 3rd Gallica centurion was called into several private audiences with the emperor Nero. From Centurion Varus, the young emperor obtained a firsthand appreciation of the state of affairs in the East. But Nero was interested most of all in his commander in the East. According to Cassius Dio, many people at Rome were saying that Corbulo would make a better emperor than Nero. Now Nero quizzed the 3rd Gallica centurion about everything the field marshal said and did. According to Tacitus, Centurion Varus offered some very unflattering observations about his commander. But he apparently put Nero's mind at rest about Corbulo's political ambitions, for Nero rewarded him with promotion to first-rank centurion, making his one of the *primi ordines* of the 3rd Gallica Legion, and sent him back to Corbulo and his legion.

Meanwhile, after Major Capito had gone to Cappadocia as chief officer of the 3rd Gallica contingent in Corbulo's army, a new commander had been appointed to the Roman garrison in Jerusalem. Claudius Lysias was his name. Of Greek background, he could have been from anywhere in the Roman East, from Macedonia to Samaria. The inference from Acts is that Lysias held the rank of camp prefect. But from what we later learn about Lysias, he is unlikely to have come up through the ranks to become a camp prefect. Lysias was almost certainly the prefect of an auxiliary unit, probably a cavalry unit. With the equivalent modern-day rank of colonel, cavalry prefects were senior to auxiliary infantry prefects and to legion centurions but subordinate to tribunes.

Two years later, in A.D. 56, Major Capito and the 3rd Gallica detachment were still in Cappadocia, training with Field Marshal Corbulo. Knowing this, an Egyptian Jewish prophet came in off the desert to the southeast in that year leading thousands of Jewish followers, with plans to overthrow the Jerusalem garrison and take over the holy city. Alerted in advance to the coming of the Egyptian, the latest Procurator of Judea, Antonius Felix, was waiting for him with the 3rd Gallica's Jerusalem garrison cohort and large numbers of auxiliaries and cavalry brought up from Caesarea. The Jewish band, numbering four thousand men (Acts) to as many as thirty thousand (Josephus), was caught in the open on Mount Scopus just outside the city and quickly broken up by a Roman charge. Four hundred of the fanatics were killed in the brief melee. Two hundred others taken prisoner were sent to slave markets and arenas. Most members of the Egyptian's mob escaped back into the desert. The Egyptian prophet himself was among those who evaded capture, but not before Prefect Lysias got an eyeful of him—the Egyptian was apparently a bald man with a dark beard.

Now, in A.D. 58, Field Marshal Corbulo had launched his Armenian operation, and Major Capito and his six 3rd Gallica cohorts were at the forefront of the Roman task force rampaging through the country. And Prefect Lysias was still in charge at Jerusalem. For this Passover of A.D. 58, Procurator Felix had come up to Jerusalem bringing the 1st Cohort of the 3rd Gallica to reinforce the garrison cohort for the usual guard duty. Passover had been without incident this year, enabling Felix and his troops to go back to Caesarea. The men of the 3rd Gallica's Jerusalem garrison had returned to more mundane duties, and gossiped about the news coming out of Armenia, which told of Field Marshal Corbulo and his task force sweeping the Armenians and Parthians before them.

That spring, a forty-eight-year-old balding, bearded Jew had journeyed from Corinth in Greece to Jerusalem together with several followers. This was the Christian apostle Paul. He had been born in about A.D. 10 in Tarsus, the capital of Cilicia, and given the Hebrew name Saul by his Jewish parents. But because his father also had Roman citizenship—all inhabitants of Tarsus and their descendants are thought likely to have been granted Roman citizenship by Caesar or Antony—he also took a Roman name, Paulus Tarsensis, or Paul of Tarsus. As a youth, Paul had learned the trade of the tentmaker, almost certainly the trade of his father. With Cilicia being a major producer of flax—for rope and canvas as well as linen—there would have been many tentmakers working in Tarsus. Paul's father was a Pharisee, the Jewish sect that believed in strict observance of the laws of Moses, and in the afterlife. As Paul's father was a descendant of Aaron, Paul was sent by his family to study to become a priest under famous Jewish scholar and rabbinical teacher Gamaliel I, at Jerusalem.

Judea had become a Roman province on the death of King Herod in 4 B.C., and at the time that Paul studied at Jerusalem the province was administered by the prefect Pontius Pilate.

By A.D. 36, several years after the crucifixion of Jesus of Nazareth, Paul was an enthusiastic pursuer of Jews who followed the new Nazarene, or Christian, cult. One such convert was a Greek-speaking Jew from Samaria named Stephanus, one of seven deacons appointed by the apostles to serve Judea's Christian flock. Stephanus preached openly that the Jerusalem Temple was operating contrary to the laws of Moses. Arrested by the Jewish Temple Guard, Stephanus had been dragged before the Great Sanhedrin, the seventy-one member council of Jewish elders. Despite a vigorous defense, Stephanus was condemned to death by stoning for blasphemy. Outside the city walls, Paul of Tarsus held the robes of Jews who carried out the sentence and killed Stephanus (Saint Stephen).

Instructed by Jewish authorities to go to Damascus to bring arrested Christians back to Jerusalem for trial, Paul had reputedly been struck by a blinding light on the road and heard the voice of Jesus telling him to go among the Gentiles and further his teachings. Three days later, while recovering, he was visited by a Damascan named Ananias, who is said to have been one of Jesus' original seventy disciples, and Ananias baptized Paul.

Now, twenty-two years later, here was Paul back in Jerusalem, having established Christian communities throughout the East. This same year, according to one Christian tradition, Mary, mother of Jesus, died at Jerusalem, and was buried in a tomb in the Kidron Valley. Again according to tradition, Thomas, one of the original twelve apostles of Jesus, turned up at Jerusalem after spending twenty years founding Christian churches in Parthia and India and reputedly dying in Madras, India, five years earlier. According to that same tradition, Thomas, ever the doubter, felt sure that Mary's corpse did not lay in the tomb, and at his insistence it was opened. The tomb, so the story goes, was empty—proof, the Christian Church was to say, that the Virgin Mary had ascended to Heaven.

Neither the Gospels nor Acts make any reference to the death of Mary or of Thomas's supposed sudden visit and subsequent disappearance. Acts, focusing on Paul's missions, says that he had come to Jerusalem in A.D. 58 with a considerable quantity of money. Collected from Christian congregations in Greece and Asia, it was intended to be a contribution to the Christian community in Jerusalem, a peace offering to the apostles James and Peter. Paul had obtained permission from the Jerusalem leadership to recruit Gentiles, non-Jews, to the Christian faith, but it was a controversial decision and many Jewish members of the congregation were opposed to Paul and his Gentile converts, especially since Paul had said that Gentiles need not be circumcised. Several times the apostle Peter—his Roman name was Simon, his Jewish name Simeon, and among Greek-speakers he was called Cephas—and other Jewish Christians had gone to churches set up by Paul and tried, with some success, to turn them away from Paul's leadership.

But now, to Paul's great disappointment, the leaders of the Jerusalem congregation refused to accept the collection that he had brought them. Instead, to assert their authority, James and Peter required Paul to immediately undergo the Nazarite Vow, a seven-day Jewish rite that involved daily prayers, abstaining from wine, and then shaving of the head as a final act indicating to all Jews that he had performed the vow. Paul agreed, apparently annoying some members of the Jerusalem congregation who were hoping he would refuse and give them reason to have him thrown out.

Starting that very afternoon, and joining four other Christian Jews who were also undertaking the Nazarite Vow, Paul went to the Temple. On the afternoon of the seventh day of this rite, during the "hour of prayer" between 2:30 and 3:45 P.M., Paul was recognized by Jewish pilgrims from the provinces of Asia, who had seen him preach in their part of the world. They quickly spread the rumor that Trophimus, a member of Paul's party who was a Gentile Christian from Ephesus in Asia, had been admitted by Paul to the inner part of the Temple, which was out of bounds to Gentiles. Non-Jews were permitted to go only as far as the Court of the Gentiles. The inscription at the entrance to the inner Temple read, ominously: "Whoever is caught will be responsible for his own death, which will ensue." Paul was quickly mobbed by angry Jews. The leaders of the mob grabbed Paul and dragged him outside as the Temple's one hundred doorkeepers swung the massive Temple doors shut. There, outside, as Jews converged on the scene from throughout the city, blows were rained on Paul.

Up on a tower of the Antonia Fortress, a Roman soldier on guard duty spied the fracas, and word was quickly sent downstairs to Prefect Lysias. Fearing a riot, Lysias ordered a 3rd Gallica detachment to assemble immediately. Because Acts says that centurions were in this detachment, we know it comprised at least two centuries—160 legionaries. The detachment quickly followed Lysias down the steps from the Antonia to the street outside. Along the street pounded the men of the 3rd Gallica, armed with swords, having left their shields back inside the Antonia.

Those shields, with their bull motifs, could not be exposed in the city. Besides, even at Rome the troops of the various guard units stationed there did not carry shields on guard duty.

The rowdy crowd parted as the Roman troops came up, to reveal Paul lying battered and bloodied on the paving stones. Prefect Lysias pulled Paul to his feet, then commanded his men to secure him with double chains. Persons in Roman custody were secured with manacles around the wrists, the equivalent of handcuffs, with a chain leading to a single soldier of the escort. That chain was secured to the soldier's left side, leaving his right side, his sword side, free. In this case, Paul was secured to two legionaries. What follows, including the conversations, is recorded in Acts.

"Who is he?" the prefect asked the mob. "What's he done?"

Everyone spoke at once, all with different stories. As Paul sagged back to the ground, Lysias impatiently ordered his men to lift him up and carry him to the Antonia for further questioning. Four legionaries carried Paul toward the fortress, and the other troops fell in behind, holding back the crowd, who followed along, clamoring for Paul to be removed from Jerusalem. At the bottom of the flight of steps leading sixty-five feet up to the Antonia entrance, the legionaries set Paul down, and motioned for him to climb the steps under his own steam. The chained prisoner slowly shuffled his way to the top. There, Paul looked at Major Lysias, who stood waiting for him by the door.

"May I speak to you?" he asked the camp prefect in Greek. Paul would have heard the legionaries address the officer by name and guessed Lysias's Greek background.

The major was surprised. "You can speak Greek?" Then he frowned as he surveyed the bald, bearded Jew. "Aren't you that Egyptian who caused an uproar and led four thousand murderers out of the wilderness to attack Jerusalem?"

Paul shook his head. "I'm a Jew from Tarsus, a substantial city in Cilicia. It's no mere country town, I assure you." He nodded toward the rowdy mob crowding around the bottom of the stairs. "Please, may I address the people?"

Lysias shrugged. "Go ahead. If they'll give you a hearing."

Standing on the Antonia stairs, Paul put up his chained hands for quiet, and the mob gradually quieted, although not entirely. Speaking in the Hebrew tongue, he told them that he was a Jew who had been born in Tarsus but brought up there in Jerusalem, where he had been taught the Jewish law by the leading Pharisee teacher, Gamaliel. The crowd was silenced by this, having been unaware of his credentials. He told them how he had persecuted both men and women who transgressed Jewish law, chaining them and dragging them off to prisons. He told them how he had been sent by the Jewish elders of Jerusalem to collect prisoners awaiting trial in Damascus, and how on the road to Damascus he had been blinded and heard the voice of Jesus of Nazareth, and as a result had become one of Jesus' followers. And of how, in Damascus, he had been commanded to go out and convert the Gentiles to the faith. At the mention of bringing Gentiles into Judaism many in the crowd exploded with indignant rage. This was a sacrilege of the worst order. Calling for the prisoner's death, angry Jews cast off their clothes and threw dust into the air—normally the symbolic prelude to a stoning.

Prefect Lysias had seen and heard enough. He ordered his men to bring the prisoner into the Antonia. Paul was carried into the fortress. As the heavy door thudded closed behind them, shutting out the noise of the yelling crowd, Lysias ordered the centurion of the guard to have Paul questioned under whipping, until the facts of the matter could be established. As the prefect returned to his quarters, the centurion had Paul taken to the main courtyard within the Antonia complex, where a whipping post stood. Christian tradition holds that it was one of the columns of the colonnade, fitted for the role of whipping post with iron rings where the prisoner's hands could be secured.

As legionaries were tying Paul to the whipping post, Paul said to the centurion in charge, "Is it legal for you to flog a Roman, without a trial or a conviction?"

The centurion looked suddenly worried. "What do you mean?" he demanded.

"I am Paulus Tarsensis, a Roman citizen," said Paul.

They both knew that under the Valerian and Porcian Laws no Roman citizen could legally undergo punishment without first being convicted in a court of law, a right that was not accorded noncitizens. Roman citizenship bestowed certain inalienable rights on the holder. A fair trial was one of them. In the Roman Empire, it was a capital offense to ignore those rights. It was also a capital offense, punishable by a flogging followed by death by crucifixion, to claim you were a Roman citizen when you weren't. Both Paul and the centurion knew that Paul's claim could be readily checked—a dispatch could be sent via the Cursus Publicus to the office of the Procurator of Cilicia in Tarsus seeking confirmation from the city records. If such a check were ordered, it might take a week or ten days—the emperor Tiberius had boasted that no part of the empire was more than ten days distant from Rome through the agency of the efficient couriers of the Cursus. During that time, Paul would be kept in custody. If a negative answer were to come back, Paul would be crucified. The false claim of citizenship was so easily exposed that it very rarely occurred. Very occasionally, escaped slaves falsely claimed citizenship and joined legions, but they were usually caught, sooner or later. One escaped slave actually reached the rank of centurion before he was found out, after which he was returned to his master.

Now the 3rd Gallica centurion ordered his men to wait, while he hurried off to Prefect Lysias. "Sir," said the centurion to his superior when he found him, "you'd better be careful what you do. This Jew says he's a Roman citizen."

This wasn't the first time that Paul had sprung his citizenship on Roman jailers. Initially, for years, he had tried to keep his Roman citizenship a secret—after all, it wasn't something that could be expected to endear him to fellow Jews or other noncitizens, for it set him above them in the eyes of the law. The last time he'd revealed his secret had been at Philippi in Macedonia, which had grown into a large and prosperous town after Octavian and Antony's victory over Brutus and Cassius there in 42 B.C.

Paul personally tells, in one of his letters, Second Corinthians, that he'd allowed himself to be beaten with rods by Roman authorities three times in the past. Only after he'd been beaten and thrown into prison with a death sentence hanging over him, at Philippi, had he finally revealed his citizenship and that of his companion at the time, Silas, whose Roman name was Silvanus. The city's magistrates had quickly come to him in prison, and, terrified that they themselves might be prosecuted for breaking Roman law, had set him and his companion on the road and gladly watched him leave.

Now Prefect Lysias returned to the Jewish prisoner with the centurion.

"Tell me," said Lysias to Paul, "are you a Roman citizen?"

Paul nodded. "I am."

"Are you sure? I had to buy the freedom that comes with citizenship, and it cost me a considerable sum."

Technically, you couldn't buy Roman citizenship. It was granted by the emperor on the recommendation of a respectable sponsor. Provincial governors frequently sent to Rome the names of people in their provinces whom they recommended for citizenship. Pliny the Younger, when governor of Bithynia-Pontus, recommended the granting of citizenship to numerous applicants in his letters to the emperor Trajan. Pliny's recommendations were based on merit, but avaricious officials such as Procurator

Felix of Judea made applicants pay them large fees to forward their recommendations to Rome.

The profiteering from citizenship hadn't stopped there. During the early part of the emperor Claudius's reign, his third wife, Valeria Messalina, was infamous for secretly charging to arrange for her husband to grant citizenship. All an aspirant had to do was contact one of the freedmen on her staff and pay the required amount. Citizenship could be bought so easily at the time that the people of Rome joked that a man could become a citizen simply by giving the right person a few pieces of broken glass. But in reality, buying citizenship would not have been cheap. It is probable that Lysias's family had been successful in business and could afford to buy the citizenship for him.

"I was born with the rights of Roman citizenship," Paul replied.

"Unbind him," Prefect Lysias instructed.

"What do you want to do with him, sir?" asked the centurion as Gallican legionaries freed Paul from his chains.

"Keep him in here overnight," the prefect instructed. "We'll see what the Jews who accuse him have to say tomorrow."

Prefect Lysias wasted no time in sending an instruction to the chief priests and members of their Jewish governing council, the Great Sanhedrin, requiring them to convene a hearing the next morning. Since the sixth century B.C., the Great Sanhedrin had fulfilled the role of the Jews' "house of judgment," their supreme judicial body, responsible for teaching, interpreting, and upholding Jewish law.

The Sanhedrin duly assembled at their judgment hall within the Temple enclosure the following day, and the Roman garrison commander brought Paul before them. Permitted to speak, Paul asked what he had been accused of, declaring that he had offended neither Jewish law nor the laws of Rome. There were two factions among the priests on the council, the Sadducees and the Pharisees. The Pharisees believed in resurrection and angels; the Sadducees didn't. As far as the Sadducees were concerned, when you were dead, you were dead. Paul had been raised a Pharisee, and the members of his sect declared that if an angel (Jesus) had spoken to Paul then that was fine by them, as they weren't going to fight the will of Jehovah. Predictably, the Sadducees were all for Paul's stoning. When angry voices were raised and things looked like they were getting out of hand, with Sadducees pulling Paul one way, and Pharisees pulling him the other, Prefect Lysias instructed his legionaries to take him back to the Antonia.

What Paul didn't tell Prefect Lysias was that this wasn't the first time he'd been arrested during his preaching career. Five times he had been apprehended by Jewish authorities. He'd been lashed each time, and had been left for dead after a stoning. He'd been in Roman custody three times previously, having a close escape from the executioner at Philippi. On another occasion, Paul himself was to write, he had been thrown into an arena with wild beasts, but somehow he had survived. The last time that Paul had been in hot water with the Roman authorities had been seven years back, in A.D. 51, at Corinth in the province of Achaea, fifty miles west of Athens. Paul had been preaching his Christian doctrine in the local synagogue when Jewish leaders had accused him of blasphemy. The Roman proconsul of the province of Achaea at the time had been Junius Gallio, brother of Seneca—now the emperor Nero's chief minister— and uncle of the poet Lucan. Governor Gallio had dismissed the charges on the basis that Paul, a Roman citizen, had broken no Roman law. But Paul now kept quiet about these earlier arrests and favorable verdicts, in case they weighed against him. After all, someone who was regularly brought before Roman courts might be considered an habitual offender and a troublemaker, whatever the outcome of the previous hearings.

Besides, there was the little matter of an outstanding charge of treason hanging over Paul's head that no one in Judea knew about. Years before, in Thessalonika in northeastern Greece, during the early days of his mission when his sermons had been a lot more fiery and a little more incautious than now, Paul had proclaimed Christ a rival emperor to Caesar. That was a matter significant enough to trouble a sitting of a Roman court and to encourage a death sentence. Paul had gotten out of town fast at the time, and steered clear of Thessalonika from then on.

On the night of his arrest in Jerusalem, not long after dark, Paul's nephew came to the Antonia fortress and asked to see his uncle. This young man was a son of Paul's sister, who lived in Jerusalem. Conscious of what had gone on earlier, and of Paul's status as a Roman citizen, the centurion of the guard took the young man to see Paul. Uncle and nephew spoke briefly, before Paul called the centurion and asked him to take his nephew to Prefect Lysias, as he had vital information. So the centurion escorted the youth to Lysias. Paul's nephew informed the prefect that his mother had learned that a band of more than forty Sadducees had gone to their leaders on the Sanhedrin and told them they had vowed not to eat or drink until they had killed Paul. To give them an opportunity to commit the murder, they asked the priests to ask for Paul to be brought back before the Great Sanhedrin for further questioning the next day. The assassins would lurk in the crowd attending the hearing, and would pounce on Paul and kill him.

Lysias had already received just such a request for a second hearing, although he had yet to agree to it, and this led him to suspect that Paul's nephew was telling the truth. He wasn't prepared to take the risk that he wasn't. There were few Roman citizens in Jerusalem apart from the men of the 3rd Gallica. The prefect was not going to permit any citizen to be murdered by the Jews.

"Don't breathe a word to anyone about what you've revealed to me," Acts says Lysias told the young man, knowing that Paul's nephew had put his life on the line to bring him this information. He then sent him on his way with a promise he would look after Paul, and swiftly summoned two of his centurions.

X

SAVING THE APOSTLE PAUL A SECOND TIME

laudius Lysias, commander of the Roman garrison at Jerusalem, had acted quickly. The news from a Jewish informant that a Sadducee murder squad had vowed to kill his prisoner Paul of Tarsus the next day meant that he had to act fast. Prefect Lysias knew that if he simply kept the prisoner inside the Antonia Fortress, the Orthodox Jews of the city might riot. The garrison commanded by Lysias would have consisted of little more than 1,200 men: 480 legionaries, 480 auxiliary light infantry, and 124 to 248 auxiliary cavalry. With such a relatively small force, Prefect Lysias knew he had no way of controlling a crowd of tens of thousands of rioting Jews within the city's narrow streets. Wisely, he decided that the best way to defuse the situation was to spirit Paul away as soon as possible and get him down to the provincial capital, Caesarea, on the coast, a city with a larger Roman garrison and a much smaller Jewish population than Jerusalem. That would be easier said than done. There were many Jewish towns and villages between Jerusalem and Caesarea. Lysias would have to use the cover of darkness if he was to succeed.

In the early evening, Prefect Lysias summoned two of his 3rd Gallica Legion centurions and told them of the plot to kill their prisoner. He then instructed the centurions to prepare a detachment for immediate action. Acts says that force consisted of 200 legionaries plus 200 auxiliary infantry and 70 cavalrymen. Classical authors habitually rounded the figures when referring to the number of men in Roman legions and cohorts, and invariably referred to a century as containing 100 men and a cohort containing 500 men. The actual numbers were 80 and 480 men, respectively. So the force swiftly assembled by Lysias's centurions this summer's night of A.D. 57 is likely to have actually been made up of 160 legionaries, 160 auxiliaries, and 70 cavalry troopers.

The legionaries were men of the 3rd Gallica Legion. We don't know the precise identity of the auxiliary unit, but the author of Acts, who is thought by most historians to have been the physician Lucius of Antioch—Saint Luke, the Gospel writer—describes them as spearmen. This indicates that they were German auxiliaries, who were equipped with spears, their national weapon. Originating from a tribe such as the Frisii or the Cannefates, they would have been tall, fair, and bearded—unlike the clean-shaven legionaries, and they wore breeches, unlike the barelegged legionaries.

Prefect Lysias told his centurions to have the troops ready to depart for Caesarea at nine o'clock that night—about an hour away, once darkness had fallen. As the centurions hurried away to organize the detachment, the prefect called in his secretary, a male freedman, and dictated a letter to Procurator Felix in Caesarea. The contents of the letter have been recorded word for word in Acts, suggesting that Paul was subsequently given a copy of the letter so he was fully acquainted with the case as the prefect saw it, and this copy was later passed on to Luke, the Acts author. This, says Acts, is what Lysias wrote:

> From Claudius Lysias, to His Excellency Antonius Felix, Procurator, Greetings.
>
> This man was taken from among the Jews, who would have killed him if I had not intervened with an armed force. I rescued him, understanding him to be a Roman citizen. To determine what the Jews were accusing him of I brought him before their ruling council. From this I perceived that he was accused of questions relating to their law, but I felt that no charge was laid against him that justified a death penalty or imprisonment. Then when I was informed that the Jews intended to lay in wait for the man and murder him I immediately sent him to you, at the same time commanding his accusers to say before you what they had against him. Farewell.

A little after 9:00 P.M., Paul, handcuffed and attached to a soldier of his escort by a chain and probably disguised in a hooded farmer's cloak, was hustled out of the Antonia Fortress. Down the long flight of steps to the street below he was taken, to be surrounded by the 320 foot soldiers of his escort. Prefect Lysias was obviously concerned that the Sadducee assassination squad might be watching the Antonia for Paul to emerge, and that's why he'd allocated such a large number of troops to the mission.

The two centurions in charge had explicit orders from Lysias to convey Paul safely to Procurator Felix. One of them carried the prefect's letter for the governor. Now the pair gave hushed orders for the troops to move out. Making the minimum of noise, Paul and his escort passed along the narrow Via Dolorossa, the Street of Sorrows, toward the city's Genath Gate. As they went, the soldiers watched the shadows with a hand resting on the hilt of their sheathed swords. Ironically, this was the same route followed by Christ on the way to his execution two decades before.

At the Genath or Water Gate, they were met by the cavalry. The seventy auxiliary troopers of the cavalry detachment had slipped their horses from the stables at the Palace of Herod and were waiting, looking anxious as they surveyed the darkness for signs of the Jewish murder squad they had been warned to be on the lookout for. The troopers took up their positions in front of and behind the main body. From the back of his horse the centurion in charge would have quietly ordered the party to move off. The soldiers stepped out; the cavalrymen urged their steeds forward at the walk.

Two roads split away from the Genath Gate. The road to the left ran beside the old wall, then swung away to the south, leading the traveler to the little village, five miles distant, of Bethlehem—in actuality Bet Lehem, meaning house of the baker. From there it continued on to the ancient walled town of Hebron, another twenty miles away, and then down to the Dead Sea. The road to the right was the Beth-Horon road, running down through the dusty hills to Lod and the coastal plain. The Roman military party followed the road to the right.

Tense and expectant they marched, leaving Jerusalem behind, with equipment rattling and horses making an occasional snort or whinny, but otherwise silent and tense, for the Jews were experts at laying ambushes. Along the road the soldiers briskly went, down through the hills past the two darkened Beth-Horon villages, past Lod, coming down out of the hills and continuing on to the predominantly Greek town of Antipatras. There, in the early hours, they halted, and rested for the remainder of the night.

At dawn, Paul was transferred to a horse. He was then taken on to Caesarea via the coast road by one centurion and the cavalry detachment, moving at speed. In the meantime, the second centurion turned around and marched his infantrymen back the way they had come, in daylight now. This was all according to Prefect Lysias's instructions. If the Jewish assassination squad in Jerusalem had by then discovered that Paul had been smuggled out of the city and came rushing down the road after him, they would have barged straight into the Roman infantry, who would have barred their way.

Paul reached Caesarea safely, and the centurion in charge of the escort brought the prisoner before Procurator Felix in King Herod's old Judgment Hall that same day. Antonius Felix had been appointed by the emperor Claudius in A.D. 52 on the recommendation of his brother, Pallas. A freedman, Pallas had been Claudius's powerful secretary for finances, but he was later executed by Nero. Prior to his Judean appointment, Felix, like his brother, a former slave, had been granted membership in the Equestrian Order by Claudius. He had subsequently served in the army as a prefect of auxiliaries and a prefect of cavalry. According to Roman biographer Suetonius, the ambitious Felix married three times, always to women of royal birth. Initially, Felix had proved an able administrator. He'd cleaned up the province, sending his troops ranging through Judea's "bad lands," rounding up bandits and rebels. Among them had been a gang leader named Eleazar, who had been plundering Judea for twenty years since the time of another famous bandit leader, Bar Abbas, or "son of Abbas," the "Barabbas" of the New Testament.

Nero had reconfirmed Procurator Felix's appointment when he took the throne on Claudius's death in A.D. 54. But now, six years into the job, Felix had realized that he was never going to become rich on his salary—procurators earned 60,000 to 100,000 sesterces a year, the amount depending on the importance of the posting. Even 100,000 was not much when a first-rank centurion of the legions earned 35,000 sesterces a year. Felix had begun to routinely charge for his favors, and was growing wealthy as a result. In the view of Josephus, Felix became one of the most corrupt men ever to administer Judea.

Paul was arraigned in front of the judgment seat in Herod's Judgment Hall, and the centurion passed Prefect Lysias's letter up to the procurator. Felix quickly read Lysias's note. Then he looked down at Paul, who stood manacled before him and flanked by the centurion and the soldier of the 3rd Gallica to whom he was chained.

"Which province are you from?" Felix asked.

"Cilicia, Your Excellency," Paul replied.

Felix nodded. "Very well, I'll hear your case when your accusers also come before me." He turned to the centurion. "He is to be kept here at the Judgment Hall."

There was a prison wing attached to the Judgment Hall, and Paul was kept in a cell there for the next five days. At the end of that time Ananias, the Jewish high priest, came down from Jerusalem with the Sadducee elders of the Great Sanhedrin, to appear before the procurator and prosecute Paul. To put the best case possible, the Sanhedrin had employed an advocate named Tertulus.

Advocate Tertulus told Felix: "My Lord, this fellow is a ringleader of the Jewish sect called the Nazarenes and he has profaned the Jewish Temple." He went on to say that in the normal course of events the Jewish authorities would have judged the man according to their own law, but the Roman prefect Lysias had preempted their action by interfering "with great violence" and taking him away. The Jewish priests all voiced their agreement.

Procurator Felix beckoned Paul forward. "Prisoner, what do you have to say in your own defense?" he asked.

"Excellency, because I know that for many years you have been a judge of the Jewish people," Paul began, "I am more than happy to speak for myself before you. Twelve days ago, I went up to Jerusalem to worship. My accusers didn't find me in the Temple in dispute with anyone, or rousing the people in any way. Not in the synagogues either, or even in the street. Nor can they prove the things they accuse me of." He then explained that what his Sadducee accusers called heresy, the belief in resurrection of the dead, he had always believed in, as a Pharisee. He went on, "Now, after many years, I came to bring alms to my people and offerings for the Temple. Certain Jews from Asia saw me in the Temple, purified, without a crowd around me, and not making a noise. It is they who should be here today, to accuse me." He pointed to the Sadducee priests. "Instead, it's they who accuse me. And all they can accuse me of is referring to the resurrection of the dead when I stood before their council."

Felix had learned to tread warily when it came to the Jews. "When Prefect Lysias comes down from Jerusalem," he said, "I'll learn the heart of the matter." He then ordered the centurion of the guard to keep Paul in custody, although without being chained. Paul would also be permitted to receive visitors.

A few days later, while he was waiting for his garrison commander to come down from Jerusalem, Procurator Felix sent for Paul and held a private meeting with him. There were just three people present—Paul, Felix, and Felix's Jewish wife, Drusilla, who was the youngest daughter of Herod Agrippa I and reputedly a great beauty. The procurator then asked Paul to tell them about his faith. This audience, and Felix's unusual request, seem to have been sponsored by Drusilla, who as a Jew was curious about Paul's teachings. Paul apparently used the opportunity to deliver a fire-and-brimstone sermon, because Felix was visibly shaken as a result and had Paul taken back into custody, saying he'd see him again another time.

Every now and then over the months that followed, Governor Felix would send for Paul, but not to hear another sermon. It seems that Prefect Lysias did go down to Caesarea to provide his report on Paul's original arrest at Jerusalem, repeating his view that Paul was innocent of any crime under Roman law. But the greedy Felix, knowing that Paul had come to Judea with a large sum of money that he had not given to his brethren in Jerusalem, let Paul know that in exchange for a large payment the charges against him would be dropped and he would be set free. But the apostle wasn't interested in bribing his way to freedom, standing on his rights and the strength of his case. What he wanted was a ruling in his favor, which would have been a slap in the face for the Sanhedrin. Each time Felix's offer was made, Paul refused to pay. And each time, he was returned to the cells, continuing in prison at the procurator's pleasure. He was to remain in custody at Caesarea for the next two years.

XI

TO CAESAR YOU SHALL GO

S itting at their garrisons throughout Judea in late A.D. 59, men of the 3rd Gallica cohorts who had remained in Judea plied their comrades who had served with Field Marshal Corbulo with questions. Undoubtedly the returned soldiers would have boasted about their exploits, and inflated their role in Corbulo's crushing success. As the Romans said, victory has many fathers, while defeat is an orphan. But the 3rd Gallica had performed up to Corbulo's expectations, and more. In March A.D. 58 his task force had swept into Armenia. Marching with the men of his three legions were the infantry and cavalry of regional allies King Agrippa II of Chalcis and King Antiochis of Commagene, the archers of King Soaemus of Emessa, a full siege train, and plenty of supplies. Corbulo, determined not to make the same mistakes Mark Antony had made in this same part of the world a century before, had spent four years preparing for this mission.

Aware of Corbulo's formidable reputation, and hearing that he had just crossed the border into Armenia with an army, Tiridates, the Parthian king of Armenia, had quickly asked for a meeting as he marched the Armenian army west from his capital, Artaxata, to confront the Roman threat. On the Armenian plain, the two leaders came together for a tense meeting. Corbulo arrived with the 6th Ferrata Legion and the three thousand men of the 3rd Gallica Legion detachment, all under one eagle. The 3rd Gallica's eagle was, of course, back in Caesarea, but Corbulo's intent was to give the impression he had less men than he did, suspecting that the enemy leader was only trying to size up his forces. He was right—Tiridates canceled the meeting, and the two sides warily parted.

Corbulo split his army in two. He led a legion in one direction and assaulted the fortress of Volandum. Meanwhile, Brigadier General Cornelius Flaccus took the other legion and the 3rd Gallica cohorts and proceeded to overrun one Parthian fortress after another—three in one day. The two forces then linked to advance on Artaxata, in the far northwest of the country. Forty years before, Germanicus Caesar had taken Artaxata bloodlessly, using his charisma to gain Armenian submission. Corbulo was hoping to emulate the almost mythical Germanicus.

Trying to head him off, Tiridates's fast mounted bowmen and lancers repeatedly fell on the Roman column, in which the 3rd Gallica cohorts had responsibility for protecting the right flank. The Roman army plowed relentlessly on. After several skirmishes, Tiridates fell back, eventually withdrawing with his army into Media, which was ruled by his brother Pacorus—named for the famous Prince Pacorus of Mark Antony's time. As Corbulo's army appeared on the plain outside Artaxata, a city on the Aras River, the inhabitants opened the city gates and surrendered. The Roman general spared the lives of all the residents but had them evacuate. He then ordered his legionaries to destroy the city—unable to garrison such a large city so far from the nearest Roman base, he'd decided to deny it to the enemy. The legionaries stripped the city bare, burned it, then leveled the ruins, stone by stone. Messages were sent to Antioch by mounted courier, and from there to Rome by the Cursus Publicus, to announce that the Armenian capital was no more and that King Tiridates had been driven from the country. At Rome, the Senate voted numerous honors to the emperor Nero in celebration of Corbulo's success.

But the job was not finished. The field marshal and his legions spent the winter of A.D. 58–59 in eastern Armenia. In the spring of A.D. 59 they resumed the task of taking cities, towns, and fortresses in a push to the southwest, aiming for the next principal city of Armenia, Tigranocerta. Not unlike Mark Antony during his Median campaign, Corbulo found his supplies becoming stretched, and his legionaries were forced to eat beef instead of their normal bread ration, which they were not at all happy about. While Corbulo was concentrating on Tigranocerta in the south, news reached him that Tiridates had crossed the border back into Armenia with his troops. By sending a large part of his army east, Corbulo frightened Tiridates into quickly retreating the way he had come. With his kinsmen the Parthians engaged in a war with neighbors to the south, Tiridates had no hope of support from that quarter, and he went into hiding in Media. By the fall, Corbulo had taken Tigranocerta, and all Armenia was in Roman hands.

On Nero's orders, Field Marshal Corbulo installed the Cappadocian prince Tigranes, who had been brought up in Rome, as the new king of Armenia. Providing him with a force of a thousand legionaries from the 6th Ferrata and 10th Legions plus three cohorts of allied infantry and some cavalry, Corbulo left Tigranes on the throne in Tigranocerta, the new capital of Armenia, and marched his legions out of the country. He quartered the 6th and the 10th just across the border, in Cappadocia, in winter camps from where they could quickly strike into Armenia again if the need arose, but he sent the 3rd Gallica back south. While Corbulo had been campaigning in Armenia, his rival the governor of Syria, Ummidius Quadratus, had died in office. Corbulo now found his gubernatorial authority extended by the Palatium to also take in Syria and Judea. So, while he now based himself in Antioch, knowing the 3rd Gallica was soon due for discharge and reenlistment, he sent its six cohorts marching back to their regular station.

By the time these cohorts returned to their old posts in Judea late in the year, all the men of the 3rd Gallica would have been thinking about their discharge the following spring. Already, officials throughout Syria were requiring young men with citizenship who were age seventeen or above to submit their names for military service. In the late fall, those young men were summoned to a muster at which centurions of the 3rd Gallica quickly weeded out the physically and mentally unfit and assigned the recruits to cohorts. Men from the same region were kept together, so that a large contingent from the city of Beirut would constitute a cohort or two.

On January 1, A.D. 60, the cohorts of the legion assembled at their various bases throughout Judea and, as tradition required, swore allegiance to the emperor—in this case Nero. Several weeks later, the new Syrian recruits, who had signed their enlistment contracts and had been outfitted locally, were marched down to the legion's headquarters at Caesarea. There they would undergo basic training, to be ready by the spring to fill the shoes of the men who were retiring. Some legion veterans would voluntarily sign up for another twenty-year enlistment, and many of these men would go into the legion's 1st and 2nd Cohorts, the senior cohorts. Other would be promoted and spread throughout the legion. Some centurions would be transferred to more senior positions with other legions.

But most of the legionaries of the A.D. 40 enlistment were ready for their retirement bonus and grant of land. Some would become farmers. Because they could not legally sell their land grants for twenty years, others would lease their land and move into cities and towns. Commerce was open to them, furnished as they were with savings from twenty years to invest in their future. They would become tavernkeepers, shop owners, brothelkeepers, moneylenders, factory owners, shipowners, importers. Some, ex-centurions in particular, would run for election to their local city senates. Forbidden to marry while serving in the army, most would take a wife.

As spring began, they assembled again, this time for their paying-off ceremony. Each man going into retirement was presented with his discharge certificate and a retirement bonus of 12,000 sesterces in gold. At the same ceremony, the new recruits formed up and were presented by the most senior officer present with their new cohort standards, which were blessed in the Lustration Exercise. Only the eagle would be staying with the legions. The retirees then marched off behind their old standards, to several Roman military colonies in the East, where they would take up their land grants. Those men from the last enlistment who had signed on for another twenty years with the legion moved up into the senior cohorts. As Jerusalem was such a difficult place to police, it's likely that the new 2nd Cohort was given the Jerusalem posting, because it contained mature, experienced men.

When a legion underwent its twenty-year discharge and reenlistment, the Palatium frequently also replaced the civil head of government at the same station. Now, in A.D. 60, a new procurator, Porcius Festus, arrived in Judea to take the place of Antonius Felix. When Felix departed Judea, he left Paul of Tarsus still a prisoner in Caesarea. According to the author of Acts, before he went, Felix ordered Paul placed in chains, to please the Jews. It would be up to his replacement to decide Paul's fate.

Within three days of arriving in Caesarea, Procurator Festus traveled up to Jerusalem to see the city for himself and to meet the Jewish leadership. He spent ten days in Jerusalem, staying at the Palace of Herod. While he was there, the high priest Ananias and other Jewish leaders came to pay their respects. They soon raised the subject of the troublesome Paul of Tarsus and asked a favor of the new procurator—send Paul up to Jerusalem to be tried, with a light escort, and they would lay in wait along the way and kill him, getting rid of a man who was a problem for them all. Festus said he would review the case on his return to Caesarea and told the priests to accompany him to Caesarea, where they could level their accusations against Paul to his face.

The day after his return to Caesarea, Festus convened a hearing in the Judgment Hall. As he took his seat, Jewish priests of the Sanhedrin appeared, and Paul was brought in. Several Jews spoke against Paul, making a variety of accusations but offering no proof of their claims. When

Paul was allowed to speak in his own defense, he said that he hadn't offended the law of the Jews, or against the Temple, or against Caesar.

Festus, obviously prepared to render the Jews the favor that they had asked of him, then asked Paul, "Will you go up to Jerusalem and be judged there?"

"I stand before Nero Caesar's judgment seat," Paul responded, "where I should be judged, as a Roman citizen. I've done the Jews no wrong, as you very well know. If I'm an offender and have committed anything worthy of the death penalty, I'll submit to execution. But if there's nothing to these charges they bring against me, no man has the right to hand me over to them." Then he played his trump card, the card he so often had held up his sleeve. "I appeal to Caesar," he now declared, "under the law of Augustus."

Early in the reign of Augustus, the Senate had legislated that Augustus was from that time forward the chief judge of Rome, which, under the Valerian Law and Porcian Law, meant that any Roman citizen accused of a crime had the ultimate right to appeal directly to him. This right had continued through the reigns of all subsequent emperors, as Augustus's successors had inherited his titles, powers, and responsibilities. As a final court of appeal, appearance before the emperor was the Roman equivalent of going before today's U.S. Supreme Court or Britain's Privy Council.

Festus called the members of the Sanhedrin forward and told them that under Roman law he had no choice now that Paul had sought to appeal to the emperor. He then straightened, looked at Paul, and said: "You say you wish to have your appeal heard by Caesar? Then to Caesar you shall go."

Paul was returned to the custody of a 3rd Gallica centurion until circumstances permitted his journey to Rome. A few days later, thirty-one-year-old King Herod Agrippa II of Chalcis and his sister, the beautiful and smart thirty-year-old Queen Berenice, arrived in Caesarea. They had been in Jerusalem celebrating the Passover, staying in their own residence there, the Hasmonaean Palace beside the Temple Mount. Now they were on their way back to Chalcis, their realm in northern Galilee. Agrippa was a Jew, but was a firm adherent to Rome. To show his loyalty to Nero, he had personally led several thousand of his own troops in Field Marshal Corbulo's Armenian task force. Agrippa and Berenice stayed with Procurator Festus for some days, during the course of which Festus told the couple about Paul's case. Intrigued, Agrippa asked to hear Paul speak.

So the next day Paul was brought before the procurator, the king, and his sister the queen. He found the Judgment Hall crowded with Roman officials, members of the royal entourage, and military officers. Festus announced to all present that Paul had applied to have his appeal heard by Caesar under the law of Augustus, and that accordingly he would send him to Nero Caesar at Rome. But, said Festus, he was uncertain what he should write in the indictment that accompanied Paul. So now he asked King Agrippa for his advice regarding the charges against which Paul was appealing.

King Agrippa invited Paul to speak for himself, so Paul proceeded to tell of his life, his education, and his religious training, which would have included instruction in Greek, Latin, and Hebrew. He spoke of his career as a Pharisee, of his conversion on the road to Damascus, and of his work converting Jews and Gentiles throughout the East since. Then he began to talk of how Christ had been the first to rise from the dead. He obviously became very impassioned by this point, because the governor loudly interrupted him.

"Enough!" he called. "Paul, you're not making sense! Too much learning has obviously sent you crazy."

"With respect, most noble Festus, I'm not crazy," Paul replied. "I speak nothing but the sober truth." Paul then fixed his eyes on Agrippa, and told the king that he knew what Paul had said was the truth. He asked him if the prophets of old hadn't predicted the coming of the Messiah, and his death and rising from the dead.

"You have almost persuaded me to become a Nazarene," Agrippa responded, perhaps with a smile. He then went into a huddle with his sister and the procurator. All agreed that Paul had done nothing to justify a death sentence or imprisonment.

So, still uncertain what to write in the indictment that accompanied Paul to Rome, Procurator Festus had the accused taken back into custody until there were enough prisoners bound for Rome to warrant detaching troops from the Caesarea garrison to escort them.

XII

THE CENTURION'S DECISION

This was not the best time of year to be sailing to Italy. It was September, and before long, the seasonal winds would change, fierce storms would brew, and after that the winds would blow the wrong way entirely. All sailing to Italy from the East would then be suspended until after the winter, when the favorable south wind, the "fast wind," returned.

The 3rd Gallica Legion detachment preparing to make the voyage, escorting prisoners from Caesarea to Rome, would have come from one of its newly recruited cohorts, one of the five based at Caesarea. At the very most, there were eighty of them—an entire century, or platoon. They were all Syrian, and all were conscripts, many as young as seventeen. Many would never have left their hometowns before joining the army. Now they were setting off for the very center of the Roman world.

According to Acts, the detachment's leader was a Centurion Julius. We don't know his age, but his subsequent wisdom and fortitude on the difficult journey suggest he was a man of mature years. He may have been in his forties, but could have been older. We know of Petronius Fortunatus, a centurion of the 1st Italica Legion several decades later, who was still serving at age sixty-six, so the concept of Centurion Julius being a tough old bird of sixty or so is not beyond the realms of possibility. Julian was not necessarily Syrian or a worshipper of Baal. Centurions underwent many transfers during their careers. Just as Centurion Fortunatus was promoted and transferred twelve times during his career, all centurions were transferred between a number of legions during their careers as they went up the ladder of seniority. Some, too, were detached from legions, to be assigned to provinces to command local police forces of freedmen or to new auxiliary units as instructors.

Centurion Julius would have two other noncommissioned officers to help him. One, an *optio*, or sergeant major, was the training and records officer of a century. The other was a *tesserarius*, or orderly sergeant. His title came from his duty of distributing the *tessera*, a wax tablet on which was written the watchword, or password for the next twenty-four hours. At sunset every evening, the tribune of the watch reported to the most senior officer in camp and advised him of the number of men fit for duty. The commander gave him the watchword, which was distributed on the tessera to all guard posts.

Earlier in the year Julius had put his cohort of raw, naive Syrian youths through tough physical training, using the business end of his centurion's vine stick to enforce discipline. He had made each man pick a buddy from the ranks who would be executor of his comrade's will when he died, and who would fight at his back in combat. The centurion taught his men how to swiftly take up textbook combat formations, and put them through weapons training. The legions' drills, says Josephus, were so intense they were like bloodless battles, while their battles resembled bloody drills.

Legion training methods were based partly on fear, with some infringements of military law punishable by death. As a result, Josephus was to say, legionaries' ears were constantly ready for orders and their eyes ready for signals. The iron discipline and machinelike routine saw the men of the 3rd Gallica up before dawn every day. They learned how to dig entrenchments, erect tents, build camps, bridges, and siege equipment, and how to site and fire artillery. Now, in theory, Centurion Julius's men were equipped for whatever the gods threw at them. Now, through fear and blind trust, they should obey their centurion's every command without question, without hesitation.

Now, six months after officially joining their legion, which was renowned in Syria as the legion that had saved Mark Antony, the 3rd Gallica's new recruits, the *tiros*, were ready for action. Already they had been called out several times to settle civil disturbances between people of Greek background and Jews in the province. According to Josephus, the legionaries always favored the Greeks in these disputes, because, he said, they were of similar background to themselves.

But this police work was no preparation for the journey upon which the men of the prisoner escort were about to embark. That journey would be by sea. Few if any of the young legionaries could swim, few had been to sea before. They would have been very conscious that there was a chance their ship might be wrecked. So, many of the 3rd Gallica youngsters in Centurion Julius's party would have had mixed emotions—excitement at the prospect of seeing mighty Rome, apprehension about the terrors of a lengthy sea voyage.

Paul of Tarsus would have been looking forward to the journey. Not only would it free him from the Caesarea cell he had occupied for the past two years, it also would allow him to visit the Christian congregations in and around Rome. During the reign of Claudius, all Jews had been banned from Rome—and Christians were then considered a Jewish sect. Only recently, in the reign of Nero, had Jews been permitted to once more live in the capital, and Christians, including a number who had been converted by Paul and his subordinates, had relocated there from the East. Paul was an experienced sea traveler, having made a number of voyages around the eastern Mediterranean during his mission to the Gentiles over the past twenty-four years. And, according to his letters, he had been shipwrecked on at least one occasion prior to this. By this time he had survived so many trials and tribulations that another sea voyage would not have worried him. Besides, he would not be alone—as the journey would be undertaken on passenger-carrying cargo vessels, it would be possible for Paul to take along several companions as long as they paid their own way.

Paul chose three companions for the journey. One was Luke the physician. A native of Thebes in Greece and longtime resident of Antioch, Luke was a well-educated man and a trained doctor—learned Greeks dominated the medical profession of the Roman Empire. Paul would have met and possibly converted Luke in Antioch, for a number of years the base for Paul's evangelical work. Luke, who had accompanied Paul since his earliest missions in the East, would remain unmarried throughout his life, until, unlike many of the early Christian preachers, he died of natural causes in his eighties. According to Luke, in Acts, another of Paul's companions for the journey to Rome was Aristarchus of Thessalonika, a Macedonian Greek. And according to tradition, the third was Trophimus of Ephesus, the catalyst for Paul's arrest in Jerusalem.

On a fine fall day, passengers boarded a coastal freighter from Adramyttium that lay at the busy Caesarea docks. The ship was due to sail to Lycia, northwest of Caesarea, in today's southern Turkey. Cargo vessels of the day were carvel-built, with oak planks laid flush against each other over closely spaced ribs. Unlike warships, they were not equipped with oars. Freighters relied for motive power solely on the wind and a large rectangular canvas mainsail. When possible they "coasted"—following the coastline to their destination, enabling them to quickly seek a safe harbor if a storm blew up or if pirates threatened. There was no belowdeck accommodation on these ships. The master had a small enclosed space at the rear of the main deck, but with most of the space belowdeck filled with cargo, his crew slept on the hard main deck, and so did the paying passengers. Luke, Aristarchus, and Trophimus boarded with these passengers and staked out sleeping places. Apart from clothing and other personal items, passengers supplied their own food, wine, and water.

With distaste, other passengers watched as a legionary detachment came crunching down the thronging stone pier behind a cloth detachment standard of the 3rd Gallica Legion, leading chained prisoners. The prisoners came clanking up the boarding plank, led by the chain tugged by their individual escorts. The exact number of prisoners is unknown, but it is likely to have been ten or so. Some, like Paul, would be citizens going to Rome to have their appeals heard by the emperor. Others would be condemned men on their way to face execution.

Their 3rd Gallica escorts would have been deliberately terse and unfriendly. Fifty years later, another Christian prisoner sent in chains to Rome from Syria, Ignatius Theophoros, the later Saint Ignatius, bishop of Antioch, would write that his escort was made up of ten Roman soldiers who shared his escort duties. No matter how hard Ignatius tried to befriend the soldiers of his guard, he was not able to even get a smile from them. "Veritable leopards," he called them. There was a specific reason for this lack of friendliness. Centurion Julius would have warned his men in A.D. 60 that on a long journey a prisoner might befriend his guard, then through their friendship engineer his escape. If soldiers of the escort let a prisoner escape, all those soldiers were liable to suffer capital punishment.

Once satisfied that prisoners and legionaries were securely aboard, Centurion Julius gave the master permission to sail. From now on, the centurion would be in charge on board ship, and the master would have to seek his approval for everything he did. As the tide was turning, the ship's mainsail went up, lines were cast off fore and aft, and the freighter slowly sailed out between Caesarea's stone breakwaters with the tide.

Centurion Julius and his men would have admired the sight of Caesarea's handsome Roman theater running down to the beach. They would have looked up at the imposing white walls of the stone fortress of Caesarea that had become their home, and thought about Syrian relatives and comrades of the 3rd Gallica they were leaving behind. They knew it would be months before they saw them again. Early, excited conversations would have faded. Out on the Mediterranean, the only sounds were of the wind billowing the sails and the water coursing around the bow. Paul and his companions would have been experiencing mixed feelings as they watched the coast recede. Leaving behind many friends, and foes, they were heading for the lion's den, literally. There was no telling whether or when any of them would see Judea, or Jerusalem, again.

A mile or so out to sea, and with those on board still able to see a white marble temple at the center of the city glowing in the sunlight—built by Herod the Great and dedicated to the Divine Julius—the ship gradually came onto a new, northerly course and coasted north up the Phoenician coast. The next day they put into Sidon, a two-thousand-year-old trading city famous for its purple dyes and glassware. There, Centurion Julius allowed Paul to go ashore and take refreshment with friends—although still chained to a soldier. Then it was on with the voyage, coasting past Cilicia and Pamphylia, with Cyprus on their left, heading for the port city of Myra in Lycia.

Every night during the voyage all on board slept on the deck. The crew spread leather covers suspended from mast to rails. These were designed to both provide shelter in the event of rain and collect drinking water. And every morning without fail, the soldiers of the 3rd Gallica Legion detachment knelt on the swaying deck, bowed to the rising sun, and offered prayers to their sun god Baal. No mention of these ministrations to Baal are mentioned in Acts. But, likewise, there are no references to any other pagan religious observances anywhere in Acts. With most of the civilian passengers and crew on this ship being pagans, worshippers of the Greco-Roman pantheon, all around Paul and his three Christian companions on this journey people would have been offering prayers to Roman gods. Jupiter, king of the gods, would have been called on to bless the travelers, as would Neptune, god of the sea. Meanwhile, members of the crew would have been offering prayers to Castor and Pollux, patron deities of sailors.

After an uneventful voyage, the ship docked in Myra, at the mouth of the Andriacus River. Today's Demre, the city was overlooked by an acropolis whose western side was carved with pillared facades representing temples and houses. A magnificent drama theater sat at the foot of the acropolis. Here at the Myra docks the ship unloaded, and Centurion Julius went looking for another suitable vessel for the next leg of the journey. He soon found a heavily laden ship of the grain fleet out of Alexandria. Bound for Italy, making one of the last runs of the year, it was lying low in the water with its precious cargo of wheat belowdeck.

Grain ships were built to a common design—typically 90 feet long and 28 feet wide, they had high, pointed prows and sterns. They could carry 250 tons of cargo below and up to 300 deck passengers. Because of their squat, curved appearance, the tubby grain ships were nicknamed "round ships" by Romans. The grain ship was powered by a mainsail, a bowsail, and a small topsail. A century earlier, the orator Cicero had written to a friend that people had flooded to the docks every spring when the first ships from the East had begun to arrive at the port of Puteoli, modern Pozzuoli. Lining the shoreline around the bay, spectators had watched the ships coming in, bringing the grain they depended on for their survival and all the luxury good from the East that enhanced their lives. Because of the importance of grain ships, Cicero had said, they alone were permitted by port authorities to keep their topsails up when they came into the harbor.

When the grain ship carrying Paul of Tarsus and his 3rd Gallica escort sailed from Myra, it was, according to Acts, carrying 276 passengers—crew, prisoners, legionaries, and paying travelers. A naval frigate of the same period, a vessel of a similar size to these grain ships with a length of 108 feet and a beam of 12 feet, carried a crew of 144 rowers for its two banks of oars and 10 to 15 sailors to handle the sail and rigging and to man the rudders, as well as 40 marines. So with only the sails to handle, the crew of this freighter would have comprised about 15 men. Acts says that in addition to the skipper, the ship's owner was aboard. It was the habit of Italian merchants to sail to Alexandria at the start of the sailing season to supervise the acquisition of cargoes, then return home to Italy at the end of the season.

Paul was still chained to his escort day and night during the voyage. A Roman citizen awaiting appeal was, technically, not permitted to have his freedom impaired. In practice, such a prisoner was permitted to receive any visitors he chose while in custody, and he did not have his feet placed in stocks, but while on the move his wrists were enclosed by manacles. There was no lock—manacles were closed by a metal pin, and could be opened only by that pin being driven out of its slot using a hammer and chisel. The term "having his chains knocked off" derived from this act. If the ship carrying a chained prisoner were to sink, there would be neither the time nor the incentive for the guards to release him from his chains.

In one of his letters, Paul writes that because he was chained on the journey, apart from his three Christian companions he was shunned by all other free passengers but one. The exception was Onesiphorus, who, like Trophimus, was from Ephesus in Asia. Onesiphorus would regularly chat with Paul during the journey, ignoring his prisoner status. From later references it seems that Onesiphorus became a Christian convert and firm follower of Paul as a result of the time they spent together on this journey.

All went well as the ship coasted west between the island of Rhodes and the mainland. But then the winds became contrary, and the master was forced to swing farther south in search of a consistent breeze from the east. This took the ship into exposed waters below Crete, instead of the safer route through the islands of the Cyclades. Even so, they were now repeatedly becalmed. It was obvious that the fast wind had departed for the year. The ship's master and owner agreed that they should spend the winter at a sheltered harbor they were familiar with, on the southern coast of Crete, called the Fair Havens, near the city of Lasea. From there they could set off again in the new year when the fast wind returned.

But once they reached the Fair Havens, the crew decided that the cove wasn't sheltered enough, and spoke of continuing to another harbor, Phenice (Phoenix), on the western coast of Crete. When he heard this, Paul began to worry that if they continued any farther, the ship and all in it would perish in the storms that raged in this part of the world late in the year. Calling over Centurion Julius, Paul urged him to order the master to turn back. But Centurion Julius went along with the crew's professional judgment. They sailed on.

As if to vindicate the seamen, the south wind blew gently at first. But as they passed the southwestern tip of Crete and turned to head up the western coast of the island, a tempest sprang up, a wild wind from the east the locals called Euroclydon. It was too strong to fight, and the skipper decided to run before it. As the ship plowed west in the gale, wallowing in the huge seas, young soldiers of the 3rd Gallica would have hung over the sides, being violently seasick. The master now ordered all sails struck, and prayed to his gods, as they were carried along with no control over their course or their fate.

The tempest continued unabated through the night and into the next day. As water washed over the deck, the master ordered all unnecessary baggage tossed over the side to lighten the ship. The next day, the weather was no better, and passengers were called on to help the sailors cut away the ship's tackle and heave it overboard. As the storm-tossed days passed, they saw neither the sun nor the stars.

One night, Paul had a dream that an angel stood beside him and assured him that he would survive to appear before the emperor, and everyone else on board also would survive, although the ship would be lost. This, Paul told anyone who would listen, meant that they would be wrecked on an island. But no one took any notice of this Jewish spiritualist, a man who was, reputedly, the subject of often violent headaches.

For fourteen days they were at the mercy of the gale. Then, finally, on the fourteenth night, the wind dropped considerably, and at about midnight the experienced seamen on board became convinced they were near land. Dropping a lead weight to sound their depth, they found they had

20 fathoms, or 120 feet, of water beneath them. A little later the depth was down to 90 feet, and the crew began to worry they would soon be driven onto a rocky shore. Four canvas sea anchors were cast over the stern to slow their progress, and as the black of night shrouded the ship, everyone on board waited impatiently for the dawn.

But some of the crew began to fear that the ship would be dashed on rocks before the sun came up, so under the pretext of going to cast more sea anchors from the bow, they lowered the ship's boat forward, planning to make their escape.

Paul now called out to Centurion Julius and his legionaries, "If they don't remain on the ship, none of you will survive."

Centurion Julius ordered the crewmen away from the rail, and told his men to cut the dinghy adrift. Drawing their swords, several legionaries cleaved through the ropes holding the boat fast. With crewmen glumly watching, the boat was last seen astern, drifting into the darkness.

At Paul's urging everyone ate a proper meal for the first time in two weeks—bread and salted meat. As they ate, they agreed that it was either them or the ship's cargo now. So, to lighten the ship, all hands set to work bringing up the wheat from belowdeck and casting it into the sea. The ship's owner would not have been a happy man, losing his valuable cargo, but it was now literally a matter of life or death.

As the sun rose into a grimy sky, and the legionaries dropped to their knees and offered fervent prayers to Baal for their salvation, all on board saw that they were near land. The wind and current were pushing them into a long, thin bay—where, no one knew. Spotting a creek entering the sea on a rocky, sea-pounded coast, the ship's master decided that their best chance of survival was to try to run the ship aground in the creek. So as the four sea anchors were dragged back on board, the mainsail was run up. The tiller, which had been lashed in place till now, was unfastened. The ship headed for the shore.

They came in riding the waves, with the steersman straining to keep the ship from broaching, and with soldiers of the 3rd Gallica hanging onto the tiller with him to maintain a straight course. With a giant shudder the ship hit land at the mouth of the creek. Here, where the waters of the creek and ocean collided, they lodged on a sandbank still some distance from shore. The bow was stuck fast, with the sea swirling around the sides and waves pounding into the stern. Now, too, heavy rain lashed the ship, and it was bitterly cold. At first those on board huddled out of the rain under the night covers. But as the violence of the waves took effect, with frightening creaks and cracks, the ship's stern began to break up. Clearly, it would be only a matter of time before the entire ship was wrenched apart by the force of the waves.

The 3rd Gallica soldiers held a quick conference. They knew that if their prisoners were to escape they would pay with their lives. All agreed on what they had to do. The soldiers went to Centurion Julius. Standing around him on the shuddering deck, the grim-faced legionaries urged their centurion to allow them to kill the prisoners, to prevent any of them from swimming away and escaping. It was, they said, with hands on the hilts of their sheathed swords, them or the prisoners.

XIII

CAST UP ON MALTA

enturion Julius shook his head. No prisoners would be killed while he was in charge. The author of Acts says that Julius made this decision specifically to save the life of Paul. The centurion ordered his unhappy men to knock off the manacles of all the prisoners. Acts says he then told all aboard who could swim to take to the water and make for the shore. As for the rest, they should pull up decking planks and timber fittings.

As the few swimmers aboard plunged into the boiling sea and made for shore, the 3rd Gallica soldiers removed their helmets, sword belts, and heavy, segmented armor. Then the legionaries gingerly climbed over the side, and with sword and dagger scabbards on planks, they allowed the incoming waves to take them toward the land. When Centurion Julius was sure the prisoners and his own men had left the ship, he, too, would have taken to the water, with his sword and the cylindrical leather dispatch case containing his orders and the indictments against the prisoners lashed to a plank. One by one, the men floating in the sea were washed ashore.

As the ship came apart on the sandbank, every one of the men who left the ship and took their chances in the water reached land safely—all 276 of them. And not a single prisoner had escaped. There, the soldiers of the 3rd Gallica strapped on their sword belts, and, feeling like soldiers once more, herded their charges together, as the rain continued to fall. With the dawn, local people appeared, rough and ready tribespeople from a nearby village, looking with pity on the shivering, bedraggled survivors. They told the shipwrecked survivors that they had landed on the island of Malta. The travelers in fact made landfall in a bay that in modern times bears the apostle's name—Saint Paul's Bay—on the northwestern tip of the island. Malta had been a Roman possession since 218 B.C. Originally administered from Sicily, Malta later became self-governing, coining its

114

own currency and sending ambassadors to Rome, but still very much as a part of the empire and answerable to Rome.

The tribespeople led the shipwrecked travelers to their village, today called San Pawl il-Bahar, on the southern shore of the bay, where they gratefully huddled around a large fire. After a meal and a good night's sleep, the shipwrecked victims were taken across the island to the city of Melita, from which the island took its name, today the town of Rabat. There the chief official of the island, Governor Publius, received the centurion and his party warmly and for the next three days provided lodgings in his spacious villa for soldiers and prisoners. On the fourth day at Melita, the party moved into their own quarters in the city, which had been arranged by Centurion Julius. As Roman law required, he was to permit Paul to receive visitors throughout his stay.

The 3rd Gallica party waited three months on Malta—for the winter to pass and for favorable winds to return. Centurion Julius found another northbound Alexandrian grain ship that had arrived ahead of them and was wintering at anchor in one of the island's sheltered coves, and arranged passage for his party. As the spring of A.D. 61 approached, the ship prepared to sail. Over the winter, the local authorities had reequipped the soldiers of the 3rd Gallica detachment, and now they provided them with provisions for the next leg of the journey. As the centurion put his prisoners and escort aboard the ship, fee-paying passengers joined them once again.

This grain ship sailed under a flag bearing the insignia of Castor and Pollux, the patron deities of Roman seafarers, who were believed to protect shipwrecked sailors and bring favorable winds. With a good following wind, the ship departed Malta early in the spring, and sailed north, to Syracuse in Sicily, without incident. After three days at Syracuse, waiting for the wind to freshen, they again set sail and soon landed at Rhegium, today's city of Reggio on the tip of the boot of Italy. The following day, a strong wind blew afresh from the south, and they put to sea once more.

Now they ran up the western coast of Italy to the Bay of Naples, heading for Pozzuoli in Campania, near modern Naples. From the ship's deck, the soldiers of the escort would have gazed at places they had heard about in the East. They passed the isle of Capri, close on their left quarter. The emperor Tiberius had kept twelve villas on Capri and spent the last years of his life there. To their right, conical Mount Vesuvius stood tall behind the busy little port town of Pompeii. Vesuvius had become famous as one of the strongholds of the rebel gladiator Spartacus and his slave army in 73 B.C., before Pompey's 3rd Legion had helped terminate their bloody revolt. The Vesuvius the travelers saw in the spring of A.D. 61 had two summits, not the one we see today. Away to the northeast, the semiactive volcano Solfatara, known to Romans as Forum Vulcan, was actively emitting sulfurous gases. No one on board that ship as it crossed the Bay of Naples in March of A.D. 61 could have imagined that eighteen years later Pompeii and nearby Stabiae and Herculaneum would be wiped from the map as Vesuvius literally blew one of its two tops in a devastating eruption.

Pozzuoli was one of Italy's busiest commercial ports, and the grain ship docked amid scores of unloading cargo vessels from all around the Mediterranean. Just around the bay, at Micenum, the warships of Rome's Tyrrhenian Fleet were based, and as the travelers from Judea came ashore, there were probably one or two frigates and cruisers out on the bay exercising, their oars dipping and flashing in the spring sunshine. Centurion Julius and his 3rd Gallica detachment herded their prisoners onto the Italian shore. The last stage of the journey to Rome would be undertaken on foot.

They stayed in Pozzuoli for seven days, which suited Paul, as there were Christians in the town, and Luke and his traveling companions sought them out. The local Christian community, which had no idea Paul was coming to town, greeted him warmly. Meanwhile, Centurion Julius reported to the tribune of the 17th Cohort of the City Guard of Rome, then based in Pozzuoli, producing his written orders from Procurator Festus in Caesarea. The tribune would have sent a dispatch to Rome. When a reply came back, it would have been in the form of written orders from the Prefect of the Praetorian Guard, Sextus Burrus, instructing the centurion to proceed with his party to Rome and report to the Praetorian tribune of the watch in the capital. The Gallic-born prefect Burrus, able, honest, and fair—attributes usually lacking in a colonel of the Praetorian Guard—had been Praetorian commander for a decade, after forging an impressive career as a tough soldier despite a withered left hand. He was no man's fool. Nero's senior military appointments, like that of Field Marshal Corbulo in the East, had been strongly influenced by Burrus. But in A.D. 61, Prefect Burrus was in the advanced stages of the throat cancer that would kill him the following year. His orders would have been accompanied by written authority from Flavius Sabinus, City prefect, granting Centurion Julius and his detachment permission to enter Rome under arms.

At the same time that Centurion Julius sent his dispatch to Rome, the Christians in Pozzuoli sent a messenger to the congregation in Rome, alerting them of Paul's imminent arrival. For years, Paul had been promising to come to the Christians in Rome, writing them letters of comfort, encouragement, and guidance. Now, at last, he was fulfilling his vow, although not quite in the manner he would have wished. One day in March or early April, surrounded by his armed guards of the 3rd Gallica Legion and his fellow prisoners, and in chains, Paul set out from Pozzuoli on the road to Rome. That road, the Appian Way, was a stone-paved 330-mile highway that ran all the way from Brindisi, on the southeast coast, to the capital. At its broadest, the Appian Way was only eighteen feet wide. Designed by military engineers as all-weather thoroughfares along which Rome's legions could travel quickly, they were as straight as a die. Their paving stones were deliberately laid in a slight camber, higher at the middle of the road, lower at the edges to allow rainwater to run off into roadside culverts. The party from Caesarea marched along the busy Appian Way, with the banner of the 3rd Gallica detachment going on before them. People traveling the highway would have quickly moved aside and looked with disdain at the chained prisoners in the legionaries' midst.

Beside a canal, 43 miles from Rome, at Forum Appii, a market village full of boatmen and cheating innkeepers, according to Horace, the party was met by Christians who had come from Rome to welcome Paul, forewarned by the Pozzuoli congregation's message. Paul's spirits had sunk lower the closer he came to Rome. But now, says Acts, the sight of fellow Christians, many of whose faces he knew from the East or whose names he knew from correspondence, did his heart good, and he found new courage. The Christians from the capital joined Paul's companions in the rear of the column, and the enlarged party spent the night at Forum Appii before moving on shortly after dawn the next day. Eighteen miles farther on, at the next night halt, Tres Tabernae, where a tavern, general store, and blacksmith's sat at a crossroads, another band of Christians from Rome greeted Paul and also fell in with the party. With the new day, the journey saw the party passing tombs of wealthy Romans that lined the Appian Way for many miles from the outskirts of Rome. By midmorning they were within sight of Rome's famed seven hills.

In through the suburbs they marched, to the old city wall, halting by the twin openings of the Appian Gate—just wide enough for a chariot or wagon to pass through. At the gate stood sentries of the City Guard, wearing the same uniform and equipment as legionaries. But City Guard troops were freedmen, former slaves, not citizens. The young legionaries would have looked from the massive city walls, dating back hundreds of years to the time of Servius Tullius, sixth king of Rome, to the giant gates of wood and iron suspended in the arches above the gateways. At a moment's notice guards would chop the ropes that held them in place. The gates would come rushing down, to crush anyone standing beneath—just as they had in the civil war between the consuls Sulla and Marius 150 years before.

While his men were gazing wide-eyed at the sights, and as civilians flooded in and out around them, Centurion Julius produced his authorities. The centurion of the guard would have then given explicit instructions on where to go. And, with precise steps, the young soldiers from the other side of the empire marched into Rome with their prisoners.

XIV

IN NERO'S ROME

P roceeding through the massive "in" gate, with the Tiber River on their left, the 3rd Gallica party marched through Rome's 1st Precinct toward the Circus Maximus. If it was a race day, they would have heard Rome before they saw it, with 255,000 voices in the Circus Maximus roaring as one like the voice of an angry god as four chariot teams pounded around the track in one of the day's twenty-four races, each seven circuits long. The teams—the Whites, the Blues, the Reds, and the Greens—were run by corporations. Stock in those corporations was so valuable it was passed from father to son. The corporations were so powerful that they operated stud farms throughout the provinces, and their horse buyers had first call over any horses on sale, even having precedence over remount buyers acting for the army. Romans, the original sports fans, were fanatical supporters of their chariot-racing teams, and families followed their team from one generation to the next. Some fans even had the name of their team inscribed on their tombs. Successful charioteers, usually former slaves, became rich, and were the rock stars of their day.

The soldiers of the 3rd Gallica would have been aware that their emperor loved chariot racing. A follower of the Greens, Nero drove four-horse chariots in competition, always taking the winner's prize even if he didn't come first. Before long he would add two more teams to the competition—the Golds and the Purples. His uncle, the emperor Caligula, also had raced chariots. At this time the Circus Maximus stadium was constructed entirely from timber—to this day it is the largest wooden structure ever built. It would burn down several times until, under Domitian and later emperors, its lower sections would be rebuilt in brick, stone, and marble and seat as many as 385,000 spectators. No modern stadium has ever been built that could seat as many. On a race day, the deserted city streets were patrolled by the City Guard to discourage burglaries. But on a normal business day, like today, you could hardly move in Rome's narrow, pedestrian-clogged thoroughfares.

After passing beneath the towering Marcian Aqueduct, which brought running water from miles away to the public baths and fountains, the legionaries of the 3rd Gallica turned right and marched along the Triumphal Way. Rising to their left, the Capitoline Hill was adorned with Rome's largest temple, the Temple of Capitoline Jove. As the legionaries marched along the base of the Palatine Hill, they could see, on the summit, the rear of the original palace of the first emperor, Mark Antony's nemesis Augustus, its white marble gleaming in the spring sunshine. By this time Augustus's palace was called the Old Palatium. Most succeeding emperors had built their own palaces on the Palatine, and they now ranged down the northern slope of the hill toward the Forum—the palace of Tiberius, the surprisingly small palace of Caligula, Nero's palace, even a palace that had been the home of Nero's famous grandfather Germanicus Caesar, Tiberius's murdered heir.

On the Sacred Way, they passed the circular Temple of Vesta, where the six Vestal Virgins maintained the sacred eternal flame twenty-four hours a day. The more learned among the Gallicans would have been aware that the palace next to it was the traditional residence of the Pontifus Maximus and had been Julius Caesar's home at Rome for many years. To their left now the soldiers saw the entrance to the Forum of Rome, with its famous temples and meeting places, the courts where justice was dispensed, and the Senate House where the "conscript fathers," the senators of Rome, met to debate and make the laws of Rome.

Turning right, the Gallicans marched along narrow streets lined with sidewalk stores whose goods spilled onto the paving stones. Here the young soldiers saw live birds in cages caught in reed traps outside the city overnight, jars of cosmetics from Egypt, African olive oil in huge clay amphorae, fresh fish from the Tyrrhenian Sea, and farm produce from Italian estates. There were kitchen pottery and wooden shoes and sandals from Gaul, leather belts from Germany, cuts of meat and live rabbits and fowl at the butchers' stores, and gleaming sharp knives displayed in knife stores. There were even live monkeys from Africa sitting forlornly chained to one store's countertop.

The party passed busy cafés and aggressive melon sellers who would have tried to sell the legionaries fruit as they passed. There were wine bars with laughing patrons sitting on stone stools and playing checkers. Lines of slaves toting wicker baskets to fill their masters' orders trailed away from busy bakeries. Scribes with quill pens could be seen writing letters for illiterate customers. Others sat at bookstore desks mass-producing copies of the latest works of a leading poet or playwright. For 20 sesterces you could buy the memoirs of a general, a Greek history, the treatise of a scholar on matters agricultural or scientific, or an epic true tale told in verse, such as the adventures of Germanicus Caesar by Albiovanus Pedo.

Blacksmiths pounded anvils to make kitchen tools, barbers shaved customers who sat on pavement stools, craftsmen beat copper and worked silver in their open doorways. Jewelers fashioned jewelry. Schoolteachers sat on stools with their classes, their schoolroom windows and doors open to all the passing parade. All this activity was in the shadow of brick apartment buildings, none less than four stories tall and as many as seven stories. And all around the visitors, builders were knocking down buildings to erect larger ones so landlords could charge higher rents.

The city bathhouses were closed. In the afternoon, their bells would toll and their doors would be flung open to admit impatient bathers. There were several large public bathhouses, where entry was free. Even so, the more than one thousand commercial bathhouses in Rome were inexpensive, with an entry fee of just one-sixteenth of a sesterce, and children free. It would be another half century before the emperor Hadrian decreed that men and women must bathe separately. The Roman bathhouse was for more than bathing: it was the social hub of daily life. In the vast public bathhouses you could discuss business and politics, visit a library, see an exhibition in the bathhouse museum, or shop in the arcades. Within little more than a decade, as the legion's winter bases around the empire were improved, every legion would have its own private bathhouse.

The assault on the visitors' senses extended to the dust in the air from construction work, the drifting smoke from thousands of workshop fires, the aromas of sweaty bodies, rare spices, freshly baked bread and stale wine, the pungent odor of ammonia wafting out from side alley tanneries to burn the soldiers' nostrils.

Their course took them toward another city wall entrance, the Viminalis Gate. On their left now rose the Qurinal Hill, a crowded residential quarter. Up there, in Pomegranate Street, stood the modest house of General Titus Vespasianus, who had come to fame during the conquest of Britain seventeen years back. Rome had long ago overflowed its old walls, and now the Gallicans passed out into the suburbs of the 4th Precinct. Their final destination, the Castra Praetoria, the massive gray-brown complex of stone and brick and concrete that was the headquarters of the Praetorian Guard, stood to the left of the Nomentian Way. Today the National Library occupies part of the site. In A.D. 61 it contained a fortress that combined barracks and training facilities for the Praetorian and City Guard cohorts then stationed in Rome. The high stone walls of the complex were equipped with stone guard towers with conical roofs. There was a gate in each of the four walls. At the southeast-facing front entrance, the decuman gate, two large arched gateways, side by side, stood open, with Praetorians on duty at each. Much like the Carabinieri in Italy today, the Praetorian Guard was part military unit, part police force. In one-thousand-man cohorts commanded by a tribune, the Praetorians were the Roman Army's elite troops. In recognition of their status, they served only sixteen years, as opposed to the twenty-year enlistments of legionaries. The current Praetorians were six years into their latest enlistment. When they retired, they were to receive a bonus of 20,000 sesterces, 8,000 sesterces more than legionaries.

Now, as the 3rd Gallica detachment halted at the gate, Centurion Julius produced the scroll containing his orders from the Procurator of Judea. The centurion of the duty cohort inspected the orders and attached list of prisoners, then inspected the prisoners. He ordered Centurion Julius and his party to make their way to the tribune in charge of the duty cohort. While Paul's followers remained outside, the men of the 3rd Gallica marched Paul and the other prisoners into the complex. When Centurion Julius reported to the tribune of the watch, he would have handed over the indictments against Paul and his other prisoners that he had brought from Procurator Festus, having kept them safe even through the Malta shipwreck. It seems that Procurator Festus recommended that Paul be kept under house arrest in the city. The recommendation was accepted, and Paul was told to provide his own accommodation in the city while awaiting his appeal. He would not be permitted to leave the house, and would be constantly chained to a single Praetorian soldier. But he was granted unrestricted access to visitors, as was his right as a citizen.

At this point, Centurion Julius and his men parted company with Paul. Julius and his men would have spent that night at the Praetorian compound. Whether they got any sleep is debatable. They would have discovered that night why Rome was called "the city that never sleeps"—a title borrowed much later by New York City. The traffic that was banned from Rome during the day, the thousands of merchant carts and wagons bringing in and taking out the products that sustained the capital, rolled along the cobbled streets throughout the night. From sundown to sunup, the rumble of wheels and the cries of wagon drivers and muleteers were on the air, along with the crack of whips and the chatter and laughter of Rome's night owls who partied the night away. Many a provincial accustomed to silent nights back home was to complain about their inability to sleep when they stayed at Rome.

Next morning, yawning from lack of sleep, the men of the 3rd Gallica detachment would have formed up in their ranks and then marched back the way they had come. No time off for sightseeing. They had a long way to go to rejoin their legion in Judea. And with the winds against eastbound maritime travel at that time of year, they would have to walk all the way, arriving back in Judea in time for the summer, full of stories for their comrades of the 3rd Gallica about surviving a shipwreck and seeing the wonders of Rome.

Paul's friends, meanwhile, quickly arranged the rental of a house in the city. Later Christian writers were to say that the house was in a residential block later occupied by the Colosseum, at or near the intersection of the Sacred Way and the Triumphal Way. A city *domus*, the property of a wealthy landowner, it was sizable enough to accommodate the meetings that Paul soon began conducting, with the city's few Christians but also with the Jewish residents of Rome, whom he hoped to convert to Christianity. Within three days of his arrival in Rome, Paul was addressing large groups at the rented house. There, attached by chain to his Praetorian sentry, Paul lectured Rome's Jewry on the life and death of Jesus Christ. The Jews of Rome told him that they had not received any warning from the Great Sanhedrin at Jerusalem of his coming to Rome, but they said they had heard of the Nazarene sect, and they told him that Jews everywhere spoke adversely of it.

Acts says that Paul spent the next two years awaiting his hearing before Nero. Some later writers affirm that when he did appear, Nero dismissed the vague charges against him. Driven by guilt and remorse, Nero was going through a quest for spirituality at the time, following his A.D. 59 murder of his mother, Agrippina the Younger, and tried numerous religions and religious leaders, including the Jew Simon Magus. Obsessed with his matricide, he was particularly interested in those cults involving the birth of a deity from a virgin mother, a common theme in ancient religions of the East. It has been suggested that he spoke privately with Paul several times, hoping to find what he was looking for in Christianity. Nero did not convert to Christianity, but his mistress the freedwoman Acte, who stayed with him to the end, playing Eva Braun to his Hitler, was said to have been a Christian. She is also supposed to have introduced a number of people close to Nero to Paul and to Christianity while the apostle was living at Rome, including the emperor's cupbearer and an officer of the Palatium guard, the German Guard.

By the time Paul was released, in A.D. 63, and returned to his mission of spreading the word about Jesus of Nazareth, the men of the 3rd Gallica Legion, the legion that had twice been responsible for saving Paul's life in Jerusalem, and had, through the agency of Centurion Julius, spared his life in Malta, were preparing for another war.

<h1 style="text-align:center">XV</h1>

<h1 style="text-align:center">FANNING THE
FLAMES OF REVOLT</h1>

I t had been coming for a long time. In A.D. 66, Jewish resentment at greedy rule by Roman procurators finally exploded into revolt in Judea. And the 3rd Gallica Legion, occupying the garrisons of Judea, was in the thick of it, and about to bleed.

Romans throughout the empire had been distracted. In A.D. 64 the Parthians had again invaded Armenia, and after Field Marshal Corbulo's deputy, General Paetus, had botched the counterattack, Corbulo had led his army, including six cohorts of the 3rd Augusta, in routing the enemy. To settle the Armenian issue, the Parthian prince Tiridates was permitted by Corbulo to ascend the Armenian throne, but only after he swore loyalty to Nero, emperor of Rome. Then, even as the people of Rome were celebrating Corbulo's swift victory, the city of Rome had been ravaged by fire.

There were always house fires in Rome; part of the job of the City Guard and the Night Watch was to serve as firemen. But the Great Fire of A.D. 64 was different—three-fourths of the city was destroyed. The human toll was only light, for most people had been able to escape the flames, but the inferno had swept through the closely packed buildings. The fire raged for days. Nero, on the western coast of Italy competing on a lyre in a musical contest, came rushing back and led recovery efforts, bringing in food, tents, and other resources. He then oversaw planning for the reconstruction of the capital. The cities of the empire would vie with each other to provide money, materials, and craftsmen for the rebuilding of Rome, a task that would continue for decades.

Compared to the disaster at the capital, affairs in the provinces seemed petty, and Judea rated little interest at the Palatium. For decades, violence in the province of Judea had been confined to feuds between Jews and

Gentiles, to banditry on the roads, to insurgent attempts to destabilize the Jewish priestly hierarchy, who were seen as Roman collaborators, and to the efforts of Orthodox Jews to eliminate the growing Christian cult. In A.D. 62, the Great Sanhedrin had taken advantage of the fact that the replacement for Procurator Festus had yet to reach Judea by arresting Christian leader James, brother of Jesus of Nazareth, and having him stoned to death for blasphemy.

By A.D. 66 the latest Procurator of Judea, Gessius Florus, had been in the job for two years. When he first took up his Judean appointment, Florus had felt his way. But, says Josephus, as the opportunities for filling his own purse became apparent, the handsome young Florus, greedy for the good life and determined to make the most of his assignment, as his predecessors had done, found every opportunity to fleece communities and individuals. His activities became so oppressive, according to Josephus, that some residents packed up and moved to other Roman provinces.

Complaints from the Jews of Judea about the bullying tactics of the new procurator and his lack of respect for Jewish ways and traditions had been reaching his superior the new governor of Syria, Gaius Cestius Gallus, for months. Gallus, a native of Camerinum, a town in Umbria in central Italy a little to the northwest of Rome, had replaced Field Marshal Corbulo. Governor Gallus was no Corbulo, although of a similar age. A senator for thirty-eight years and a consul in A.D. 35, Gallus was enjoying the fruits of a long career of service to Rome. The Syrian appointment was the most prestigious and the highest-paid of any governorship of an imperial province—400,000 sesterces a year. Now, early in A.D. 66, Gallus feared that if he wasn't seen to act on complaints from Judea, the Jews would take their case to the emperor at Rome, which could result in his recall. The governor decided to visit Jerusalem to mollify the complaining Jews. So that he didn't appear to be stepping on the toes of Florus, Gallus said he was merely coming down to Jerusalem to be in attendance during the Passover festival.

When Governor Gallus reached Caesarea, Procurator Florus joined him with four cohorts of the 3rd Gallica Legion. They traveled up to Jerusalem together, and took up residence at the Herodian Palace. On the eve of Passover, Gallus appeared in public, with Florus at his side, going up to the Temple forecourt, where the Jews mobbed him. Josephus says that at least 3 million people crowded into the city for the Passover of A.D. 66. Flocking around Governor Gallus, Procurator Florus, and their strong bodyguard of 3rd Gallica legionaries and auxiliary spearmen, Jewish men shouted to the governor that Florus was ruining them and their

country, and begged his help in getting rid of the greedy procurator. Josephus says that Florus only laughed when he heard this, but his grin
quickly faded when he saw that Gallus was not amused. Governor Gallus
quieted the crowd as, from a dais, he assured his listeners that all would be
well in the future.

"You have my personal guarantee that you can expect more reasonable
conduct from your procurator from now on," Gallus declared, according to
Josephus.

The public mood lightened, and budding rebels among the crowd
found that their whispered message of revolt fell on barren ground. Following the Passover, before Gallus took his leave of the young procurator
for the return trip up to Antioch, he urged Florus to act with measured
restraint with the Jews, to be firm but fair. But there was no reprimand for
the procurator. Josephus says Florus considered Governor Gallus an old
fool, neither respecting nor fearing him. Late in the spring, the procurator
ordered Camp Prefect Capito—who had resumed his post as Jerusalem
garrison commander following the Armenian campaigns with Field Marshal Corbulo—to remove a significant amount of cash from the Jewish
Temple treasury. Capito marched into the treasury with 3rd Gallica troops
and removed the equivalent of 4 million sesterces.

Josephus says that when the Jewish priests of the Temple asked why
the procurator was taking the money, Camp Prefect Capito replied, "Caesar requires it."

The Jews had in fact failed to make their annual tax payment to
Rome, which was collected throughout Judea and the worldwide Jewish
Diaspora and then funneled to the Temple treasury. They were deliberately dragging their feet as part of a concerted plan to force Rome to replace Florus. The procurator, meanwhile, with Rome in need of funds for
the postfire rebuilding program, was worried how this would reflect on
him. Playing into the hands of Jewish rebels, the intemperate and impatient Florus had decided to simply take the tax money from their Temple
treasury. As it was, the outstanding tax was still three times the amount
removed by Capito from the Temple.

Predictably, the Jews rioted. Major Capito hurriedly left town with a
cavalry escort, taking the confiscated millions on packhorses to the procurator. He found Florus at the heavily fortified inland Samarian town of
Sebaste, today's Sabastiya. Florus had withdrawn there with an escort of
two 3rd Gallica cohorts plus cavalry, leaving enmity simmering between
Jews and Gentiles over a building dispute. The tribune of the 3rd Gallica
Legion sent cavalry decurion Aemilius Jucundus with a party of troopers

from the 3rd Gallica's own cavalry squadron to sort out that problem. But they couldn't stop the fighting that now broke out between thousands on both sides.

When, in the last days of May, Florus heard from Major Capito that the Jews had rioted at Jerusalem and taken his name in vain after the treasury raid, he determined to steer them back into line. Sending orders for two more 3rd Gallica cohorts to meet him at Jerusalem, he set off for Jerusalem with his two Gallican cohorts. Accompanied by Camp Prefect Capito, he marched along the mountain road from Damascus.

Early in the afternoon of June 2, A.D. 66, Florus's force of a little over a thousand men neared Jerusalem. Major Capito pushed on ahead with fifty cavalrymen and orders to ensure that no surprises lay in their path, and as Capito came up to Jerusalem's Damascus Gate he found a large crowd of Jewish men gathered quietly outside the gate with their chief priests, as if to welcome Florus. But the major didn't trust them, and led his troopers in a charge against them, scattering them. Capito then rejoined Procurator Florus as he skirted around the city walls and approached along the Beth-Horon road from the west, right beside Herod's Palace. The procurator and his troops were able to enter the Herodian Palace without incident. As Florus made himself at home in a royal apartment in either the Caesarium or Agrippinarium wing, the men of the two 3rd Gallica cohorts who had arrived with him set up their tents in a walled palace enclosure.

At this time a royal Jewish visitor was staying at Jerusalem—the unwell Queen Berenice, sister of King Agrippa II of Chalcis. While her brother traveled to Egypt, she was performing a holy vow made by Jews who were sick or in distress. Accompanied by a small bodyguard of royal Chalcian cavalry and infantry, Berenice spent the night of June 3 at her own Hasmonaean Palace in the city.

The next morning, when the priests of the Sanhedrin refused to give up those Jews who had previously defamed Florus after the treasury raid, Florus had Major Capito lead a 3rd Gallica Cohort to sack the Jerusalem marketplace and arrest all stallholders. The manacled merchants were led to Herod's Palace. As the priests watched, the merchants were stripped, whipped, then nailed to crosses. Josephus says that even though they were Jews, some of these victims had been granted Equestrian rank by Rome, making their punishment strictly illegal. But Florus ignored the niceties of the law, the protests of the leading Jews, and even pleas for mercy from Queen Berenice.

As the sun rose on the morning of June 4, thousands of people swarmed into the destroyed marketplace in the Upper City. According to Josephus, between the sacking of the Upper Market and the executions at the Herodian Palace, thirty-six hundred Jewish men, women, and children were killed by Florus's troops on June 3. Not surprisingly, the public mood now was one of anger. It was a mood that Jews in the city described by Josephus as "insurgents" set out to exploit. Rome called them Sicari, or dagger men. They called themselves Canaanites, after the ancient name for Palestine. In Greek this translated as Zealots, by which name history has come to know them. In the A.D. 50s, a splinter group based in Galilee had broken away from the main Zealot party. While Zealots usually restricted their activities to highway holdups and raids in the countryside to annoy the Roman authorities, this more aggressive breakaway group went into cities and towns with daggers under their clothes, assassinating rivals and collaborators. At least two of Jesus of Nazareth's twelve apostles are thought to have been Sicari or former Sicari. Now the Sicari mingled with distraught residents, urging them to rise against the Romans. But for now, the ordinary people were calmed by the priests and civic leaders.

During the morning, a mounted courier arrived from Centurion Metilius, commander of the two 3rd Gallica cohorts marching up from Caesarea as ordered, informing Florus that his column would arrive via the northern road later that morning. Florus again sent for the prominent Jews of the city. In the palace courtyard, with its collection of dead men hanging from their crosses around them, Florus glowered down at the leaders. "The only way to prove to me that there will be no repeat of the previous lawlessness is to lead your people out to greet my legionaries who are at this moment approaching the city from Caesarea. Show them, and me, that you're ready to obey."

As the leaders hurried away to gather a welcoming party, Florus sent the courier back with written instructions for Centurion Metilius: instruct his men not to reply if greeted by Jews on the road into the city. And if any Jew uttered an abusive word against the procurator, they were to employ their wooden batons against them.

The priests led thousands of Jews out the Damascus Gate and along the road to greet the approaching troops, hot, tired, thirsty men of junior cohorts of the legion, possibly including Centurion Julius and the men who had taken the apostle Paul to Rome. Although they were mostly only in their early twenties, these Syrian legionaries were experienced soldiers hardened by combat in Armenia with Field Marshal Corbulo. And they knew that the Jews considered them barbarians and inferior beings.

As the tramping soldiers drew level with the civilians lining both sides of the road, the Jews began to hail the legionaries with friendly greetings. The Syrians of the 3rd Gallica followed orders and remained silent and stern-faced. After prolonged silence from the troops, insurgents among the crowd began to call out insults and curses against Procurator Florus, which was exactly what Florus had been hoping for. The centurion riding at the head of the leading cohort snapped an order. His troops swung to face the crowd, some turning left, some right, and, drawing batons from their belts, they charged. There was soon massive congestion around the two gateways of the Damascus Gate, and in their panic, fleeing Jews fell. Some were trampled. Legionaries of the leading cohort pursued the crowd through the Damascus Gate and drove into the New City, the Bezetha suburb in northern Jerusalem, as the remaining troops came on, escorting their baggage.

By now, rebels in the city had rounded up thousands of people to resist the few hundred legionaries in Bezetha, spreading the rumor that the Romans had orders from Florus to occupy the Temple. The baton-wielding legionaries found their way blocked by walls of angry Jews who fought back with staves, stones, and bare fists. From the high ramparts of the Antonia Fortress, 3rd Gallica guards could see that the men of the newly arrived column were in trouble, and Camp Prefect Capito sent messengers scurrying to the Herodian Palace to inform Procurator Florus of the situation. Before long, Florus was personally leading two 3rd Gallica cohorts from the palace on the double, determined to open the way up for Metilius's column and scatter the rioting crowd.

Many of those in the crowd barring the progress of the 3rd Gallica men from the north now turned and dashed south to block the procurator's way. Growing bolder, the insurgents in the crowd gained entry to houses overlooking the narrow Street of the Cheesemakers, south of the Antonia Fortress and the Hasmonean Palace, as Florus came marching down it. Pulling out roof tiles, they began raining them down on Florus and his 3rd Gallica reinforcements. Without shields, the legionaries were soon bloodied and bruised. When the troops tried alternative routes via side streets, they found the Jews on the rooftops there, too. Realizing he had insufficient numbers to push his way forward through the vast mob now in his path, the procurator ordered a withdrawal.

To the cheers of the rioters, the 3rd Gallica men retreated to Herod's Palace with Florus. Taking their injured with them, they manned the palace walls. Even as the Jews in the south of the city were celebrating this victory, cries of alarm went up from Bezetha. Centurion Metilius had formed up the two 3rd Gallica cohorts from Caesarea in close order and was making a concerted push to reach the safety of the Antonia. As the legionaries and their dismounted cavalry companions forced their way forward in tight formation, the mob that had forced Florus to retreat turned and streamed along beside the Temple's western wall to support the Jews in the New City. When Jewish reinforcements arrived too late to prevent the cohorts from reaching the Antonia, the radicals in the mob convinced the others that the Romans would try to occupy their Temple via the Antonia. To prevent this, Jews in their thousands tore down the colonnades linking the two.

An uneasy calm settled over Jerusalem, with the Roman troops split between the Antonia and the Herodian Palace. During the afternoon, Florus sent for the Jewish high priest and all seventy members of the Great Sanhedrin. Warily, worriedly, Ananias the high priest and the Sadducees and Pharisees of the Sanhedrin came to the Herodian Palace to meet with the procurator. They found Florus pragmatic and conciliatory.

"I'm going to quit the city," Josephus says that Florus announced to the surprised Jewish leaders. He had realized that he simply didn't have enough troops. His secret plan was to withdraw to Caesarea and seek massive reinforcement from Governor Gallus at Antioch, before returning to Jerusalem with thousands of troops to show these Jews who was boss. "I'll leave you a legionary garrison as large as you feel is necessary," he told the priests, "if I have your guarantee that you will maintain order and ensure that your people don't become involved in demonstrations of lawlessness of the kind we've seen over recent days."

The priests gave their solemn promise that they would keep order, and told Florus that it would be enough to leave a single legionary cohort as garrison in the city, as in the past. But, they said, it must not be the cohort responsible for the destruction and killing in the Upper Marketplace the previous day—the people hated that cohort now.

Florus agreed. He gave orders for the 3rd Gallica's 2nd Cohort and Major Capito, the garrison commander who'd led the Upper Marketplace mission, to prepare to march along with three of the cohorts he'd brought up from Caesarea and all the auxiliaries at Jerusalem, including cavalry. A junior cohort of the 3rd Gallica that had arrived from Caesarea that day was assigned the task of garrisoning Jerusalem. For the time being, cohort commander Centurion Metilius would act as camp prefect in the city, with Florus assuring Metilius he would soon be back in Jerusalem with more legionary muscle.

Shortly after dawn the next morning, Camp Prefect Capito and the 2nd Cohort of the 3rd Gallica came out of the Antonia Fortress in marching

order, watched by suspicious civilians from doorways, windows, and rooftops. Accompanied by Centurion Metilius and half his men from the newly
resident cohort, they tramped across the city to the Herodian Palace,
along streets littered with broken roof tiles and other debris from the riots.
At the palace, Capito and the 2nd Cohort joined the three other cohorts
departing the city and all the auxiliaries and cavalry then at Jerusalem.
Metilius and the men with him took over guard duty at the palace, having left the remaining troops of the cohort at the Antonia.

As the sun rose over the Judean hills, Procurator Florus, Camp Prefect
Capito, and their column of three thousand men marched from Jerusalem.
Centurion Metilius and his men watched them go from the Palace of
Herod and the Antonia Fortress. The men of the 3rd Gallica Legion's 2nd
Cohort, marching down to Caesarea with Florus and Capito after six years
stationed in Jerusalem, had no idea how lucky they were to be leaving, or
that their replacements, Centurion Metilius and his 3rd Gallica men, were
doomed.

XVI

VICTIMS OF THE
JEWISH UPRISING

With surrender negotiations concluded, Centurion Metilius and his men of the 3rd Gallica filed down from the tower in Herod's Palace and lay down their arms. The Jewish rebels had just succeeded in capturing Jerusalem.

It had taken only weeks to reach this point. Once Procurator Florus had returned to Caesarea he had written to Governor Gallus at Antioch to tell him of the problem he had encountered at Jerusalem, expecting him to send the legions of Syria to restore order in Judea and punish those who defied Florus. But Gallus didn't send troops. He knew that very moment the emperor Nero was in Greece, preparing two top-secret military operations for the new year. A small Roman expeditionary force was to push south from Egypt into Ethiopia and expand the empire into East Africa. For this, the 15th Apollonaris Legion had been transferred from Armenia to Egypt, militia troops had been assembled in Alexandria, and two thousand young men had been conscripted in Libya to join three thousand recruits who were to come from Europe to fill the re-formed 18th Legion.

Nero's second operation was even more ambitious: an invasion of Parthia via the Caspian Gates. For this operation, the famous 14th Gemina, the legion that had put down the revolt of Queen Boudicca and the Britons six years back, had been transferred east, and a new legion, the 1st Italica, raised in Italy. The majority of the legions in Syria and Judea also were slated to take part. Gallus, knowing that marching Syria's legions to Jerusalem didn't fit in with the Palatium's top-secret plans, sent a tribune to Jerusalem to conduct an inquiry. He was joined there by King Agrippa of Chalcis. The tribune reported back to Gallus that the Jews had tried to blackmail him into removing Florus by promising to bring their taxes up to date once he'd been removed.

Once the tribune departed Jerusalem, at a rowdy public meeting in sight of Centurion Metilius and his men in the Antonia, the Jews of Jerusalem begged King Agrippa and High Priest Ananias to send envoys to Nero to put the case for the removal of Procurator Florus. The alternative, said the people, was taking things into their own hands. They shouted that it wasn't Rome they were against but Florus. In tears, Agrippa tried to talk his fellow Jews out of an uprising, and was at first successful. But soon the insurgents held sway, and Agrippa was banned from the city. As the king and his sister Berenice departed for their home at the head of the Jordan River, the road to revolt opened up to the revolutionaries.

When Eleazar, son of Ananias the high priest, and commander of the Temple Guard, tried to seize the Temple with his ten-thousand-man guard, King Agrippa sent a detachment of two thousand cavalry led by the chief of Agrippa's army, General Philip bar Jacimus, to reinforce the 3rd Gallica cohort in Jerusalem and prevent a full-scale revolt. But it was too late. When Agrippa had still been in the city, a frustrated group of insurgents had quietly slipped through the Genath Gate and headed south. Galilean Sicari led by Menahem bar Judas, a hard-line rabbi who had been fighting Rome just as his father and grandfather had before him, surprised the 3rd Gallica cohort guarding the Masada fortress on the southwestern shore of the Dead Sea. Cutting the legionaries' throats, the rebels seized the fortress and the storehouses where Herod the Great had squirreled away enough weapons to arm ten thousand men.

Menahem's men returned to Jerusalem with the weapons and joined the hostilities against Centurion Metilius's Gallicans and King Agrippa's troopers that had been launched by Eleazar and the Temple Guard. As Eleazar besieged the Antonia Fortress and Herod's Palace and tried to break through the huge doors of the Temple, which had been closed by fearful priests, ordinary people came flocking to the uprising.

For eight days the battle raged around the three strongpoints before the attackers tricked their way into the Temple. Most of Agrippa's troops fought their way through the streets to join the legionaries at Herod's Palace. The attackers then concentrated their assault on the massive but lightly defended Antonia Fortress, and two days later, the 250 men of the 3rd Gallica defending the Antonia were overwhelmed by the tens of thousands of besiegers. Every Gallican legionary in the fortress was put to the sword. Eleazar and his gleeful followers stripped the Roman dead, emptied the fortress's arsenal, set the fortress on fire, then turned to the defenders of Herod's Palace—Centurion Metilius and the remaining 230 men of his 3rd Gallica cohort and King Agrippa's 2,000 men.

Day and night, besiegers under Menahem threw themselves at the palace's walls, only to be beaten back by Roman artillery. Menahem then mined one of the palace towers, set fire to the tunnel's wooden support, and collapsed the tower. But the defenders hastily threw up an inner wall. Soon King Agrippa's officers and the priests in Herod's Palace lost heart, and negotiated their withdrawal from the palace. Many of Agrippa's men then went over to the rebels. Centurion Metilius and his 3rd Gallica men, angry, bitterly disappointed, and knowing they could not defend the entire palace on their own, wearily withdrew to the remaining three palace towers. The Jewish assault resumed.

Internal rivalry saw Eleazar murder Menahem to take sole command. Meanwhile, not knowing that the Jews were fighting among themselves, the 3rd Gallica troops saw their cause as hopeless—out of food, water, and ammunition, trapped in the three towers and with no hope of rescue. On a Saturday morning, Centurion Metilius sent out a message offering to discuss capitulation terms. Three of Eleazar's lieutenants met with the centurion, and among them they agreed that the legionaries could depart Jerusalem on condition that they leave the palace at once and lay down their arms. To seal the agreement both sides exchanged sacred oaths, swearing on their individual gods. It was, after all, the rebel lieutenants would have reminded Metilius, the Jewish Sabbath day.

So now the surviving Roman soldiers—about two hundred of them—came down from the towers and formed up in good order in front of thousands of Jewish rebels. One by one the 3rd Gallica legionaries lay down their weapons and removed their armor. Then they began to march toward the Genath Gate, passing between lines of smiling partisans. Suddenly Eleazar's men rushed forward, fell on the unarmed prisoners, and cut their throats. The legionaries were so shocked by the violation of the surrender agreement that they didn't even resist. Roman soldiers considered three things inviolable: their legionary eagles, the sanctity of ambassadors, and their holy oaths.

"The oaths!" Josephus says the Syrian legionaries cried as they died.

Every unarmed legionary was cut down. A sacred Jewish oath to "barbarian" sun-worshippers, it seems, did not count. Only one Roman was spared: Centurion Metilius begged for his life and swore he would convert to Judaism and submit to circumcision. He kept his life, for the moment; but Centurion Metilius was never heard of again.

XVII

THE HEROES OF ASCALON

 t the outbreak of the revolt, the men of the 3rd Gallica cohort at the Herodian fortress at Cypros, sitting on a rocky rise overlooking Jericho, were unaware of the uprising only several miles away at Jerusalem. They were caught off guard by a rebel force, probably with their gates still open. Partisans were able to surprise the Cypros cohort and, in the words of Jewish historian Josephus, "exterminate" every man in the unit.

The legionaries of the 3rd Gallica cohort stationed at the hilltop Herodian fortress of Machaerus, to the east of the Dead Sea, were either more alert or received warning of the uprising. They were prepared for the partisans who surrounded Machaerus. Their gates were closed and their walls defended. So the Jews called for a truce and agreed to let the legionaries depart in peace if they gave up the fortress. Preferring to live to fight another day, the 3rd Gallica cohort at Machaerus abandoned the fortress. But unlike their comrades at Jerusalem, they refused to disarm. Leaving their fortress fully armed, and in the chaos that swept the Judean Hills following the uprising, they made a forced march overland and reached the safety of the legion headquarters at Caesarea.

So far the revolt had gone well for the Jews and badly for Rome, in particular for its 3rd Gallica Legion. Three of the legion's cohorts had been wiped out. Jerusalem and three fortresses in the south had fallen. Much of Judea was now in the hands of the rebels.

Just one last major asset remained in Roman hands, the city of Ascalon, in Idumaea. To the southwest, on the Mediterranean coast, Ascalon guarded the highway between Syria and Egypt, and provided shelter and provisions for Roman vessels coasting between the provinces. A handsome two-thousand-year-old city, Ascalon had been the hometown of Antipater, father of Herod the Great. Herod had endowed the city with a number of fine buildings, and a palace there had been gifted to Queen Salome by the emperor Augustus. Today the ruins of Ascalon, in southern Palestine, are called Tel Ashquelon. At the outset of the Jewish Revolt, the majority of Ascalon residents were Idumaeans, but the population also included several thousand Jews.

In the first flush of the revolt, after Masada was taken, uncoordinated bands of Jewish rebels had flooded throughout Idumaea, killing Gentiles and causing considerable property damage. At Ascalon they set fire to the buildings outside the city walls, burning them to the ground. But the rebels didn't stay around to take on the Roman garrison manning the city walls. That garrison at Ascalon was made up of a 3rd Gallica Legion cohort led by a Centurion Antonius, supported by a squadron of auxiliary cavalry. Leaving Ascalon isolated, the Jewish partisans attacked other undefended cities, towns, and villages in the region, sacked them, killed their inhabitants, and destroyed them. Gaza was one of the many towns of Idumaea left in smoking, corpse-strewn ruins.

Behind the closed gates of Ascalon, the non-Jewish residents embarked on furious and bloody revenge for the destruction wrought on the city by the marauding partisans. They butchered twenty-five hundred Jewish residents and threw the remainder into the city prison. Centurion Antonius and his men of the garrison went on high alert, expecting the rebels to soon return in greater numbers. They were not to be disappointed, but it would be many months before the expected assault came. In the meantime, the people of Ascalon, like their garrison, remained behind the locked city gates, cut off by land by the partisans but able to receive supplies by sea.

Rome's answer to the Jewish Revolt came slowly at first. Some of King Agrippa's fleeing cavalrymen brought the news of the uprising to Procurator Florus at Caesarea. Florus quickly put the remainder of the 3rd Gallica on full alert and sent a messenger flying to Governor Gallus in Antioch. Privately, Florus would have crowed that he had been proven right by events. Meanwhile, the Samaritans of Caesarea, learning of the uprising at Jerusalem and fearing the Jews in their own community, took up arms against their Jewish neighbors and, says Josephus, killed thousands of them.

Three months passed, during which Jewish partisans flooded throughout Judea, Idumaea, Samaria, and Galilee, and even up into southern Syria, attacking Gentile towns, cities, and villages. In the Egyptian capital, Alexandria, the large Jewish population, encouraged by the success of their brethren in Jerusalem, ran riot. But this was not Jerusalem, with just a small legionary garrison. The Roman governor of Egypt, Prefect Tiberius Alexander, called out the troops garrisoned in Egypt and let them loose. The ten thousand men of the 3rd Cyrenaica and 22nd Deiotariana Legions and two thousand young Libyan recruits of the 18th Legion surged into Alexandria's Jewish quarter and killed thousands. Order was quickly restored in the Egyptian capital.

While, during these months, Florus and his troops stayed behind their fortress walls at Caesarea, in Syria and Samaria, the locals in Tyre, Ptolemais, and Gadara killed Jewish residents and threw many more into prison. In contrast, at Antioch, Sidon, and Apamea, the locals would not permit the Jews in their cities to be killed or imprisoned.

In expectation of an inevitable Roman response, the Jewish leadership at Jerusalem appointed seven generals to command in the regions, to conscript Jewish fighters and to fortify their main centers. The general appointed to command in Galilee was Joseph bar Matthias, the later historian Josephus, who conscripted a hundred thousand Galilean partisans and tried to teach them Roman discipline and tactics.

Finally, in September, wearing his sword and armor and displaying the consular standard of a lieutenant general, Governor Gallus ventured south with a force centered on the 12th Fulminata Legion, whose men were looking forward to their twenty-year discharge in the new year. Backing the 12th, says Josephus, were four legionary cohorts from each of "the rest"—that is, the other legions then in Syria, the 4th Scythica, 5th Macedonica, 6th Ferrata, and the 10th. To this force of twelve thousand legionaries Gallus added three thousand auxiliary light infantry and a wing of five hundred auxiliary cavalry. The force was supported by five thousand infantry and cavalry from King Agrippa of Chalcis, whose loyalty to Rome was stronger than his loyalty to his fellow Jews. There also were five thousand archers from King Antiochus of Commagene, and four thousand foot and mounted troops, mostly archers, from Soaemus, king and chief priest of Emesa. Altogether, Governor Gallus's force totaled more than twenty-six thousand men.

Following the Mediterranean coast, Cestius Gallus's column marched south. Entering southern Galilee, he burned and looted every deserted Jewish village before reaching Caesarea. There, four of the surviving seven cohorts of the 3rd Gallica would have been added to Gallus's army.

Once an advance force had killed two thousand partisans on Mount Asamon, left a small garrison at the friendly inland city of Sepphoris, and took the Jewish city of Joppa, Governor Gallus swung up into the Judean Hills. In early November, with winter just around the corner, the Roman army reached the village of Gaba, eight miles north of Jerusalem. In Jerusalem itself, the people were celebrating the Feast of the Tabernacles. With months to prepare for a Roman counterattack, excited partisans streamed out of the city and headed north in their tens of thousands. Coming under attack, Gallus built a fortified camp at Gaba. From there, King Agrippa sent envoys to the Jewish leaders, seeking peace talks. Three days later the reply came in the form of a wounded ambassador—the Jews had cut the throat of his colleague before he escaped.

"Non-hostile communications between belligerents must be conducted with scrupulous good faith," says the British Army's *Field Service Regulations* of 1914 on the subject of peace parleys. Some Jerusalem Jews who held similar views protested to the partisan leadership that ambassadors should not be attacked. In response, the Jewish protesters were themselves clubbed to death on the orders of their leaders.

Advancing on Jerusalem, Gallus's force occupied Mount Scopus, overlooking the city. After pausing for three days, Gallus then bypassed the city's incomplete Third Wall and, burning the northern suburb of Bezetha, advanced to the city's inner Second Wall. The Jewish defenders prepared to defend the Second Wall and the major bastions of the city—the Temple, the Antonia, and the three remaining towers of the Palace of Herod. Rejecting a Jewish offer to open the gates and let the Romans enter if Gallus would agree to peace terms, the Roman commander commenced an assault on the northern wall of the Temple. For five days his legionaries attempted to scale the wall. But the defenders rained down arrows, spears, and stones on the men below trying to use assault ladders, and continually drove them back. Only then did Gallus bring up his artillery. Eventually the deadly accurate fire of Gallus's catapults swept the wall of defenders long enough for a testudo to go into action. On the sixth day, led by Gallus himself and supported by volleys from the bowmen from Emesa and Commagene, several hundred legionaries were able to reach the base of the wall under cover of their shields. Working feverishly, they undermined the wall and set a fire at the northern gate.

Many Jews panicked, certain that the Romans would breach the wall at any moment. Some Jews who tried to escape were killed by fanatical partisans. Others advocated surrender. But, convinced of ultimate success, the Jewish war party prevailed. Sure enough, the fire at the gate didn't take hold, and the mining work was not a success. Defenders returned to the north wall. Governor Gallus was no farther advanced.

Now the Roman commander did a strange thing. Josephus was to claim that Florus the procurator bribed several of Gallus's leading officers to convince him to give up the siege; why he would do that, we aren't told. Winter was coming on, and perhaps that influenced Gallus's decision. Whatever the reason, Gallus suspended the siege and withdrew all his forces to Mount Scopus. The next day, to the astonishment of the people of Jerusalem, the entire Roman army pulled out and began marching north, back the way it had come. Thousands of elated partisans poured out of the city and attacked the retreating troops every step of the way with arrows and sling stones. Under orders not to break formation, the Romans lost hundreds of men.

Dragging their heavy equipment with them, the legionaries gratefully gained the walls of their previous camp at Gaba. For two days the men of the legions strengthened the camp walls while General Gallus and his senior officers met in a council of war and anguished over what to do next. All the while, more and more armed Jews gathered on the hillsides around the camp. In the end, Gallus decided to make for the coast, to retrace the route that had brought them to this place. Once out of the hills, which were ideal for the hit-and-run guerrilla tactics at which the lightly armed Jewish partisans excelled, the Roman infantry could form up in battle order and fight on clear, level ground, where the cavalry would also be able to ride down attackers. At least that was the plan. Setting his initial objective as Lod, and after that the safety of Caesarea, Gallus marched his army out of Gaba shortly after dawn on November 23, A.D. 66, and turned west. It was a date the Jews would always remember and celebrate.

The road that Gallus chose to lead his soldiers along dipped five hundred feet into a valley beyond Gaba, then swung to the right. There were two villages in the valley: Beth-Horon Superior and Beth-Horon Inferior. The Jews couldn't believe their luck; twice in their history, Jewish armies had defeated foreign invaders in the Beth-Horon Valley. Now it seemed that Jehovah was delivering another great victory to them. A large Jewish force hurried through the hills, passing the enemy and posting itself in front of the approaching Romans. Other partisans took up positions on the hillsides beside the road. Another force followed behind the slow-moving Roman column as it struggled along the narrow road with all its animals and heavily laden wagons.

As the column wound down into the Beth-Horon Valley, the Jews sprang their trap. The force in front attacked. The force behind launched an assault. The Jews on the hillsides rained missiles onto the Roman flanks. The Roman troops found themselves trapped on a narrow road with precipices on either side. There was nowhere to run. Gallus issued orders for the heavy equipment to be left behind and urged his men to keep advancing; if they stopped, they were dead. Mules and horses were killed so the Jews couldn't use them. Personal items were dumped. But Gallus insisted the legions bring the carts and mules carrying their remaining ammunition and artillery; he was determined not to answer in Rome for letting that fall into enemy hands to be used against Roman troops.

All the while, the air was filled with spears, arrows, and stones. Wounded cavalry horses tumbled into ravines, carrying their riders with them. The infantry were too busy protecting themselves with their shields to return fire. All around them the Jews were yelling with exhilaration, letting go their missiles with blood-curdling war whoops. Every now and then parties of Jews would suddenly dash in among the Romans on the road, striking fast, then spring away again, having observed that the Roman troops were under orders to retain formation and not chase after them. The men of the 12th Fulminata and 6th Ferrata Legions were coming in for particular attention. Both marched behind their golden eagle standards, and the Jews were determined to seize those prized eagles.

The 12th Fulminata fared worst; its second-enlistment men of the senior cohorts were tired veterans in their late fifties. Between the missiles and the hit-and-run attacks, legionaries, auxiliaries, and allied troops fell like flies as they strove to make their way down the dusty road. They progressed at a snail's pace, leaving dead comrades at the roadside. As the hours passed, the pressure on the 12th Fulminata told. A surge of partisans overwhelmed the 1st Cohort men defending the legion's eagle standard— the 12th's most experienced legionaries, older men from northern Italy who had sworn to defend the eagle, fell dead all around it. The eagle bearer was cut down. Another grizzled legionary stepped up to grab the eagle standard and hold it high. He, too, was overwhelmed and killed in the vicious close-in fighting. The eagle was snatched from its dying bearer by an elated Jewish partisan. With a cheer, the attackers withdrew, carrying away the eagle of the 12th. The 12th Fulminata men were shattered; to lose your eagle to the enemy was a huge disgrace to a Roman legion. The shame would last for generations.

Only the coming of night saved the Roman army from complete annihilation. Carrying their wounded and what little equipment they'd been able to salvage, pushing and pulling carts bearing their useless artillery, the legionaries staggered into the village of Beth-Horon Inferior and took up defensive positions around its walls. The Jewish partisans surrounded the village in the darkness and waited for the dawn.

Gallus now called for volunteers for a suicide mission. From the many men who stepped forward he chose four hundred legionaries, who were posted on the village rooftops and given extra ammunition. All through the night, the doomed four hundred called the watches and talked loudly to give the impression that the entire army was still in the village. Meanwhile, abandoning his artillery at last, Gallus led his surviving men from the village in the early hours of the morning, creeping through the darkness and past sleeping partisans.

At sunup, the Jews attacked the village. The four hundred legionary volunteers put up stiff resistance, but they were overrun by the tens of thousands of attackers as one rooftop after another was cleared of defenders in bloody hand-to-hand fighting. The delaying tactic worked. Gallus had stolen the march on the Jews, and without the encumbrance of the artillery he was able to make much better time. Despite resumed attacks on his rear he kept ahead of his pursuers and led his surviving troops into the city of Lod. The partisans decided not to pursue the Romans any farther. Singing victory songs and carrying away their spoils, which included the eagle of the 12th and many other captured Roman standards and the Roman army's artillery and fully laden pay chest, the Jewish fighters marched back to Jerusalem, where they would be greeted as heroes.

General Gallus and his savaged army struggled north across the Plain of Samaria to the sanctuary of Caesarea. Total casualties in Gallus's ill-fated and poorly led Judean expedition, according to Josephus, were 5,300 infantrymen and 480 cavalrymen. Among the dead were Brigadier General Tyrannius Priscus, commander of the 6th Ferrata Legion and the task force's chief of staff, as well as Colonel Longinus, a senior tribune and quite probably commanding officer of the shattered 12th Fulminata Legion, and Colonel Aemilius Jucundus, a prefect of cavalry. Governor Gallus himself died shortly after. Tacitus suggests that Gallus either committed suicide or died of shame.

Now that they had driven the Romans out of Judea with their tails between their legs, the Jews turned their attention to the one nut that remained to be cracked: Ascalon, and the lone cohort of the 3rd Gallica Legion holding the coastal city. Niger of Persaea, appointed Jewish governor in the Idumaea district by the rebel leadership at Jerusalem, and the Jewish general John the Essene, whose new revolutionary command covered the towns of Thamna, Lod, Emmaus, and Joppa, joined forces with the objective of taking Ascalon. One of their senior officers was Silas the Babylonian, the only trained soldier among them, who had been a cavalry officer in the army of King Agrippa before defecting to the rebels. Silas had just distinguished himself against Governor Gallus's troops in the Battle of Beth-Horon Valley. According to Josephus, the attacking force led against Ascalon by this trio numbered well in excess of 20,000 men. All were lightly armed conscripts with little training. Yet, pitted against just 480 legionaries of the 3rd Gallica and their 124 cavalry companions at Ascalon, the Jewish numbers and the momentum of victory after Beth-Horon seemed to guarantee success.

At Ascalon, Centurion Antonius was ready and waiting when a cavalry scout came pounding up to the main city gate with the news he had been expecting since the summer: "The Jews are coming!" As the cohort's trumpeter blared "To Arms," the 3rd Gallica sentries in the city's guard towers could soon see the dust raised by thousands of feet tramping across the plain from the Idumaean Hills to the east. Below, in the city, while the remainder of the cohort came running to man the walls, Centurion Antonius mounted up and led his cavalry squadron out a city gate. As Antonius and the troopers galloped off to the south, the thick gate thudded into the closed position.

Yelling encouragement to each other and waving their weapons in the air, Jewish partisans flooded through the blackened buildings on the city outskirts and surrounded the city walls on the three landward sides. As the rebels launched an assault against the walls, the legionaries of the 3rd Gallica opened up a hail of missiles—handheld javelins and arrows from artillery pieces mounted on the ramparts.

Suddenly, seemingly from out of nowhere, Antonius and his cavalry swept in and charged the attackers' rear. Caught totally by surprise, the Jews fell into disorder. Their lines broke up. They separated into groups, which the Roman cavalry surrounded, then mowed down, a group at a time. Two of the Jewish commanders, John the Essene and Silas the Babylonian, were killed early in the fighting. Without their senior officers, partisans fled across the plain in wild disorder, with Roman troopers chasing them all the way to the hills. The Romans cut down rebels until night fell. Josephus says the Jews lost ten thousand men that day. The number may have been exaggerated, but there can be no doubting that Centurion Antonius and his men raised havoc among the partisan force. Meanwhile, a handful of legionaries on the walls of Ascalon were wounded by missiles; but not a single Roman soldier was killed in the day's action.

The surviving Jewish commander, Niger, regrouped at the Idumaean hill town of Chaalis. Several days later, even before their wounds had healed, the surviving Jewish fighters set off to renew the attack on Ascalon. Expecting the partisans to try again, Centurion Antonius moved his troops up into the hills and established ambushes in the passes. The partisans walked straight into the Roman trap. After brutal close-in fighting, Antonius's troops drove Niger's men back to the village of Belzedek, where many took refuge behind the palisades of a wooden fort. The Romans set fire to the fort, and when they were sure that no one could escape the inferno, they withdrew to Ascalon.

According to Josephus, another eight thousand Jews died during this day's fighting, but again this may be an exaggerated figure. In Republican times, a Roman general who killed ten thousand enemies of Rome was entitled to a Triumph. And here Antonius the centurion and his six hundred men had reportedly killed eighteen thousand Jewish rebels in two days of fighting! Three days later, partisans sneaked to Belzedek to locate the body of their commander, Niger, only to discover to their joy that he had survived by hiding in a cave beneath the burned-out fort.

No more Jewish attempts were made to take Ascalon. After Centurion Antonius's 3rd Gallica men delivered the first blows in revenge for their comrades who had died at Jerusalem, Masada, and Cypros, Ascalon would stay in Roman hands for the remaining four years of the revolt. The 3rd Gallica Legion lost some fifteen hundred men in the early stages of the Jewish Revolt. And with cohorts also involved in the Gallus disaster, the legion would have suffered more killed and wounded. After the unit's almost bloodless successes in Armenia under Field Marshal Corbulo, the losses in Judea must have come as a shock to the surviving Gallicans. Despite the Ascalon victory, the legion's pride would have been dented. Not the least for the ignominious surrender of Machaerus: not since Mark Antony's time had the 3rd Gallica Legion been forced to retreat.

XVIII

THE EXECUTION OF
A TROUBLESOME JEW

On a morning in the spring of A.D. 67, a detachment of grim-faced, steely-eyed Praetorian Guards marched along the paving stones of the Appian Way, heading south, away from Rome, as travelers in their path quickly moved aside. In the soldiers' midst, a Praetorian dragged a fifty-seven-year-old, pale, balding, bearded Jew at the end of a chain—the Christian apostle Paul of Tarsus.

Acts says that Paul spent two years under house arrest at Rome following his delivery by Centurion Julius and his men. Most scholars agree that Paul was acquitted by Nero and resumed his Christian mission. It is generally believed that his later travels took him to Greece and Asia once more, and to Cyprus. There is also a belief in some quarters that he fulfilled a wish expressed in one of his letters—to take his message to Spain. The Christian church in Tarragona in northeastern Spain firmly credits its foundation to Paul, in partnership with a follower named Thecla, in A.D. 60, when Paul was under house arrest at Rome. Perhaps the Spanish date is wrong. By most accounts, he returned to Rome after several more years, and there, in about A.D. 66, he was arrested on new charges and lodged in prison with the apostle Peter.

Some think Paul's new arrest was because he reputedly converted Nero's mistress Acte to Christianity and convinced her to refuse to have sex with the emperor. Another story says that Paul and Peter had tried to destroy the influence of Jewish "magician" and miracle worker Simon Magus, to whom Nero is supposed to have turned for spiritual enlightenment in the years following his mother's murder. While no reliable historical evidence exists to prove that either Paul or Peter were at Rome at this time, most Christian scholars believe that both were condemned to death at Rome in the A.D. 60s.

Peter, being a noncitizen, was crucified—according to tradition, upside down, at his own request. Paul, as a Roman citizen, had the privilege of a swift death via decapitation. According to tradition, both were cast into the underground condemned cell of the Tullianum, or Tullian Keep, also called the Mamertime Prison. Jailers lowered food and water through a hole in the roof. Paul and Peter were said to have been imprisoned for nine months, converting forty-seven fellow prisoners to Christianity as well as two freedmen jailers, Process and Martinian. Their execution dates are disputed. Some accounts say Peter died first, on February 22, and Paul several months later. To further confuse matters, the Catholic feast commemorating their deaths is celebrated in June. But the spring is given by many Christian writers as the time of Paul's execution.

In traditional accounts, the year each died ranges between A.D. 64 and A.D. 69. The latter, during the mayhem of the civil wars following Nero's demise, is unlikely. Advocates for the A.D. 64 date for Paul's execution link this to the Great Fire, pointing out that in Tacitus it is claimed that Nero blamed the Christians at Rome for the Great Fire and brutally executed a number of them in his gardens. Many historians take the view that this paragraph in Tacitus was a later Christian interpolation, and that Tacitus never wrote it and Nero never did it. A number of scholars favor A.D. 67 as the year of Paul's execution, and there are good reasons to support that view. If Paul was executed in early A.D. 67, it would have been in the wake of the news of Governor Gallus's bloody repulse by the insurgents in Judea. Anti-Jewish feeling was then running high around the empire. It seems probable that Nero, in Greece by late A.D. 66, angrily issued death warrants for many condemned Jews around the empire once he had heard about the humiliation of Gallus's Roman army by the Jewish rebels in Judea.

Now, in March, the Praetorian Guard was carrying out the execution of Paul of Tarsus as part of Nero's slate of Jewish punishments. Under Roman law, funerals, cremations, and executions all took place outside the city walls. Just as the tombs of wealthy and famous Romans lined the Appian Way, along this same tree-lined avenue criminals were executed. Six thousand survivors of Spartacus's slave army had been crucified along this road for a hundred miles after the defeat of the rebels in 71 B.C.

According to tradition, when Paul's execution party reached a milestone three miles from the golden pillar in the Forum at Rome from which all distances were measured, they turned off the highway, at a place named Aqua Salviea. Ironically, there was a natural spa here renowned for the healing power of its waters. Paul, in manacles, was led by his escort into the Glade of the Tombs, called today by Italians the Tre Fontane, or Three

Fountains. Paul was forced to his knees. Because of the nature of Paul's execution, the sword is a symbol associated by the later Christian church with the apostle. With most executions carried out by the Praetorian Guard the death blow was delivered by the centurion in charge using his twenty-inch gladius. Modern-day research has shown that it is possible for a strong man to cleave off a head at the neck with a single blow of the Roman short sword. Even so, there are a number of Roman executions on record where the swordsman had to make several hacking blows to finish the job.

In his letters from Rome, Paul had written that he had been expecting his execution for some time and was resigned to it. He even seems to have welcomed it. Not in the way that the likes of Saint Ignatius would be determined to make a martyr of himself fifty years later. Paul seems to have been physically and mentally exhausted. Perhaps permitted by the centurion in charge to say his final prayer to God, he then lifted his head. The centurion lifted his weapon. The blade came crashing down onto Paul's neck. The blow cleanly severed head from shoulders. The head tumbled to the earth amid a spray of blood from the victim's neck—which would sponsor a later Christian story that a fountain a blood arose from the spot where Paul's head fell. The centurion would have jammed the head onto a javelin and raised it high, announcing that so died another criminal. The men of the escort would have cheered. According to one Christian tradition, three soldiers from the execution party and the executioner himself all later converted to Christianity, although there is no proof of this.

The heads of executed citizens were taken back into the city and displayed in the Forum or on the Gemonian Stairs nearby, as proof that the sentence had been carried out and they had been put to death. Romans rarely buried their dead. That was a Jewish custom. The Romans cremated their dead. Roman tombs merely housed caskets containing the ashes and charred bones of the dead. According to Christian tradition, Paul was cremated, and his ashes are said to be in a marble urn in the Basilica of Saint Paul Outside the Walls in Rome. This church superseded one built in A.D. 318 by the emperor Constantine. Two miles from the city, on the Via Ostiensis, the road to the port of Ostia, the Basilica of Saint Paul Outside the Walls is said to be over the tomb erected by Christians at Rome to contain Paul's remains, on land donated by a wealthy female believer. The myth grew that it was there that Paul was also executed. As for Paul's head, it is said to have ended up at the Saint John Lateran Church on Rome's Caelian Hill.

XIX

BLOOD FOR BLOOD

A t Caesarea, the legionaries of the six surviving cohorts and cavalry squadron of the 3rd Gallica Legion were spoiling for a chance to revenge themselves on the Jews, for the extermination of their colleagues at Jerusalem, Masada, and Cypros. They wanted blood for the blood of their Syrian comrades, brothers, cousins, and fellow townsmen. On January 1, A.D. 67, when they stood in their ranks in a courtyard of the Caesarea citadel and loudly reaffirmed their oaths of loyalty to the emperor Nero, the Galli-cans could only hope that after Governor Gallus's failed bid to recover Judea, the Palatium would appoint a real general to terminate the Jewish Revolt.

At about the time when the apostle Paul was executed just outside Rome, the men of the 3rd Gallica Legion got their wish: an able new commander in chief. The new military commander was not to be Corbulo, the general under whom the 3rd Gallica had conquered Armenia. The previous fall, Nero had summoned Corbulo to meet him. Corbulo had gone to Greece under the impression that he was to receive a new appointment. But his son-in-law Vinianus Annius, who had been one of Corbulo's legion commanders in Armenia, had been executed in Italy for joining a plot to murder the emperor. Succumbing to fears that Corbulo was also plotting against him, Nero had issued orders for Corbulo to be put to death. When Corbulo stepped ashore in Greece, he was met by a centurion leading an execution squad. Grabbing a sword, Corbulo had ended his own life. According to Cassius Dio, with his last words Corbulo bitterly regretted going to see Nero without his legions.

Nero had taken Lieutenant General Titus Flavius Vespasianus—Vespasian, as we know him—to Greece with him. It's clear that Vespasian had been slated to lead one of the Palatium's two major military operations for A.D. 67, either the Caspian Gates operation or the Ethiopian expedition. With both those missions now on hold, and with the focus firmly on reclaiming Judea from the Jewish rebels, Vespasian was an obvious choice to lead the counteroffensive in Judea.

Fifty-eight-year-old Vespasian, grandson of a centurion in Pompey the Great's army, younger brother of Flavius Sabinus, Rome's longtime City Prefect, was a blunt, coarse, down-to-earth soldier with a formidable military reputation. For leading the 2nd Augusta Legion with distinction in the A.D. 43 invasion of Britain, he had been awarded Triumphal Decorations by the emperor Claudius. He had been made a consul in A.D. 51 and governor of Africa in A.D. 63. It was common for commanders to take their military-age sons with them to their new appointments, and Vespasian's twenty-seven-year-old son Titus was with him in Greece with the rank of senior tribune when the emperor gave Vespasian his new command. Vespasian sent Titus in a fast frigate to Egypt to collect the 15th Apollonaris Legion for the Judean offensive while he himself traveled overland to Antioch. At the Syrian capital, Vespasian was met by his senior officers and by King Herod Agrippa II, who, despite the bloody nose he had received from the Jews during Governor Gallus's expedition and retreat, had brought his Chalcian army to the Syrian capital to participate in Vespasian's offensive.

Vespasian had already decided the makeup of his Judean task force. For his legions, in addition to the 15th Apollonaris, which his son was bringing up from Egypt, he would use the 5th Macedonica and the 10th. The 12th Fulminata, in disgrace since losing its eagle to the Jewish partisans in the Beth-Horon Valley, had been dispatched to the Mediterranean port city of Laodicea, a little west of Antioch. There it was undergoing its scheduled discharge and reenlistment; it would play no part in Vespasian's offensive. The 4th Scythica, meanwhile, was building a new legion base high on an escarpment at Zeugma, to the east of Antioch. Its job was to guard what was by far the easiest crossing of the Euphrates against any repeat of the Parthian incursions under Quintus Labienus and Prince Pacorus in Mark Antony's day. The 6th Ferrata was farther south in Syria, at the Raphanaea base, also facing the Parthians across the Euphrates.

The Parthians had been quiet since their Armenian humiliation at the hands of Corbulo. In A.D. 66, Tiridates, brother of the Parthian king, had traveled to Rome in a vast caravan including a bodyguard of two thousand Parthian cavalrymen—an astonishing sight for the people of Rome. There, bearded Tiridates had bowed down to Nero, declaring that he would worship him as a god just as he worshiped the eastern god Mithras. And Nero had officially crowned him vassal king of Armenia. But the Parthians might well take advantage of Rome's problems in Judea, so the 4th

Scythica and 6th Ferrata would have to be on their guard while the other legions dealt with the Jewish rebels.

For the moment, the men of the 3rd Gallica at Caesarea waited to see what role General Vespasian would have for them in his offensive, and quizzed each mounted legion courier who arrived at Caesarea from the north for information about the general's movements. In the late spring they learned that, from Antioch, Vespasian had marched swiftly south down the Syrian coast with the 5th Macedonica and 10th Legions and King Agrippa's army, as allied forces from Commagene and Emesa hurried from farther north to join him. Basing himself at Ptolemais, just above the border between Syria and Samaria, and west of Galilee, he sent a seven-thousand-man garrison to the largest city in Galilee, Sephoris, which had remained loyal to Rome throughout the revolt. From Sephoris, these troops harassed Jewish-held towns and villages throughout Galilee.

As the Gallicans had hoped, five of the six 3rd Gallica cohorts at Caesarea now received orders to march up the coast to General Vespasian's assembly point at Ptolemais. They would be accompanied by the Gallica's own cavalry squadron and the five squadrons of the legion's associated auxiliary cavalry wing that had been based at Caesarea. Leaving just the legion's 1st Cohort to garrison Caesarea, the Gallica's infantry and cavalry quickly made their way north to join General Vespasian. A total of eighteen cohorts of Roman auxiliaries from Syrian bases also joined Vespasian at Ptolemais. Ten of those were *equitatae* cohorts. From today's Luxembourg, Belgium, northern Holland, and from western Germany, these equitatae units ranged between six hundred and a thousand men strong. Emulating German national military tactics, some of an equitatae cohort's men were cavalrymen, some were foot soldiers armed with spears. They were trained to work closely together. Sometimes a foot soldier would mount up behind a trooper, while in other situations a cavalryman would push his horse through an enemy formation, with an infantry colleague hanging onto the horse's tail until he had been delivered into the thick of the fighting. These auxiliaries wore beards just like their countrymen back home, tended to be several inches taller than the average Roman legionary, and were more lightly armed, carrying flat, round or oval shields.

At much the same time that all these units were assembling at Ptolemais, in the south, the 3rd Gallica Legion's lone cohort at Ascalon welcomed Vespasian's son Colonel Titus Vespasianus. Titus had marched up the coast road from Egypt at the head of the 15th Apollonaris Legion and a thousand allied cavalry and five thousand archers from Nabataea. Titus had pushed his column hard and was making record time on the march north. Apparently Titus took the 3rd Gallica's Centurion Antonius into his column, so that he could be rewarded by Vespasian for his spirited defense of Ascalon. His cohort was left to continue to garrison Ascalon as Titus pressed on with his column. With his large number of cavalry, Titus was not troubled by partisans—with no cavalry of their own, the Jews had learned not to take on Roman mounted troops in the open after the earlier bloody lesson outside Ascalon. Skirting Joppa, which Jewish partisans had reoccupied, Titus soon linked up with his father at Ptolemais.

Once his son joined him with the 15th Apollonaris and the Nabataean troops, Vespasian marched with upward of sixty thousand men. As the combined Roman army turned east and crossed the frontier into southern Galilee, more than thirty thousand Jewish partisans under thirty-year-old Josephus, the later defector and historian, were lying in wait nearby. But the approaching Roman army was so daunting that most of Josephus's conscripts simply melted away. Josephus was forced to retreat southeast to the fortified town of Tiberias, on the western shore of the Sea of Galilee.

While King Agrippa led his troops toward partisan-occupied towns in eastern Judea, in what is today Jordan, Vespasian concentrated on Galilee. His first objective was the town of Gabara. Only lightly defended, it fell to the Romans within hours. All the occupants other than children were killed, and the town and surrounding villages were burned to the ground. The task force swung south and marched on Jotapata, modern Jefat, a town harboring a large number of resistance fighters. The chosen route was via a stony mountain track, so a group of roadmakers went ahead of the main advance and created a highway for the army to pass over.

Five days later, Jewish general Josephus slipped out of Tiberias and galloped down to Jefat, where he took command of the town's defense. That same day, a Roman cavalry force arrived outside the town and surrounded it. The following afternoon, just as the sun was setting, Vespasian arrived at Jefat with the main battle group. The siege that followed was to last forty-seven days. Roman artillery sited on mounds and in siege towers on wheels lobbed arrows and rounded stones half the size of modern bowling balls into the defenses. To wreck this artillery, Josephus sent assault parties surging out the gates. The 5th Macedonia and 10th Legions took the brunt of the Jewish counterattacks outside the walls. And then they endured the missiles and boiling oil the defenders sent down from the towers and ramparts as the legionaries struggled to breach the walls with siege towers equipped at ground level with battering rams. The men of the 3rd Gallica and 15th Apollonaris Legions, held back for the final assault, waited impatiently for the order to go in en masse to storm the city. But it never came.

After weeks of this grueling stuff, a Jewish deserter suggested the best time and place for a surprise attack. Vespasian's son Titus led an assault group that crept up to the city wall in the hour before dawn. With him went Colonel Domitius Sabinus and a handful of men from his 15th Apollonaris Legion. Behind them, auxiliaries led by a pair of tribunes waited for the way to be cleared. Titus and his small commando group from the 15th silently placed ladders against the wall and pulled themselves up the rungs to the top, hoping all the while that the deserter hadn't set them up, that they weren't climbing into a trap. But all went according to plan. They mounted the wall and quickly silenced the sleepy sentries, then entered the town. With a signal from the wall that all was well, the waiting auxiliaries swarmed up the ladders and into the town. The Jefat citadel was quickly taken. When the sun rose, the town was in Roman hands.

Forty thousand people in Jefat died during the seven-week siege and twelve hundred were taken prisoner at its close. Roman casualties also had been heavy. Those casualties included a number who had been horribly burned by the boiling oil used by the defenders, and, right at the end, one notable member of the 3rd Gallica Legion. As the Roman troops were scouring the city for any Jew who remained in hiding, including the partisans' commander, Josephus, who had yet to be found, they came on a number of people who had taken refuge in caves. Centurion Antonius, who had made a name for himself as commander of the 3rd Gallica cohort that had successfully defended Ascalon, and who had probably been decorated by Vespasian, called down to the people in one of the caves to come out, promising they wouldn't be hurt if they did.

In response to the centurion, a Jew in the cave—a mere hole in the ground—came to the entrance and looked up to the 3rd Gallica legionaries above. He asked for Centurion Antonius's hand, as a pledge of sincerity and to help him climb out. The centurion reached down to give the man his right hand—his sword hand. As he did, the Jew grabbed it with his left, produced a sword in the other, and savagely thrust up into the Roman. The sword's blade entered Antonius's body at the groin and pierced his vital organs. The celebrated Centurion Antonius fell back and was soon dead. Josephus provides no account of what Antonius's men did to the Jew and his companions in response to that piece of treachery, but we can well imagine.

For three days, Roman troops searched Jefat for Josephus. They finally caught a woman emerging from a hiding place, and when they looked inside they discovered the man they were looking for skulking in a cave with forty of the city's leading citizens. While his troops wanted to burn them out, Vespasian tried to have the Jews talked out, sending several tribunes to discuss surrender with Josephus. The Jewish commander was all for giving up and saving his neck, but those with him threatened to kill him if he tried. Finally he agreed to commit suicide with the forty others. Most of the forty kept their pact and killed each other, but Josephus managed to talk the man who was supposed to kill him into surrendering with him.

Josephus was dragged to Vespasian by Roman troops. The general was going to send him to Nero in Rome, but according to Josephus he predicted to Vespasian that he and his son Titus would each become emperor of Rome one day. This was apparently enough to convince Vespasian to keep him around, although it's likely that Josephus also promised to advise him on how to beat his former Jewish compatriots, particularly when it came time to attack Jerusalem. Josephus was kept under close guard, chained to a centurion, but treated well. Vespasian's son Titus even gave him clothes and other gifts.

While the siege of Jefat was taking place, a force of thirty-six hundred infantry and cavalry under Brigadier General Sextus Cerialis, commander of the 5th Macedonica Legion, was sent by Vespasian to deal with a gathering of Samaritans at a temple on Mount Gerizim, halfway between Jefat and Jerusalem. Inspired by the Jews, these Samaritans had decided they would revolt from Roman rule as well. After they refused to surrender, General Cerialis and his force wiped them out—all 11,600 of them, says Josephus.

Although it was only August, and the summer had yet to run its course, Vespasian now decided to end offensive operations for the year. He had just received instructions from the Palatium to detach the men of the 3rd Gallica Legion from his task force and send them to the province of Moesia in Europe. Sarmatian raiders had crossed the Danube and killed a thousand Roman troops in a savage surprise attack before pillaging the countryside and retreating across the river. We aren't told whether those Roman casualties were suffered by either of the two legions then stationed in Moesia, the 7th Claudia and the 8th Augusta, or came from auxiliary cohorts stationed at one or more of the many Roman fortresses built along the southern bank of the Danube. But the losses caused alarm in Moesia and at Rome. To reinforce these embattled units, Rome had decided to withdraw the six cohorts of the 3rd Gallica currently marching with General Vespasian and send them to Moesia.

Throughout the first century it was not uncommon for the Palatium to transfer units that had suffered heavy casualties to new stations. Why the Palatium felt Vespasian could spare three thousand legionaries we don't know. It seems that Vespasian was furious at being ordered to give up crack troops, men with a determination to revenge themselves on the Jews who had killed so many of their comrades, and this may have influenced his decision to cease operations for the year.

Vespasian marched his army down to Caesarea. There, the 5th Macedonica and 10th Legions were told to settle into the city's citadel to enjoy a long break until the following spring, as the five returned cohorts of the 3rd Gallica linked up with the legion's 1st Cohort and all six prepared to march to the Danube. At the same time, the 15th Apollonaris Legion was ordered to march inland to winter at the friendly Greek city of Scythopolis, near the Jordan River. As his legions hung up their swords and shields, Vespasian, taking a large bodyguard of auxiliaries and cavalry with him, proceeded north to Caesarea Philippi. This inland city near the head of the Jordan River, occupying a similar latitude to Tyre, was the capital of King Agrippa's little kingdom of Chalcis.

There, Vespasian and his son Titus spent three weeks enjoying the generous hospitality of Agrippa and Berenice. During this sojourn, young Titus fell in love with the beautiful Berenice, who was thirteen years his senior, and the pair began an affair. But the vacation was rudely interrupted. A message arrived to inform Vespasian that there was a major concentration of Jewish partisans at Tiberias on the western shore of the Sea of Galilee, and that Tarichaeae on the southern shore had gone over to the rebels and barred its gates to Romans. Vespasian immediately sent Titus hurrying to Caesarea to fetch the main body of the army.

Titus brought the troops of the 3rd Gallica, 5th Macedonica, and 10th Legions to Scythopolis, linking up there with his father and the 15th Legion. Vespasian then advanced on Tiberias. When the city was given an opportunity to surrender, the leading townspeople threw open the city gates to the general, and the Jewish partisans there fled to Tarichaeae. This town sat at the foot of mountains at the southern tip of the Sea of Galilee. It was well fortified, and thronging with resistance fighters. While the main Roman force marched toward Tarichaeae, Titus led a large cavalry formation on ahead at a gallop. Titus and his cavalry routed a Jewish force sent out to intercept them, then fought their way into the town. According to Roman biographer Suetonius, Titus had his horse shot from under him during this action and subsequently mounted the horse of a trooper who'd been killed beside him.

Thousands of partisans escaped from Tarichaeae onto the Sea of Galilee in small boats. Not to be denied, Titus and his men built large rafts, went out onto the inland sea after them, and destroyed all resistance. The Sea of Galilee turned red with blood, and corpses and parts of corpses were being washed up on the lake's sandy shores for days afterward. Tens of thousands more Jews surrendered at Tarichaeae. They were instructed to leave the city, and at first they thought they were being allowed to go free. But as they passed out the city gate they found the road ahead lined by Roman troops—the men of Vespasian's legions and their associated auxiliaries—all the way to Tiberias. There the Jews were herded into the town's stadium. More than thirty thousand prisoners were auctioned off as slaves. Thousands more were selected to go to Rome to work on building projects. Twelve hundred old and infirm men were put to death.

At this point, September of A.D. 67, Vespasian sent his son Titus on a secret mission to Gaius Mucianus, governor of Syria, in Antioch. Vespasian and Mucianus were old enemies. Mucianus had disliked Vespasian for years for kowtowing to emperors such as Caligula, Claudius, and Nero to get where he was, and had not made a secret of it. Yet Mucianus liked young Titus. Suetonius claimed that Mucianus was homosexual, and perhaps he was attracted to Titus, a handsome, virile young man. Titus now acted as go-between, smoothing the waters between his father and Mucianus.

The reason for Titus's quick dash up to Antioch to see Mucianus has never been revealed. It is probable that Vespasian had received a letter from Julius Vindex, Roman governor of the Gallic province of Lugdunensis. Vindex was planning to revolt against the emperor Nero. We know that Vindex wrote to Galba, governor of Farther Spain, seeking support for his scheme. In the end, Galba did support him, but he was the only provincial governor to do so—publicly, anyway. Vindex launched his rebellion in March of A.D. 68, only for it to be crushed in May by the legions of the Army of the Upper Rhine, which remained loyal to Nero.

It's probable that not only did Vindex write to Galba in advance of his move, but he also wrote to a select group of Roman governors and generals whom he felt would support a revolt against Nero—including Mucianus and Vespasian, in which case Vespasian probably sent Titus to Antioch to literally compare notes with Mucianus and discuss a response to Vindex, if any. There was another consideration. According to the Roman biographer Suetonius, in the wake of Vindex's revolt and Galba's support for him, Nero considered arresting all his provincial governors and army commanders, and rumor of this potential threat may have reached the ears of both Vespasian and Mucianus. In the event, neither of them supported

Vindex and both remained loyal to Nero. But while the subject of Titus's meeting with Mucianus remained a secret, the very fact that Vespasian may have discussed such a revolutionary proposal was not something he would have wanted to leak out. Later, Vespasian would be at pains to claim he had not conspired for the throne; it was thrust on him by his troops, he would say.

While Titus was away, Vespasian wasn't idle. Determined to terminate resistance throughout the region before winter set in, the general marched on Gamala, a Jewish city well to the east of the Sea of Galilee in dry, inhospitable territory, in the vicinity of Al-Karak in present-day Jordan. For seven months, troops of King Agrippa of Chalcis had kept Gamala under siege, but it had refused to submit. Now the unstoppable General Vespasian and his Roman army came up to see if they couldn't do better.

Built into a massive hill that resembled a camel's hump, the town seemed to hang on the side of the dusty slope, with the buildings sitting almost on top of each other, clinging to the hillside. Because of the terrain, alternating between hills and ravines, it was impossible to ring the town with troops, so Vespasian had to settle for placing sentries at key points to watch all escape routes. On a hill overlooking the town, the legions built their fortified camps. Then they began building siege works. While the 5th Macedonica began construction of a ramp of earth against the central part of the town wall, the 15th Apollonaris threw another ramp up at the eastern end of the town, and the 10th filled in ravines and trenches leading up to Gamala. At the same time, the men of the 3rd Gallica prepared to lead the upcoming assault. The men of the Gallica knew that this would probably be their last opportunity to come to grips with the Jews before Vespasian ordered the other legions into their winter camps again and finally sent the Gallicans marching to Moesia as the Palatium required.

Three massive battering rams went to work on the walls of Gamala, and after weeks of effort all three broke through at the same time. The trumpets of the legions sounded the charge, the legionaries bellowed a frightening war cry, and then the men of the 3rd Gallica led the way through the breaches. At first they drove the defenders back, step by steep step up the narrow alleys. But the partisans regrouped, and charged back down the slope; the men of the 3rd Gallica were driven back by their impetus.

Thinking they could outflank the Jews, the Syrian legionaries clambered onto rooftops. Tiles gave way under legionary feet. Roofs caved in. Homes collapsed down the hill, like houses of cards. Legionaries were buried in the rubble. Hardly able to believe their luck, partisans poured through the ruins, killing trapped Romans, using the rubble to bombard troops coming through the breaches in the wall. Dazed legionaries of the 3rd Gallica, covered in dust, some with broken limbs, stumbled back into advancing comrades.

Vespasian himself rushed up into the town when he saw his troops in difficulties. Taking personal command on the spot, he ordered his troops to lock shields, then conducted a gradual, orderly withdrawal. That night legionaries of the 3rd Gallica licked their wounds back in their camp. They had lost a number of men in the day's unsuccessful assault, and more still had been injured. Other were missing.

A Centurion Gallus and ten of his 3rd Gallica legionaries had been cut off during Vespasian's withdrawal. Gallus, Syrian-born like his men but probably a descendant of a legionary veteran from Gaul who had settled in Syria at the time of the discharge of 33 B.C.—the name Gallus refers to Gaul—had the presence of mind to lead his group into a house and then hide for the night in the roof. Before long, the eleven soldiers of the Gallica heard Jewish partisans come in down below, and with rumbling stomachs heard and smelled them make supper. Over their meal, the partisans spoke loudly and confidently of how they were going to deal with the Romans the next day. Centurion Gallus and his men waited in the rafters until the early hours of the morning. Then they stealthily came down from their hiding place, crept up to the sleeping partisans, and slit their throats. The eleven 3rd Gallica men then tiptoed through the streets, taking slow, deliberate steps. Slipping out a gap in the wall without being spotted by Jewish sentries, they succeeded in returning to their own lines.

After this aborted assault, Vespasian held back his storm troops and concentrated on building his ramps and siege towers higher. At the same time, he sent cavalry commander Colonel Placidus with six hundred troopers to handle a large band of partisans who had taken refuge on Mount Tabor, near Scythopolis. Once he arrived, Placidus called on the Jews to come down to discuss a truce. The partisans came down, apparently unarmed, then produced weapons from under their cloaks and attacked the troopers. Placidus led his men away, and the Jews gave chase. On a trumpet call, the cavalrymen suddenly wheeled about and charged the pursuing partisans. After all the trickery employed by Jews against Roman troops over the past year, Placidus had been expecting the partisans to do precisely what they'd done, and he had led them into a prearranged ambush. A few partisans escaped to Jerusalem to fight another day, but most were mown down by the cavalrymen. When they'd finished, Mount Tabor was no longer a problem.

In the night, three men of the 15th Apollonaris Legion quietly worked away at the base of a tower in the Gamala town wall. Unseen by the sentries, they were able to pull five large stones free. The tower above gave way with an almighty crash. But when the besiegers subsequently made no attempt to enter the city, the Jews began to think that the Romans were afraid to try another assault, after the way the last one had ended.

The next day, Titus returned from his mission to Antioch. After consulting with his father, discussing his meeting with Mucianus, and getting an update on the situation at Gamala, he selected two hundred cavalrymen and some infantry for a night attack on the town. That night, while the rest of the army quietly moved into position, Titus and his assault group crept up to the city wall and then waited for the hours to pass.

In the early hours of the morning Titus sprang forward, with his men close behind. They slipped through the breach created by the 15th Legion trio. The Jewish sentries were overwhelmed, and the Romans poured into the lower town. Legion trumpets blared, signaling the main attack. With a roar, and with Vespasian at their head, thousands more waiting Roman troops swarmed into Gamala. The partisans tumbled out of their houses and fought a rearguard action all the way to the top of the hill. There, those who didn't die on Roman swords flung their wives and children from a clifftop, then jumped to their deaths after them. Between Romans and suicide there were only two Jewish survivors of the storming of Gamala, both women.

Sending Titus with a thousand cavalry to deal with the last Jewish stronghold in Galilee, the small town of Gishala, Vespasian withdrew the rest of the army for the winter. Ordering the 10th Legion to Scythopolis by the Jordan, he led the remainder of the task force to Caesarea. From there, while one of their cohorts remained in Ascalon, the men of the six remaining cohorts of the 3rd Gallica Legion and those of the legion's cavalry squadron finally set off on the march to Moesia. Their year's pay, they were told, would be waiting for them at their new station.

From Josephus we have a description of a Roman column on the march in Judea, and from this we can picture the makeup of the 3rd Gallica Legion column as it headed into Syria on the first leg of its overland journey to the Danube. At the column's head rode part of their cavalry squadron and a cohort of legionaries ready for action. Before the day's march, the centurions commanding each cohort had drawn lots to determine where in the column the cohorts would go. The advance guard was followed by ten men from every century, led by a junior tribune, carrying measuring equipment as well as their own backpacks. This party would lay out the legion's marching camp every day on the journey to Europe. Next would have come the legion's unidentified tribune and the first-rank centurions, including Arrius Varus. Farther back came most of the cohorts, marching six men abreast, among them Centurion Gallus and the legionaries who had survived the dangerous night in Gamala, and Centurion Julius and members of the detachment that had escorted Paul of Tarsus to Rome seven years earlier.

In the vanguard came the senior men of the 2nd Cohort, who, but for the insistence of the Jews of Jerusalem that they be withdrawn, would have been butchered there, as Centurion Metilius's men had been at the outset of the uprising. In the middle of the formation, clustered together for the march, came the standard-bearers—the proud eagle-bearer with his golden eagle, and around him, the bearers of the open-handed standards of the cohorts. Next came the cohorts' young trumpeters, all in a line. The official baggage train containing all the legion's military equipment and their worldly goods was in the middle of the column. Trailing a short distance behind the main baggage train came a second baggage train. Herded by the personal servants of the officers and the more affluent soldiers, its mules and carts carried all the luxuries that their masters had collected during their years in service. One cohort would have brought up the rear, with several troops from the cavalry squadron last of all as rear guard.

As the 3rd Gallica Legion departed Judea, the Jewish commander at Gishala abandoned the town and fled to Jerusalem. Those he left behind opened the town gates to Titus. All of Galilee was once more under Roman control. The legionaries of 3rd Gallica would have regretted being deprived of the opportunity of participating in the recapture of Judea, and of continuing to march under General Vespasian, a soldier they respected and admired. Little did they know that their involvement with Vespasian was far from over; that within two years they would set out to make him emperor of Rome.

XX

SLAUGHTERING THE SARMATIANS

I n the spring of A.D. 67, the men of the six cohorts of the 3rd Gallica Legion who had marched all the way from Judea settled into new quarters in the province of Moesia. Of the two existing legions in the province, the 7th Claudia was at Viminacium, today's Kostolac in Serbia, and the 8th Augusta was farther to the east, at Novae, the modern-day town of Svistov in Bulgaria. There were numerous other Roman fortresses dotted along the southern bank of the Danube, occupied by auxiliary units. It is unclear which of these bases became the temporary Moesian home to the 3rd Gallica.

Conquered by Rome in 29 B.C., Moesia had been made a Roman province early in the first century. Encompassing today's Bulgaria and much of Serbia, and stretching from Dalmatia in the west to the Black Sea in the east, the province was sandwiched between Thrace and the Danube River. North of the river lay mountainous Dacia, and beyond that, the Ukraine and Russia. These unexplored lands to the north were full of enemies of Rome who had avaricious eyes on the prospering Roman cities, towns, and farms south of the Danube. The fact that Sarmatians had raided across the river the previous year and into Illyricum three years earlier was of grave concern to the Palatium. The Sarmatians, a nation of marauding horsemen, lived in southern Russia. They may have gone home after their profitable push into Roman territory the previous year; no one knew for sure. But it was just as likely that they were still in the mountains just to the north, beyond the river, and planning another transdanube raid soon.

As the Syrians of the Gallica became accustomed to their new base beside the broad blue Danube and adjusted to the temperate climate of eastern Europe after the hot climes of Judea, they were joined by their first commander of general rank in decades. The limitation put on the legion's command by the Judean posting—the need to be commanded only by an officer of tribune rank—no longer existed. Up from Rome came Brigadier General Fulvius Aurelius. In the normal promotion process established by Augustus Caesar and followed by his successors, General Aurelius would have been a newly appointed senator of thirty, promoted from senior tribune of another legion.

In late June, astonishing news reached the legionaries in Moesia: Nero, their emperor, was said to be dead, and Galba, the governor of Farther Spain for the past eight years, was leading an army to Rome to take the throne of the Caesars for himself. Nero had become increasingly unpopular with the Roman elite for devoting himself to chariot racing and appearing onstage while allowing a tyrannical Prefect of the Praetorian Guard, Tigellinus, to initiate a reign of terror. For months, the news from Rome had been all about how everyone in power had deserted the increasingly demented young emperor. In the first week of June, both the Praetorian Guard and the emperor's bodyguard, the German Guard, had refused to serve Nero, after being offered a huge bonus by Galba to do so. Declaring Nero an enemy of the state, the Senate ordered his arrest and execution. On June 9, the thirty-year-old emperor was said to have fled his new palace, the Golden House, to hide in the suburbs of Rome with several freedmen. There, so the story went, Nero had cut his own throat just as Praetorian cavalry arrived to arrest him.

But other stories that reached the men on the Danube spoke of Nero fleeing Italy. It was known that his most trusted freedmen had prepared ships at Ostia, the port of Rome, to take him to Egypt, and one subsequently turned up in Africa. There were stories that Nero himself was seen in Syria. According to Tacitus, a redheaded man claiming to be Nero was executed on a Greek island. Another Nero would appear in Parthia and be handed over to Rome by a reluctant King Vologases, who had come to respect Nero. And for years to come the rumor would persist that Nero was living incognito in the East. Yet another story, later committed to paper by Suetonius, the only contemporary source for the details of Nero's death, had his mistress Acte and his childhood nurses cremating his body and consigning his ashes to the tomb of his father's family, the Domitius clan.

Whatever did happen to Nero, the last Roman emperor from the Caesar family, he was gone, and the Senate recognized the legitimacy of the claim of seventy-year-old Servius Sulipicius Galba. He was of noble birth, being related to Livia, wife of Augustus, the first emperor, and had strict habits. He was also, according to Plutarch, the richest private person to become Roman emperor till his time. In July, Galba marched into Rome at the head of an army that included the new 7th Galbiana Legion, raised by him in Spain in the recruiting grounds of the 7th Claudia Legion. And throughout the empire, with a promise from Galba of a bonus to every legionary, Rome's legions, including the 3rd Gallica, assembled in their camps and swore loyalty to the new emperor. Provincial governors and army commanders such as Mucianus and Vespasian did the same.

Six months later, on January 15, A.D. 69, the empire was again convulsed: Galba had been murdered at Rome by disaffected troops. Not only had he failed to pay the promised bonuses to the soldiery, Galba had quickly lost favor with the nobility for unwise appointments and harsh treatment of opponents. Two weeks before his death, first the Army of the Upper Rhine and then the Army of the Lower Rhine had refused to swear the traditional January 1 loyal oath to Galba as emperor. Instead, they had hailed their commander, Lieutenant General Aulus Vitellius, as their new emperor.

But at Rome the soldiers of the Praetorian Guard and German Guard had chosen their own emperor: Marcus Otho. He had been Nero's best friend until Nero had taken Otho's wife, Poppae, as his own and sent Otho to Lusitania, today's Portugal, which he had ably governed for ten years. According to Plutarch, Otho had been the first provincial governor to go over to Galba, and had expected to be named his heir and successor. But Galba had turned his back on Otho. And so a campaign to ferment revolt within the Praetorians and other soldiers at Rome had taken hold, and Galba had been assassinated in the Forum. A lone centurion of his bodyguard had fought, and died, in a vain attempt to prevent the crime.

In Moesia, at an assembly on a bitter winter's day, the men of the 3rd Gallica Legion hailed Otho as their new emperor. The Gallicans had no liking for fat, lazy Vitellius, the general chosen by the Rhine legions as emperor. And there was a lingering guilt about the demise of Nero. He had been a Caesar after all, and a descendant of Mark Antony, with whom men of the 3rd Gallica had always felt a strong connection. To the minds of many Romans neither Galba nor Vitellius could become a Caesar simply by taking the title Caesar Augustus. Thirty-six year-old Otho, who had been closely connected to Nero, seemed a more worthy sovereign. The other legions in Moesia and those in neighboring Pannonia and Dalmatia followed suit and swore loyalty to Otho.

In the East, both General Vespasian and Syria's governor, Mucianus, swore loyalty to Otho, as did all the legions in the East. Vespasian had by this time retaken all of Judea from the Jewish rebels except for Jerusalem and the fortresses of Masada and Machaerus. His 10th Legion occupied Jericho, while the 5th Macedonica and the 15th Apollonaris were in camp at Emmaus, just north of Jerusalem. Suspending further offensive operations until the conflict between Otho and Vitellius was resolved, Vespasian dispatched his son Titus to Rome by sea to personally pledge to Otho the loyalty of the legions in the East on behalf of Vespasian and Mucianus.

Come February, in snowbound Moesia, just as the men of the 3rd Gallica Legion were talking about marching to Italy to support Otho against an expected threat by Vitellius and his legions from the Rhine, "To Arms" was sounded throughout their camp. When they assembled, their commander, General Aurelius, stepped up onto the tribunal and informed them that a force of thousands of Sarmatian cavalry from the Roxolani tribe had crossed the frozen Danube and commenced raiding in northern Moesia. The 3rd Gallica and 8th Augusta Legions had been ordered by the province's governor, Lieutenant General Marcus Aponius Saturninus, to immediately march to intercept the raiders.

As the 3rd Gallica cohorts moved out from their base accompanied by a unit of auxiliaries, marching along a snow-covered road with their legion's cavalry squadron galloping ahead to locate the Sarmatian raiders, their thoughts were on their new enemy. They wouldn't be up against wild Jewish partisans on this occasion. The Jews had been lightly armed and on foot. The new adversary would be heavily armored and on horseback. The Gallicans had been told by locals in Moesia what to expect when they encountered the Roxolani. Natural horsemen who had originated in Asia and migrated to the Ural Mountains from today's Iran, the Sarmatians had broad noses and slanted eyes, which made them repulsive to Romans. Overwhelming the Scythians, the original inhabitants, the Sarmatian tribes came to control southern European Russia. The large Roxolani tribe settled along the Volga River. They were seminomadic, living on horseback and in wagons, and were renowned as fast riders who hated to walk, and who loved gold. Fierce fighters, they wore body armor and used long lances but had no time for shields. According to folk tales, like the Amazons of Greek legend, unmarried Sarmatian women took up arms alongside their menfolk. With nudges and winks, many a soldier of the 3rd Gallica would have been looking forward to taking on female fighters.

By the time Roman cavalry scouts tracked the Roxolani down, the Sarmatians had pillaged towns and farms for weeks, sending Roman settlers fleeing south, east, and west for their lives. The Roxolani had set up camp over a wide, flat area at a roadside close to frozen marshes, on ground that was stony and ice-covered. Tacitus says that there were several roads in the vicinity, so the camp was probably at a crossroads. Dispersing over a wide area, the Roxolani had not bothered to build any camp defenses in the Roman style. As night fell, the light from their campfires gave them away to the Roman scouts. The Sarmatians worshipped a god of fire, so a huge central bonfire would have been burning, with many smaller campfires throughout the camp. Unhitched Roxolani wagons stood everywhere, loaded with loot taken in the latest raid. Hide covers would have spread from wagons to ground to create tents. Thousands of horses were tethered in groups.

As the dismounted Roman cavalry scouts crept in close for a reconnaissance in the night, there would have been a hubbub of conversation and gales of laughter from around Sarmatian campfires. It's likely that the 3rd Gallica's Centurion Arrius Varus, an expert horseman who frequently rode with the cavalry, was in charge of the scouts. He would have noted that the Sarmatians wore tunics, trousers tied around the ankles, and moccasin-style leather footwear. Their principal weapon, the *kontos*, a massive iron-tipped lance twenty feet long, would have stood in stacks throughout the camp. The conical Sarmatian helmet, with a neckpiece of iron mail down the back, would have been hanging on the sides of wagons, along with the armored suit worn by each fighter. These were made of overlapping fish-scale armor, sometimes of small plates of iron, in other cases of hardened leather. The horses of the tribe's nobles were also fitted with armored coats. In action, a leather quiver filled with bow and arrows hung from the left side of the Sarmatian's horse. The Sarmatian also used a giant broadsword. Wielded double-handed, it was, according to Tacitus, so long it had to be worn on a scabbard hung down the back. A Sarmatian would reach over his left shoulder with two hands to draw it.

The Sarmatians were little different from the Parthians and other nations of the East in the way they equipped and trained their fighting men. Of all the legions that would be pitted again the Roxolani, the 3rd Gallica Legion, with its experience against Parthian cavalry in Armenia, would be best prepared to combat them.

As they watched the Sarmatian camp, the eyes of the Roman scouts would have glinted greedily. Not only was there the plunder in the hundreds of Roxolani wagons—which the 3rd Gallica men would claim as their own should they defeat the enemy and seize his camp—gold was everywhere to be seen. Like Roman cavalrymen, Sarmatians decorated their steeds with gold horse ornaments. Individual Roxolani men wore gold rings, bracelets, plaques, buckles, and buttons. Even the wooden hilts of the swords of nobles had gold lacings, and were topped by a knob of valuable agate or onyx. When Centurion Varus and his fellow scouts slithered away into the darkness, they had estimated the size of the enemy force, plotted the location of the various elements of the camp, and noted the best place for an attack—assuming the Roxolani stayed put.

The Roxolani were feeling victorious, says Tacitus—once again they had plundered the Romans with impunity. Tacitus relates that the Roxolani had heard about the troubles the Romans were having with their internal politics. They had become convinced that Roman minds were fixed on their own impending civil war, and as a result foreign affairs had been disregarded, leaving Moesia open to this attack.

When General Aurelius reached the area with the 3rd Gallica, he set up camp several miles from the Roxolani, no doubt in the cover provided by forest, and issued orders for his men to prepare to launch a surprise attack the next morning. Aurelius knew that he could not wait for the 8th Augusta Legion to join him. The Roxolani might well move on before long, and Aurelius could lose his chance for a surprise attack.

So that the enemy would not be alerted to their presence, fires would have been forbidden in the Roman camp; the soldiers of the Gallica ate cold rations that night, and spoke in whispers. How much sleep they gained, stretched out on frozen ground wrapped in their cloaks, can only be guessed. Running through their minds would have been the prospects for the morning. The scouts would have reported many thousands of Roxolani cavalrymen in the enemy camp. It would later turn out there were nine thousand of them. The men of the 3rd Gallica were outnumbered by three to one. And not by infantry, but by cavalry, and Sarmatian cavalry at that. Tacitus was to say of Sarmatian cavalry: "When they charge in squadrons, scarcely any infantry line can stand against them." Young General Aurelius and his men were hoping that the element of surprise would counter the Roxolani advantage in numbers. Otherwise, the 3rd Gallica, savaged the previous year by the Jewish partisans, could be going to its doom the next day.

A damp morning dawned, with a mist overlying the silent countryside. The men of the Gallica faced east, bowed down, and prayed to Baal for victory and life, hoping that their god would hear their hushed voices. Then, without uttering another word, and following the signals of their standards, the Roman troops moved out of camp and marched over icy ground to take up their assigned positions in the mist. Tacitus says that the ice was thawing by the time the battle began, making it late morning.

The mist had risen and the sun was well up when Roman trumpets sounded "Charge."

The Sarmatians, not having posted sentries, were caught entirely off guard when the Romans appeared from the trees and came plowing through the snow with a blood-curdling roar. Desperately, they tried to pull on their armor, to saddle their horses, to grab weapons, to mount, and to fight. Because the Roxolani camp was so spread out, while the Sarmatians who took the brunt of the Roman charge were quickly mowed down, many of their comrades deeper inside the camp managed to don their armor. Some succeeded in mounting. But, says Tacitus, in their heavy armor the Roxolani were continually sinking in the soft, deep snow.

A number of Roman legionaries, finding that javelins merely bounced off the thick Sarmatian armor when thrown, kept hold of their javelins and used them as lances. Others rushed in and used their shields to knock heavily armored opponents off their feet, then quickly dispatched them with jabs of the sword to face or neck. The Roxolani were, says Tacitus, virtually defenseless once they were knocked to the ground, because the weight of their armor made it difficult for them to get up again, and, just as importantly, because they were not equipped with shields. Those Roxolani who were able to mount found their horses slipping under them on the icy ground and were unable to form up in their squadrons to charge. With the Roman troops pressing in, the Sarmatian lances were much too long to use at close quarters. By the time they resorted to their swords, they were being pulled from the back of their horses and thrown heavily to the ground. And once brought down, the vaunted courage of the Sarmatian warrior vanished. "No soldiers could show so little spirit when fighting on foot," Tacitus was to remark of them.

By nightfall it was all over. A handful of wounded Sarmatians escaped to the marshes. Every other member of the Roxolani raiding party was killed in the fighting. The men of the 3rd Gallica went through the Roxolani camp, stripping the dead and claiming enemy horses, baggage animals, and the wagons and their contents. It had been a profitable day's work. The next day, after a bitterly cold night, 3rd Gallica patrols found the Roxolani who had escaped. Seeking refuge in the marshes, all had died, either of their wounds or from exposure. All nine thousand members of the Roxolani raiding party had perished. Casualty figures for the 3rd Gallica Legion were so slight they were not recorded.

A dispatch was soon on its way to Rome with news of the Moesian battle. At the capital, when the new emperor Otho learned of the 3rd Gallica's crushing victory, he was so delighted he rewarded all the generals in Moesia. Brigadier General Aurelius of the 3rd Gallica, Major General Tettius Julianus of the 7th Claudia, and Brigadier General Numisius Lupus of the 8th Augusta were all awarded purple consular ensigns, while their superior, General Aponius, the governor of Moesia, was awarded Triumphal Decorations.

As the men of the 3rd Gallica Legion marched triumphantly back to base with their spoils, and with their reputation made as the legion that had wiped out the Roxolani, matters were coming quickly to a head in the contest between Otho and Vitellius for the Roman throne. Already, troops loyal to Vitellius had seized much of northwestern Italy, and two task forces from Vitellius's armies of the Upper Rhine and Lower Rhine were heading for Italy: one via France, one via Switzerland. On March 14 Otho marched from Rome with an army of his own to do battle with the forces of Vitellius.

XXI

TO ITALY, TO MAKE AN EMPEROR

The men of the 3rd Gallica Legion were not happy. On April 15, while they sat at their Danube garrison, the army of the new emperor they supported, Otho, had been defeated in a bloody battle at Bedriacum, near Cremona in northeastern Italy. The following day, Otho had been found dead in his tent; he had committed suicide in the night. Vitellius was the new emperor. While his victorious generals, Fabius Valens and Aulus Caecina, waited for him in northern Italy, Vitellius swaggered down from the Rhine with a cavalcade of troops, spending the Roman treasury's money on lavish banquets and entertainments to celebrate his victory. According to Cassius Dio, when Vitellius had gone to the Rhine to take up his appointment as governor of Lower Germany a year back, he had been so heavily in debt he was surrounded not by soldiers when he left Rome but by unhappy creditors. Now Vitellius was returning as emperor, and those creditors were regretting having hounded him in the past.

By the time that Vitellius joined Valens and Caecina in northern Italy in the middle of May, the 3rd Gallica Legion had a new commander. Replacing Fulvius Aurelius, the brigadier general who had led the Gallicans to their spectacular defeat of the Roxolani, was Brigadier General Dillius Aponianus. Now, when General Aponianus called the Gallicans to assembly at their Danube base and required them to swear loyalty to Vitellius as their new emperor, they refused point blank. As Tacitus was to say, Vitellius had never led an army in battle, had never won a victory against an enemy of Rome, and had merely been elevated to the throne by the unpopularity of Galba. He was not the Gallicans' idea of an emperor.

That day the men of the 3rd Gallica were called on to swear the oath of allegiance to Vitellius, and refused, the bolder among them called up to

General Aponianus on the camp tribunal that if they were going to swear loyalty to any former consul it would be to their commander in the East, Vespasian, a general who led from the front. To them, all Vitellius could lead was a life of luxury. He hadn't even been present at the battle that had delivered him the throne.

The Gallicans had become full of self-confidence since their victory over the Sarmatians, and General Aponianus, shaken by their refusal to swear for Vitellius, was unsure what to do about it, and left the assembly. He hurriedly reported to his superior, Lieutenant General Marcus Aponius Saturninus, governor of Moesia. The governor wasn't entirely sure how to handle the situation either. In his heart, Saturninus was in agreement with the men of his star legion, but for now he sent a report to the new emperor, informing Vitellius that the 3rd Gallica was refusing to swear the loyalty oath to him. But that was as much as he told Vitellius. The governor failed to inform the new emperor that the men of the 3rd Gallica were suggesting Vespasian as an alternative emperor. As it happened, Saturninus felt that suggestion had some merit; but he would keep that to himself for the time being. What was more, he instructed General Aponianus not to press the matter of the oath of allegiance with the 3rd Gallica.

When the men of the legion realized that the governor was probably in sympathy with them, their centurions, led by Arrius Varus, who had become the legion's chief centurion by this time, wrote letters to the two other legions of the Moesia station, the 7th Claudia and the 8th Augusta. Legion couriers went galloping off to deliver the letters, in which the legionaries of the 3rd Gallica declared that they were for Vespasian as emperor. They told their comrades in the other legions that Vespasian was a member of the "meritocracy," not the aristocracy. Here was a man with a humble background, just like themselves. A man who had become a general and consul through merit, not family background. Vespasian's grandfather Titus Flavius Petro had spent seventeen years in legion ranks and fought for Pompey the Great at Dyrrhachium and Pharsalus, after which he had gone back to his hometown of Sabine Reate in Italy to work as a debt collector. They told their fellow legionaries that Vespasian's father had been a farmers' agent in Asia before setting up as a money-lender back home in Reate. Vespasian himself had invested in mule farms, none too successfully. Yet, from these humble beginnings, Vespasian had risen to be a conquering legion commander in Britain, a consul of Rome, governor of Africa, and now commander in chief in the East. This was the general who had led the 2nd Augusta Legion to victory after victory through thirty battles in southern England and been awarded T.D.s by a grateful emperor. This was the general who had rolled back the Jewish partisans in Judea. This, said the Syrians of the 3rd Gallica, was the man to save the empire. A soldier's emperor.

The 3rd Gallica letters found sympathetic readers in the 7th Claudia and 8th Augusta Legions. Like the 3rd Gallica, both these units had previously sworn for Otho. And both had marched from Moesia in April to join Otho's army in central Italy. They had just entered northern Italy in the third week of April when they learned of the defeat at Bedriacum and of Otho's subsequent suicide. Sending packing the messengers who brought them this bad news, the men of the two legions had run riot. In the process they'd torn up the cloth banners on which their commanders, Generals Julianus and Lupus, had inscribed the name of Vitellius as new emperor, and had ignored the commands of their officers. A number of legionaries had broken into the legions' money chests and divided the spoils among themselves. Once they had calmed down, they returned to the authority of their officers, and turned around and set off back to Moesia. But they hadn't returned the stolen legions' funds.

On the march back to their Danube stations, the men who had robbed the money chests began to dread what would happen to them once Vitellius found out what they'd done. According to Suetonius, they were consulting the list of provincial governors of consular rank, to find a lieutenant general they could confidently give their loyalty to, one who wouldn't punish them for their thievery, when the letters from the 3rd Gallica reached them and offered the ideal candidate. Following the lead of the 3rd Gallica, the 7th Claudia and the 8th Augusta declared for Vespasian. Both their commanding generals also subsequently swore loyalty to Vespasian.

All three legions now wrote to the legions in the adjoining provinces of Pannonia and Dalmatia—the 7th Galbiana, 11th Claudia, and 13th Gemina—urging them to do as they had done. Tacitus says that the men of the 3rd Gallica and the two other pro-Vespasian legions were prepared to use force against the neighboring legions if they refused to join the movement for Vespasian. They needn't have worried. The 13th Gemina had been humiliated by Vitellius's generals following the Battle of Bedriacum, in which it was on the losing side, and was chafing for revenge. Performing badly for Otho in the battle, its men had been forced by Generals Valens and Caecina to build a wooden amphitheater outside the city of Cremona in northern Italy following their defeat. There, gladiatorial contests were celebrated for Vitellius when he arrived from the Rhine. Without hesitation, the 13th Gemina now also swore allegiance to Vespasian.

The other legion in Pannonia, the 7th Galbiana, which had also previously marched for Otho, hesitated, until a letter to the legion arrived from the East, from Vespasian himself. The 7th Galbiana's commander, Brigadier General Marcus Antonius Primus, had the letter read aloud at assembly, and when General Primus himself declared unambiguously that he was for Vespasian, his men hailed Vespasian as their new emperor with enthusiasm. In adjacent Dalmatia, the 11th Claudia Legion did likewise.

Saturninus, the governor of Moesia, now showed his true colors, also coming out for Vespasian. At the same time, he took advantage of the situation to settle a personal score, dispatching a centurion to kill the commander of the 7th Claudia Legion, Major General Tettius Julianus, on the pretext that he was a closet Vitellius supporter. When Julianus got wind of this, he fled into the hills. But Julianus was genuinely in favor of Vespasian. At first thinking of trying to go to Vespasian in the East, he decided to stay in hiding until the opportunity presented itself to safely rejoin the Vespasian party.

Simultaneously, and independent of the happenings in Moesia, Pannonia, and Dalmatia, the movement to make Vespasian emperor had gained pace in the East. In May, when Vespasian called his three legions to assembly in Judea and led them in an oath of loyalty to Vitellius, his troops had remained stubbornly silent. Instead, some in the ranks called for Vespasian to become their emperor. Publicly, Vespasian would have nothing to do with these calls. But in June, Vespasian and Mucianus, governor of Syria, met on Mount Carmel, north of Caesarea, and agreed on a strategy to put Vespasian on the throne—with Mucianus as his right-hand man.

Mucianus made a speech at the Mount Carmel meeting, in front of Vespasian and the senior Roman officers from Syria and Judea. Apparently that speech was later made public by the Flavian Palatium, for it was reprinted by Tacitus. Mucianus's aim was to show that Vespasian had been encouraged by others to take up arms against Vitellius, the emperor now recognized by the Senate. In that speech, Mucianus invited Vespasian to claim the throne. He pointed out, sagely, that Vitellius was living proof that an emperor could be made by the army. That being the case, he said, there were nine legions in the East who would back Vespasian's claim to the throne, a claim, said Mucianus, that was superior to that of Vitellius in terms of both ability and experience.

A suggestion had come, from Vitellius or his supporters, that Vespasian be anointed as his heir—an act designed to keep Vespasian from challenging Vitellius. Mucianus told Vespasian he would be a fool to accept that. "To be chosen as Vitellius's successor would be more of an insult than a compliment," said Mucianus in the Mount Carmel speech. Vespasian, he said, was duty-bound to act, to overthrow Vitellius to save Rome. "To continue to do nothing, to leave the state to degradation and ruin, would look like indolence and cowardice."

On July 1, the Prefect of Egypt, Tiberius Alexander, who was also a party to the plan agreed to by Vespasian and Mucianus, called his legions to assembly in Alexandria and required them to swear an oath to Vespasian as emperor. The men of the 3rd Cyrenaica and 22nd Deiotariana Legions and the two thousand 18th Legion recruits all enthusiastically complied and hailed Vespasian as their emperor. Two days later, the three legions of Vespasian's task force in Judea swore the oath to Vespasian, and by the middle of the month all three legions in Syria under Governor Mucianus's command had eagerly followed suit. King Agrippa and his sister Queen Berenice joined Vespasian's party, as did the kings of Emesa and Commagene. All the governors of the other eastern provinces also vowed loyalty to Vespasian. The Roman East was solidly behind him.

Vespasian then wrote letters to governors and legion commanders in Europe seeking their allegiance, and centurions sailed aboard fast frigates to deliver them. Some of Vespasian's couriers would be intercepted by Vitellius's officials, sent to Rome, and executed, but most would get through. For those who were for Vespasian, these letters strengthened their support. For those who were against him—and that included officials and military commanders in Gaul, Britain, Spain, Rhaetia, and on the Rhine—his messages generally only strengthened support for Vitellius north and west of Pannonia and Dalmatia. Waverers, meanwhile, decided to wait and see who gained the ascendancy.

In his letters to the governors of Moesia, Pannonia, and Dalmatia and their legion commanders, Vespasian said that Governor Mucianus would march to them overland with a force that he was raising in Syria. Mucianus, he said, would take command of the army that would advance into Italy to deprive Vitellius of his newly won throne. Mucianus's force was to consist of the 6th Ferrata Legion, a number of auxiliaries, and thirteen thousand retired legionaries recalled to their Evocati militia standards, including men from the A.D. 60 discharge of the 3rd Gallica Legion.

Vespasian himself was heading to Alexandria, which he would make his headquarters. From there he could control the grain supply to Rome, while Mucianus took the fight to Vitellius in Europe. By August, Mucianus, given broad-ranging powers by Vespasian that made him a cross between a field marshal and a vice emperor, was on his way from Syria overland at the head of a large force of cavalry. A second column, made up of the 6th Ferrata and Evocati militia from Syria, was not far behind.

Vespasian knew that in taking the 6th Ferrata from the Euphrates frontier he was inviting the Parthians to strike across the river behind his back. So he wrote to the Parthian ruler, King Vologases, and to his brother Tiridates, king of Armenia, explaining that he had assumed the role of emperor of Rome and sought their friendship. Vologases, wearied by the expensive wars he had been fighting over the past decade in Armenia and on his southern border with unfriendly neighbors, had lost the taste for military ventures. Besides, the reputations of both Vespasian and Titus had quickly spread to Parthia after they had retaken Galilee and most of Judea over the past three years. Vologases knew that Titus could easily leave Jerusalem for the time being and swing his task force up into Syria to counter any Parthian incursion. Not for many years had the legions of the East been so battle-tested—as a result of the Jewish Revolt and Corbulo's Armenian campaign. And in Vespasian and Titus they had courageous and clever generals. Only a very foolish Parthian ruler would go to war with Rome right now.

The meeting of commanders at Poetovio in Pannonia had been going on for hours. Clustered around the wooden legion praetorium at Poetovio, listening through open windows and doors to the discussion inside, the men of the 3rd Gallica Legion's senior cohorts were growing increasingly restless.

The 13th Gemina Legion's base at Poetovio grew into today's picturesque Slovenian town of Ptuj on the Drava River, not far from the Austrian border. There, in September of A.D. 69, legion commanders, a lieutenant general, and numerous Roman officials were locked in a conference in the 13th Gemina's praetorium. Ptuj had been chosen as a central meeting place to discuss the best course of military action in support of Vespasian against the emperor Vitellius. Never before had the administrators from three Roman provinces and representatives of their six legions come together to discuss throwing their combined weight behind a contender for the imperial throne.

Brigadier General Vedius Aquila, commander of the 13th Gemina Legion, and his deputy, the tribune Suetonius, hosted the meeting. Colonel Suetonius, in his late twenties, had left his pregnant wife at home in North Africa many months before, and she had recently borne him a son who would become Suetonius the famous biographer. The governor of

Pannonia, Lieutenant General Titus Ampius Flavianus, was the most senior officer present at the Poetovio meeting. Elderly and rich, Governor Flavianus had fled to northern Italy when the two legions in his province had declared for Vespasian, primarily because he was related to Vitellius and was afraid his men would turn against him. Once he reached Italy and heard stories of how Vitellius was leading a life of idle luxury at Rome, Governor Flavianus had decided that Vespasian was likely to be the victor in the upcoming contest and returned to Pannonia. Flavianus's deputy, the procurator Cornelius Fuscus, an enthusiastic proponent of the Vespasian-for-emperor movement, had welcomed Flavianus back. To have the province's governor endorse the Vespasian party was reason enough to promise that Flavianus would be protected.

Procurator Fuscus turned out to be a prime mover and shaker for Vespasian, second only in Pannonia to Brigadier General Primus, commander of the 7th Galbiana Legion. Both men had written letters to the famous 14th Gemina Legion, now back in Britain after unsuccessfully supporting Otho at the Battle of Bedriacum in April. Their hope was that the 14th would influence the three pro-Vitellius legions in Britain to swing behind Vespasian. The pair had also written to the 1st Adiutrix Legion, which had also fought for Otho at Bedriacum and been subsequently sent to Spain by Vitellius. Similarly the hope was that it would bring the two other legions then in Spain over to Vespasian. As part of their propaganda effort, Fuscus and Primus had arranged for leaflets to be secretly spread all over Gaul encouraging the population to come out for Vespasian.

General Primus had accompanied Procurator Festus to the Poetovio conference, hurrying down from the 7th Galbiana's base at Carnuntum in northern Pannonia, bringing with him all the squadrons of cavalry he could muster and a number of light infantry auxiliaries. Brigadier General Annius Bassus, commander of the 11th Claudia Legion, had come up from Dalmatia for the meeting, although his province's governor, Lieutenant General Poppaeus Silvanus, another aging and wealthy former consul, had stayed away as he waited to see which way the political wind blew. Another provincial leader at the conference was Sextilius Felix, the procurator who governed Noricum, the province northwest of Pannonia covering parts of today's Austria and Bavaria. Following the lead of his neighbors, Felix had brought his province into the Vespasianist fold.

Also present were several hundred men from the senior cohorts of the 3rd Gallica Legion, instigators of the pro-Vespasian movement in Europe. Chief Centurion Arrius Varus and his comrades had force-marched down from the Danube to be at the conference, to make sure the outcome was one they agreed with. It is also highly likely that the second-in-command of the 7th Claudia Legion, the senior tribune Colonel Vipstanius Messalla, had come down from the Danube for the meeting. Since General Julianus had run for the hills to avoid Saturninus's executioner, Colonel Messalla had been in command of the 7th Claudia. From a distinguished consular family, and highly distinguished himself, according to Tacitus, Messalla would lead the 7th Claudia Legion through the tumultuous months ahead. Later, Messalla would write his memoirs. Tacitus would refer to them extensively in writing his Annals and Histories. The fact that Tacitus would quote much of what was said at this conference suggests that Colonel Messalla was indeed present and noted down proceedings.

As the Poetovio conference dragged on for hour after hour, General Primus and Procurator Fuscus, the two most ardent advocates for Vespasian's cause, became increasingly frustrated. The faint hearts among the gathered officers were all for holding the passes of the Pannonian Alps with the forces now at their disposal, and waiting for General Mucianus to arrive from Syria before launching an invasion of Italy the following summer. General Primus was all for striking at once. The stories coming out of Rome told of a new administration verging on chaos. Now was the time to advance, he declared. Delay would only give the other side time to organize.

Primus, who was a striking physical presence and possessed of a commanding speaking voice, according to Tacitus, began to take center stage. Born at Tolosa—today's Toulouse in southwestern France—Primus was in his early forties, tall, and muscular. According to Suetonius, Primus's nickname as a child growing up in Toulouse had been Becco, or "rooster's beak," implying that he had a large nose and a strutting manner. The Primus part of his name meant that he was the firstborn son of his family, the Antonius family. The Marcus Antonius part literally translates as Mark Antony; and as events were to prove, like his famous namesake, Marcus Antonius Primus's military fortunes would be closely associated with those of the 3rd Gallica Legion.

General Primus now reminded his colleagues of how, in July, Vitellius had entered Rome at the head of elements from eight legions plus thirty-four auxiliary cohorts and twelve squadrons of cavalry. As Vitellius and his supporters had commenced a binge of celebration, the new emperor had dismissed the existing Praetorian Guard, disarming its cohorts and sending them to various cities in Italy before soon telling their men to go home. In their place, Vitellius had set up a new Praetorian Guard and City Guard, taking twenty thousand men from his legions to fill their ranks. He had also dismissed the German Guard, the imperial bodyguard, and filled its ranks with men from his German auxiliary cohorts. In the same manner, in July he had abolished the Praetorian Guard cavalry unit and replaced it with a new regiment, the Singularian Horse, made up of the best German cavalrymen from his auxiliary units. Vitellius's troops—sixty thousand of them, plus an equal number of camp followers—had been lounging around Rome ever since. Military duties were being ignored, discipline was breaking down, brawls and murder were reportedly common. Added to that, many of the troops were camped in the Vatican Valley, north of the Tiber River. It was infamous for malaria in the summer, and large numbers of these men were falling ill. Those infected who weren't dying were being severely weakened.

"Yet, if you give them time, even these men will regain their old strength as they prepare for war," Primus warned his colleagues, says Tacitus. Primus reminded his colleagues that Vitellius controlled Rome's two main battle fleets, at Ravenna on Italy's east coast and Misenum on the west coast, and could bring in troop reinforcements from the Rhine, Britain, and Spain. If that happened, "What good will our mountain passes be to us then? What will be the point of putting off the war until next summer?"

Those who argued for delay spoke of how many legions Vitellius possessed.

"If you calculate the number of soldiers, rather than the number of legions," Primus countered, "we outnumber them." He also pointed out that several of the Vespasianist legions had been forced to surrender after the Battle of Bedriacum. That humiliation, he said, would work in their favor, would inspire the legions involved to exact their revenge. As for their cavalry, he pointed out that one of their squadrons from Pannonia and another from Moesia had fought for Otho at Bedriacum and had actually broken through the lines of Vitellius's army in that battle. Now, he said, eighteen squadrons of cavalry waited in the Poetovio camp to show Vitellius's cavalry how to fight.

By this stage, to the consternation of some of the conference participants, the centurions and senior men of the 3rd Gallica Legion who had gathered at the praetorium's open door and windows began to call out their support for General Primus, declaring that even if no one else marched with him, they would be proud to do so. They didn't care that, ten years before, Primus had been one of several nobles convicted under the Cornelian Law of forging the will of an extremely rich man, and sent into exile. That was then; this was now. The emperor Galba had seen fit to recall Primus from exile and give him a legion command. And now, as Primus called for immediate action and an advance into Italy with the troops at their disposal, to catch the other side unprepared and win the throne for Vespasian, he was talking the Gallicans' language. The 3rd Gallica was with him, and they told Primus so.

"You are the one true man, the one general in the army!" called a soldier at the door, says Tacitus, bringing cheers of agreement and applause from those around him.

Primus nodded. With flashing eyes, and raising his voice so he could be heard by the many soldiers outside, Tacitus relates, Primus then said, "I suggested this plan. Unless anyone gets in my way, I will carry it out." He looked at the procrastinators in his audience and wagged a finger. "You, who have never suffered a reversal of fortune, can hold back the legions if you want to. The light infantry cohorts will be all I need. Before long, you'll hear that Italy has been opened up, and that Vitellius's power has been shaken. Then you'll be happy to follow after me and to tread in the footsteps of victory!"

This brought a cheer from the 3rd Gallica men, and a vow from Chief Centurion Varus that Primus could count on him and his comrades to march with him this same day.

Primus accepted Varus's offer and ordered the 3rd Gallica men and the eighteen squadrons of cavalry and the auxiliary cohorts outside to prepare to march at once. Primus then instructed the officer from Moesia who was representing Governor Saturninus—Colonel Messalla, in all likelihood—to hurry back to Moesia and urge Saturninus to march in Primus's footsteps with the remainder of the 3rd Gallica as well as the 7th Claudia and 8th Augusta and join him in Italy. Primus also sent to his deputy, Camp Prefect Minucius Justus, at Carnuntum, with orders to bring the 7th Galbiana down to Putj to link with General Aquila and the 13th Gemina for the march to Italy.

Before he left Poetovio, Primus wrote a letter to Julius Civilis, prefect of a Batavian auxiliary cohort on the Lower Rhine. Primus had served with Civilis earlier in his military career, on the Rhine or in Britain. Civilis had commanded a Batavian cohort attached to the 14th Gemina Legion, and had befriended Vespasian when he commanded the 2nd Augusta Legion. Primus knew that Civilis was a descendant of the last king of Batavia and that he and his family still held notions of one day regaining their royal status. Those notions had caused the governor of Germany prior to Vitellius's appointment to execute Civilis's brother Claudius and to imprison Civilis himself, accused of plotting against Rome. Civilis, now in his fifties, had been freed by Vitellius and given back his cohort command. Now Primus urged Civilis to create a military demonstration on the Rhine to keep Vitellius's remaining troops of the Lower and Upper Rhine armies busy while Primus was invading Italy for Vespasian, to prevent reinforcements from reaching Vitellius from the Rhine. This plan of Primus's would backfire spectacularly, in a way he could not have imagined in those last days of September.

As General Primus, Chief Centurion Varus, and Procurator Fuscus led the advance force of several hundred 3rd Gallica legionaries, auxiliary light infantry, and twenty-one hundred cavalry as it set off from Ptuj for Italy, Procurator Felix headed back to his province of Noricum. He went with orders from the Poetovio conference to take a wing of cavalry, four thousand auxiliaries, and local levies raised in Noricum and set up a defense line along the bank of the Engadin River in Rhaetia. A pro-Vitellius province, Rhaetia took in parts of modern Austria, Switzerland, and southern Germany. Felix's instructions were to prevent reinforcements from reaching Vitellius in Italy via the Rhaetian route. At the same time, General Bassus of the 11th Claudia Legion headed south to his headquarters at Burnum—Kistanje in Croatia—to convince his superior, the reticent governor, to mobilize his forces in Dalmatia to join the campaign against Vitellius in Italy.

Vespasian, in Egypt, was totally unaware of it, but the future of his campaign against Vitellius was now in the hands of a convicted fraudster and men of the 3rd Gallica Legion who were marching into Italy with a laughably small force and the determination to catch the other side unprepared.

In 1944, when the U.S. Army's General George Patton addressed his troops prior to the D-Day landings in France, he had told them what his motto was: "Audacity, audacity, always audacity." It could have been the motto of Julius Caesar. Now it was the policy of General Marcus Antonius Primus.

At Rome, the emperor Vitellius could not ignore the threat from Vespasian any longer. In July he had dismissed the news of the 3rd Gallica Legion's refusal to pledge allegiance to him in Moesia as a temporary hiccup that Governor Saturninus would soon sort out. Even when news arrived that the two other legions in Moesia had joined the 3rd Gallica in swearing for Vespasian, he had done little to counter the revolt. Instead he had banned the utterance of Vespasian's name in public and sent troops throughout Rome to arrest anyone who flouted the ban. Addressing an assembly of his troops, he declared that the men he had dismissed from the old Praetorian Guard were spreading rumors throughout Italy that were not true. There was no chance of the armies of Rome turning against him, their emperor, he said—civil war was impossible. The portly, treble-chinned, fifty-four-year-old aristocrat could not conceive of Vespasian being accepted as emperor. Vitellius was from an esteemed family; his father had been consul three times, his uncle had been a close friend and trusted general of Nero's grandfather the legendary Germanicus Caesar. Vespasian, on the other hand, was the son of a farmer's agent and grandson of a soldier from the ranks. To elitist Vitellius, there could be no comparison between his credentials and those of Vespasian. There was an old Roman saying: "Let not the cobbler go beyond his sandal." By the same token, in Vitellius's reckoning, Vespasian, the lowborn one time mule farmer, should stick to what he knew best: soldiering.

But in August, once news arrived that all the legions of the East had sworn for Vespasian, and that the legions of Moesia and Pannonia were mobilizing against him, Vitellius's advisers prompted him to act. He sent messages to Britain, Spain, and the Rhine, summoning auxiliary troops. But to ensure that it didn't look as if he was panicking, it was done at an almost leisurely pace. With the loyalty of his governor in Africa coming under suspicion, he ordered a new legion that had been enrolled in Africa during the brief reign of Galba, the 1st Macriana Liberatrix Legion (named after the then provincial governor, Clodius Macer), and subsequently disbanded, to be re-formed. And then, as information arrived from every quarter of faltering allegiance among his own provincial governors and generals and told of the activities of pro-Vespasian generals, Vitellius was convinced by those around him to act more directly. Now he commanded his chief generals, Fabius Valens and Aulus Caecina, to lead troops into northern Italy to counter any advance of pro-Vespasian legions from the Balkans. His best and most senior general, Valens, had been seriously ill and was just recovering, so Vitellius gave immediate command of the task force put together at Rome to the extrovert young General Caecina.

At Nero's fabulous Golden House, the new Palatium that flowed down the Palatine Hill into the city, Vitellius received General Caecina. Embracing him, he presented Caecina with the ensign of a lieutenant general and wished him well on his mission. Caecina, in his thirties, had been Galba's quaestor at Cordoba in Farther Spain in A.D. 68 just prior to Galba marching on Rome to take Nero's throne. Caecina had recruited and equipped the 7th Galbiana Legion in Farther Spain on Galba's orders, in the recruiting grounds of the existing 7th Claudia Legion. He had then accompanied Galba to Rome. Once Galba was on the throne, he appointed Caecina to command the 21st Rapax Legion in the Army of the Upper Rhine. Even before he took his seat in the Senate, Caecina had hurried up to the 21st Rapax's base at Vindonissa, today's Windisch in Switzerland, to take up his command. With him went his devoted young wife, Salonina, flouting the convention that a legion commander's wife remained at home.

Caecina's support for Galba had quickly evaporated. Perhaps Caecina had been a little insulted by his appointment—when he arrived at Windisch he found that the 21st Rapax consisted of only six cohorts at that time. In A.D. 61, the emperor Nero had transferred two thousand men newly arrived from Spain to join the legion's latest enlistment, sending them to Britain to make up losses the 9th Hispana Legion, another Spanish unit, had sustained in Boudicca's Revolt. The Rapax's numbers had not been made up since. According to Tacitus, in addition, Galba had received a complaint from the people of Farther Spain that Caecina had embezzled funds while quaestor there, and Galba had initiated an inquiry into Caecina's quaestorship, which, understandably, had alienated him. Caecina had soon supported the movement initiated by the Army of the Lower Rhine to make Vitellius, their provincial governor, emperor in place of Galba.

When Caecina had led an army from the Upper Rhine to Italy via Switzerland in support of Vitellius against Otho, he had taken the 21st Rapax with him. And—scandalously, in the minds of many Roman aristocrats—riding with him had been his wife, Salonina—on horseback like a man, in a purple outfit and with a personal bodyguard of cavalry. Caecina had also lost friends among the Roman elite for his own style of dress. On the Rhine he had taken to wearing Greek-style tunics, which had square necklines rather that the usual round Roman neckline, plus boots and trousers like barbarians and auxiliaries, and multicolored cloaks. This was like a U.S. Army general in twenty-first-century Iraq wearing a Bedouin costume instead of his American uniform, just as Briton Lawrence of Arabia had taken to wearing Arab clothing in the same part of the world during World War I. In the same way that T. E. Lawrence was frowned on by London for such idiosyncratic behavior, General Caecina raised disapproving eyebrows at Rome.

The weather was baking hot as Caecina led Vitellius's army north from Rome in September to counter any pro-Vespasian forces coming down from the northeast. He was still wearing his colorful costumes, but his wife remained home at the capital. Tacitus says that the army that marched with Caecina was lacking in both energy and enthusiasm. He blamed this on the sickness and idleness that had prevailed in their camps around the outskirts of Rome over the past few months. Even the horses of the cavalry were listless, he says. All the glitter that had been on display when Vitellius had triumphantly entered Rome in July had dulled, and all the Rhine legions' wild enthusiasm for the rule of Vitellius had given way to resignation. As soldiers from eight legions and numerous auxiliary units tramped up the Via Flamina, hot winds blew dust in their faces and made them irritable and unruly. There was apprehension, too, about the size of the forces that Vespasian could send against them. Vespasian had legions such as the now famous 3rd Gallica marching for him, and although that unit was under strength, the other five legions from Moesia, Pannonia, and Dalmatia were at full strength.

This was in marked contrast to the legions in Caecina's force. All were substantially under strength. After Vitellius had dismissed the old Praetorian Guard and City Guard, which had been loyal to Otho, he had filled the Praetorian cohorts and City Guard cohorts with men from his legions. On top of that, Vitellius had split his units, leaving cohorts from seven of his eight legions in their garrisons on the Rhine to guard against German incursions from across the Rhine. The only exception was the 21st Rapax Legion, which had been under strength in the first place—all six of its cohorts had fought at the Battle of Bedriacum and then come to Rome. On top of all this, there had been the losses incurred at Bedriacum, and the deaths to illness at Rome. As a result, some of the legions in Caecina's column could barely field fifteen hundred men. Only the 1st Italica Legion resembled an entire legion; it had come intact to serve Vitellius in Italy after being stationed near the city of Lugdunum, today's Lyons, in Gaul, and had suffered only the depredations of Bedriacum casualties, the summer sickness, and the levy for Vitellius's new Praetorian Guard.

That new Praetorian Guard remained at Rome with Vitellius, as did the new cavalry unit created by Vitellius in July to replace the disbanded Praetorian Cavalry, the Singularian Horse. Comprising two wings totaling some one thousand men, the Singularian Horse was commanded by Classicus, a Batavian from today's Holland who had been a former prefect of the Treveran Horse, auxiliary cavalry from Trier on the Moselle River. This meant that the German cavalry units now sent galloping ahead by General Caecina to occupy the key crossroads city of Cremona in the central north were substantially weakened by the loss of men milked from them to create the Singularian wings. The same went for the German light infantry in Caecina's force—Vitellius had dismissed Otho's German Guard, the imperial bodyguard, and replaced them with handpicked men from the auxiliary units who had come down from the Rhine with him.

As young General Caecina made his way north up the Via Flamina at the head of his trundling army, he was very much aware that this was far from the same force that had won the throne for Vitellius in April. And Caecina was having doubts about the wisdom of leading these men against Vespasian's troops. Just before he left Rome, he had been approached by a former consul, Rubrius Gallus, with a message from Flavius Sabinus, the highly respected and longtime City Prefect and elder brother of Vespasian. In his desire to win the favor of as many constituencies as possible, Vitellius had retained Sabinus in his post. Vitellius had even performed funeral rites on the Campus Martius for Nero to make himself seem more imperial and broaden his popular appeal. But keeping Sabinus on as City Prefect may not have been such a clever move. Sabinus secretly informed Caecina that if he deserted Vitellius, then his brother Vespasian would pardon him for his role in Vitellius's seizure of power and give him a senior appointment in Vespasian's administration. Knowing that General Valens had recently gained more influence with Vitellius than Caecina, Sabinus craftily added that such an offer of a pardon and acceptance into Vespasian's inner circle would not be extended to Valens.

Caecina had not accepted Sabinus's offer, but he was mulling over his options as he led the army north when a courier from Rome overtook the column. Caecina took the message, even though it was addressed to the army as a whole, recognizing the seal of General Valens. Unraveling the letter, he read Valens's instruction to the army to halt and wait for him to join it and take over command. Tacitus says that Caecina's jealousy of Valens had by now grown into a fierce hatred of his colleague. Caecina ignored Valens's order, destroyed the letter, and instructed elderly Brigadier General Titus Manlius Valens (no relation to Fabius Valens) to take his 1st Italica Legion and Caecina's own 21st Rapax Legion up the road on the double to join the cavalry holding Cremona. The remainder of the army was to proceed along behind with the baggage at all speed.

Meanwhile, Caecina himself left the column and diverted east with a small escort. He crossed the Apennine Mountains, having told his subordinates that he intended to address the Adriatic Fleet at Ravenna to ensure that they stayed loyal to Vitellius. At Ravenna, Caecina met with the fleet commander, Lucilius Bassus. Admiral Bassus, a former cavalry prefect, had been promoted by Vitellius to command both the Adriatic Fleet and the Tyrhenian Fleet. Caecina knew that despite this meteoric rise, Bassus had wanted the powerful post of commander of the Praetorian Guard, and had been resentful ever since his naval appointment. Tacitus says he couldn't be sure that Bassus and Caecina conspired together, but he was certain that both had the same self-serving motives.

Following his meeting with the fleet commander, Caecina rode on to the town of Padova, which lay directly in the line of march of any pro-Vespasian forces entering Italy from Slovenia and Austria. It was almost as if Caecina was contemplating going over to the forces of Vespasian when they marched into Italy. But then, after a pause of a day or so, General Caecina swung around and rode west to link with his legions as they approached Cremona, passing through his hometown of Vicetia, today's Vicenza, and then Verona, on his way. By early October, Caecina had rejoined his army.

General Primus, accompanied by Procurator Fuscus, Centurion Varus, the senior men of the 3rd Gallica, and their auxiliary cavalry and light infantry troops, had quickly entered Italy from Slovenia and marched into the important northeastern crossroads city of Aquileia, by the Adriatic. The Aquileians and all the people in the surrounding towns and villages joyfully welcomed Vespasian's advance force. But knowing that speed was all-important, rather than enjoy the hospitality, General Primus pushed on with most of his troops, leaving some cavalry and auxiliaries in the area to counter the Ravenna fleet should they attempt to intervene on Vitellius's behalf.

General Primus quickly entered Padua and then the old military colony of Este, where the locals again enthusiastically embraced Vespasian's cause. There, Primus learned that several miles to the south, at Forum Alieni, today's town of Ferrara, famous for its marble, a force of Vitellius's troops was taking up a defensive position to prevent him from advancing down along the east coast. Made up of three cohorts of auxiliaries supported by the five hundred cavalrymen of the Sebonian Horse, these pro-Vitellius troops had occupied the northern bank of the Po di Vilani River, a branch of the Po, the river that traditionally separated Cisalpine Gaul from Italy. As yet, the Vitellianists at Ferrara were unaware that Vespasian's troops were so near, and as a result had built no defenses around their camp. Primus decided to attack the next day.

In the night, the little force advanced quietly down the road through the hills. At dawn, once the men of the 3rd Gallica had dropped to their knees and performed their obligatory rites to the rising sun, Primus moved them up to within sight of the camp. As the unarmed opposition troops were eating their breakfast outside their tents, Primus launched a surprise attack. Primus had ordered that those Vitellianists who wanted to surrender and join him should be given the opportunity. Many did indeed surrender without a fight, prostrating themselves in front of the men of the 3rd Gallica and their auxiliary colleagues as they came charging into their camp. A number of others were cut down by the 3rd Gallica men and their comrades as they dashed to their stacked shields and javelins. But the majority managed to escape by running over the small bridge spanning the river and hacking it down behind them to prevent pursuit.

Celebrating their first victory and taking the prisoners into their ranks, Primus and his colleagues turned northeast. Their objective was the highway that would take them along the foot of the Dolomite Mountains to Vicenza and the major regional center of Verona. Founded as a Roman military colony in 89 B.C., Verona was a renowned little city with considerable wealth and influence. Beyond Verona lay Cremona, and the west coast road to Rome. As Primus headed for Verona, he sent a rider northeast with a message for the legions of Pannonia, Moesia, and Dalmatia, urging them to get a move on and join the fight now that the war had opened with first blood to Vespasian's troops. The road to Rome lay ahead, he said.

Shortly after Primus and his force had marched back into Padova, they were overjoyed to be joined by the two legions from the Pannonia station—the 13th Gemina under Brigadier General Vedius Aquila, and Primus's own 7th Galbiana, led by Camp Prefect Justus. As they rested at Padova for several days—an army approaching fourteen thousand men strong now—Primus and his most senior colleagues met to decide their next target. It was agreed that Verona offered the best prospects if they had to fight Vitellius's legions, which they had heard were marching from Rome. Verona could provide supplies and financial support, and the flat country surrounding it would be ideal for the offensive use of cavalry, in which Primus was very strong.

As the force restocked with provisions and ammunition at Padova, Primus ordered all the towns that had now come over to Vespasian in northeastern Italy to reerect the statues of the short-lived emperor Galba that had previously stood in their forums. Tacitus says this was to give some legitimacy to Primus's actions.

While Primus was preparing to move on, a delegation from the ranks of his own 7th Galbiana Legion came to him, complaining about their camp prefect, Minucius Justus. The camp prefect was far too strict with them, so the men complained with exasperation. Saying that they were on a civil war campaign, not a parade ground, they demanded that Justus be replaced by a more reasonable and realistic camp prefect. Primus knew that in a civil war entire legions had been known to change their allegiances if they felt hard done by. So instead of supporting his deputy or merely reprimanding him, Primus gave in to the troops and removed Justus from his post, sending the camp prefect to Vespasian in Egypt with dispatches. His action was to prove a dangerous precedent, one that would make things difficult for him before long.

In early October, enjoying fine fall weather, Primus led his army out of Padova and along the paving stones of the Via Postuma toward Verona. Their route took them through the town of Vicenza. This was the native territory of many men of the 14th Gemina Legion. Because the famous 14th had fought valiantly for Otho at the Battle of Bedriacum, Vitellius had ordered its best centurions executed, and then sent the unit back to Britain, its longtime station. So, in theory, Vicenza should have been against Vitellius. But as Primus and his colleagues well knew, Vicenza also was the birthplace of General Caecina, Vitellius's commander, and so the town's sympathies lay with Caecina and Vitellius. Because of the connection with Caecina, Primus was particularly pleased to secure Vicenza. The locals didn't resist, but neither did they cheer the army of Vespasian as it passed through the town. Primus didn't pause in Vicenza, just marched through the eastern gate, along the colonnaded streets lined by silent locals, then out the western gate, as he pushed on toward the richer prize of Verona.

Situated on a bend of the Adige River, Verona was a handsome and busy crossroads city. As Primus came riding through the city's century-old gate, the Arco dei Gavi, at the head of his army, the population was out in force, greeting him with cheers and applause. When the quartermaster officers sought quarters in the city for the troops, local officials vied with each other in their zeal to please Primus, putting Verona's wealth and resources at the disposal of the forces of Vespasian. This occupation of Verona would serve both tactical and strategic purposes. Primus's troops received supplies, arms, ammunition, and baggage animals from the city, while at the same time they blocked Vitellius's supply route from Rhaetia via the Julian Alps.

Primus had received several letters from General Mucianus while he was on the march, urging him to wait for the army from Syria to join him before launching an offensive in Italy. Soon after Primus reached Verona, a dispatch all the way from Egypt caught up with him. Coming via Pannonia, it was from Vespasian himself. Addressed to the commanders of the legions loyal to him in Pannonia, Moesia, and Dalmatia, the letter from Vespasian instructed them to halt at Aquileia and wait for General Mucianus to join them with his force from the East, and to then hand over command to him.

It was Vespasian's plan to conduct a bloodless civil war. By occupying Egypt, the breadbasket of Rome, he controlled much of Italy's grain supply. He also controlled all the provinces of the eastern part of the empire, all the way to Italy. If Mucianus could combine his army of some twenty thousand men with Primus and his colleagues at Aquileia, he could move to block all the alpine routes into Italy. In effect, in this way he could grasp Italy by the throat and throttle it, cutting off provisions and pay for Vitellius's troops, who, perhaps after some months, would be forced to surrender.

That was Vespasian's plan. But Primus had other ideas. Right now he had the initiative, and the opportunity to deliver Vespasian a swift military victory as opposed to a drawn-out campaign of deprivation. And Vespasian would have to reward Primus with the highest honors if he delivered a swift victory. Primus, who had left Aquileia behind the previous week, had no desire either to withdraw there or to hand over command to Mucianus. Greedy for glory, Primus had been ignoring Mucianus's letters. Now he lived up to his audacious reputation, hiding his emperor's dispatch from his fellow commanders. He would later claim that Vespasian's order reached him much later, when the civil war had already been decided.

Other dispatches told Primus that Governor Saturninus was marching from Moesia with the rest of the 3rd Gallica Legion and the 7th Claudia and 8th Augusta Legions, and should arrive to reinforce Primus within days. That news was both welcome and unwelcome to Primus. He could use the reinforcements, but once Saturninus arrived, Primus would have to yield command to him. It appears that Primus already had a plan to solve that problem. But now Primus's scouts informed him that opposition troops led by General Caecina were approaching in force from the direction of Cremona.

XXII

PRELUDE TO A DISASTER

To the relief of his subordinates, General Caecina's energy and enthusiasm seemed to have returned once he rejoined them after his Ravenna diversion. Leaving the 1st Italica and 21st Rapax Legions to hold Cremona, Vitellius's field commander led elements from six legions and a number of auxiliary light infantry and cavalry units along the Via Postumia toward the forces of Vespasian at Verona. Several miles west of Verona, Caecina chose a well-sited location for a heavily fortified camp, between the village of Hostilia, today's Villafranca di Verona, and marshland. His opponent, General Primus, sent Vespasianist cavalry that made a lightning attack on the outposts of this camp, but they soon withdrew with just a few casualties on either side once the strength of Caecina's position was appreciated.

Now, at the beginning of the last week of October, Primus was joined at Verona by Lieutenant General Saturninus, governor of Moesia, and governor Flavianus of Pannonia. Saturninus had marched down from the Danube with Colonel Messalla and the 7th Claudia Legion plus numerous auxiliary units. He had been joined by the wavering Flavianus as he passed through Pannonia. Greeted with cool politeness by Primus, Saturninus informed him that General Lupus was not far behind with the 8th Claudia Legion and the remaining men of the 3rd Gallica. In his eagerness to participate in the dethroning of Vitellius, Saturninus had taken every one of his legionaries from the garrisons of Moesia, leaving just auxiliaries on the Danube defense line, under the command of the province's procurator.

Aware of the risk he was taking in removing the legions from Moesia, Saturninus had paid two Sarmatian princes of the Iazyges tribe from north of the Danube to ride with him to Italy. He was hopeful that other Sarmatians would resist the temptation to cross the Danube while the Iazyge princes were with him. The Iazyge princes also had offered to bring mounted warriors with them, but Saturninus, worried that he might bring the wolves into the henhouse if he accepted the offer, had politely declined. He also had arranged for two German allies of Rome, King Sido of the Suevi, and King Italicus of the Cherusci, nephew and successor to Arminius, or Hermann—Rome's great German enemy half a century before—to hurry down from the Rhine. They joined him in Pannonia with their best mounted fighting men. The reinforcements were welcome, and certainly General Primus was happy to add the 7th Claudia to his force, but now he had to surrender command to Saturninus.

From behind the walls of his camp, Caecina sent envoys to Verona with a letter for the opposition commanders. The letter had no capacity to either win over or terrify the other side. In relatively mild language, Caecina admonished the Vespasianists for drawing the sword in a cause that had already been lost—at Bedriacum in April—and boasted of the valor of his troops from the armies of the Rhine. But he said little in praise of Vitellius and nothing abusive about Vespasian. Tacitus was to say it was as if Caecina had adopted a deliberately humble position and was afraid of offending Vespasian. It seemed that Caecina was stalling for time. Saturninus, Primus, and their officers were to assume Caecina was hoping to receive reinforcements from Rome or the Rhine. That was the only construction they could put on his stalling tactic, for at this moment his forces in the camp outside Verona and at Cremona substantially outnumbered the pro-Vespasian army—by some forty-five thousand men to about nineteen thousand. Tacitus was to criticize Caecina for not attacking Vespasian's army now, while he had such a numerical advantage. But Caecina was truly playing for time, and for his future.

Saturninus and his senior officers dictated a reply that praised Vespasian, criticized Vitellius, and expressed confidence in the army they had assembled. They also declared that if Caecina's army were to capitulate now, his tribunes and centurions would be permitted to retain the privileges that Vitellius had granted them. And they repeated the offer made by City Prefect Sabinus when Caecina had still been at Rome, offering him good terms if he himself were to change sides. Nothing came of the correspondence, but Saturninus had both Caecina's letter and the reply read aloud to his troops at assembly, and this increased the confidence of the rank and file in the strength of their position and the weakness of the other side's resolve.

More reinforcements reached Verona shortly after this exchange of letters. General Lupus arrived with his 8th Augusta Legion, and General Aponianus brought in the remaining men of the six cohorts of the 3rd Gallica Legion, plus large numbers of auxiliary cavalry. With smiles, embraces, and friendly jibes, the Syrians gladly reunited with their countrymen of the senior cohorts. Once again, apart from the legion's cohort still sitting in Ascalon way across the Mediterranean, the 3rd Gallica was intact. And with these arrivals, the difference in numbers between the Vespasianist forces and the Vitellianist army facing them narrowed by ten thousand men.

Also joining the pro-Vespasian forces at Verona at about this time were approximately four thousand men who had previously served in the Praetorian Guard. Because these men had marched for Otho, Vitellius had initially dispersed them throughout Italy. At least one cohort was sent to Turin, in northwestern Italy. These Praetorians had been just two years short of their sixteen-year discharge when in midsummer Vitellius had disarmed, disbanded, and dismissed all twenty thousand members of the Praetorian Guard and City Guard. Without paying them the retirement bonuses they were owed or giving them land grants, as was the usual practice, he replaced them with men from his legions. Many of the discharged men, knowing that the procurator of the province of Gallia Narbonensis in southern France, Valerius Paulinus, had once been a Praetorian Guard tribune, went to him. Paulinus and the people of Forum Julii, today's Fréjus, had armed these men, who now occupied the city for Vespasian. Other ex-Praetorians had flooded to northeastern Italy to join General Primus's advance. All in all, with the addition of these Praetorians, Vespasian's army at Verona now totaled forty-four thousand men. Half were legionaries, and four thousand were cavalry. In terms of numbers, they now almost equaled those of Vitellius's units in northern Italy.

General Primus, unhappy that stodgy Saturninus now had command of their combined forces, was quick to add General Aponianus of the 3rd Gallica and Colonel Messalla of the 7th Claudia to his circle of like minds, along with Procurator Festus and Chief Centurion Varus. None of them liked Saturninus or the other old lieutenant general, Flavianus. All would have been glad if both were out of the way, to enable Primus to continue unhindered with the good work he had begun with this Italian campaign.

An opportunity to be rid of Flavianus soon presented itself. Saturninus and Flavianus, nervous of advancing against superior numbers, chose instead to hunker down and improve the defenses of Verona. The city was partly encircled by the Adige River, but on the western side it was flanked by a flat plain. Saturninus and Flavianus decided to build a defensive trench line facing the plain, from the river, to strengthen their position. All five of their legions began work at dawn one October morning, and toiled right through the day. At twilight, when, with aching muscles and weary limbs, the soldiers were still completing trenches, walls, and a palisade, a force of cavalry came cantering up from the southwest, the direction of the enemy camp. The 7th Galbiana Legion was laboring on the southwestern side of the defenses, and as the cavalrymen bore down on them, many men of the legion who had been working unarmed on the construction dropped their tools and fled for the city walls.

Men of the 7th Galbiana who flooded back into the city spotted General Flavianus on their camp's parade square and angrily surrounded him. These men hadn't forgotten that Flavianus was related to Vitellius, and had never entirely trusted him. To the old ex-consul's astonishment, they now accused him of having betrayed the emperor Otho to support Vitellius, of embezzlement, and of deliberately sending them out to work unarmed outside the city so enemy cavalry could cut them down in the open. As the troops called for his death, Flavianus burst into tears and prostrated himself on the ground in front of them, tearing his clothes like a supplicant to the emperor, and begged for his life. His obvious fear seemed to many soldiers in the crowd to be an indication of his guilt, and the cries for his execution swelled. As the crowd of soldiers around the governor of Pannonia grew larger, General Saturninus was summoned.

In the fading light, Saturninus arrived. His twelve lictors, his official attendants as an ex-consul, pushed a way for him through the mob so he could reach the tribunal. But when he attempted to address the men, assuring them of his colleague's innocence and telling them that the cavalrymen they had seen outside the walls were their own, returning from a reconnaissance sortie, he was shouted down. With the situation verging on mutiny, the general's lictors hustled unpopular Saturninus away. Other officers attempted to reassure the men and save Flavianus. But the troops would listen to none of them.

Finally, General Primus, the 7th Galbiana's own commander, appeared in their midst. Seeing that some men had hold of Flavianus, and several had even drawn their swords to execute him, Primus dragged the victim to his feet and hauled him onto the tribunal with him. At the same time, Primus's three lictors and several of his freedmen formed a thin wall around the tribunal and folded their arms, facing the mob. Apart from the lictors' wooden staffs of office, they were unarmed. As the crowd closed in, Primus ordered that Flavianus be placed in irons. But this wasn't going to placate the ringleaders. They pushed aside the men who were attempting to guard the tribunal, and reached for Flavianus. Now Primus drew his sword, and stepped between Flavianus and the mob.

"I will die by your hands, or my own, before I let you take him!" Tacitus says Primus growled down at them, with his sword leveled and a characteristically fierce look in his eyes. Then, peering into the crowd, he spotted various men from his unit who were known to him, and summoned them by name to come forward and stand with him. Other men, whom he didn't know but who were wearing their military decorations, he pointed to, and also called on. "You, wearer of the golden torque of valor, step forward, be worthy of your decoration, and help your general."

Feeling guilty, these men pushed through the mob and turned to stand in front of the tribunal with the general's personal staff. Then Primus turned to the standards of the 7th Galbiana standing at the legion's altar, and prayed loudly to Jupiter, Mars, and Minerva, the gods of war, that they would inspire the armies of Vitellius with madness and mayhem, not his own men. This had the desired effect. Sanity began to return to the ranks, to be replaced by shame. As the last light of day subsided and servants lit the lamps of the camp, the mob fell silent. Guiltily, men slipped away to their tents.

To solve the Flavianus problem and to preserve the governor's life, Lieutenant General Saturninus decided to send him to Vespasian in Egypt. Their emperor could decide what responsibilities the governor of Pannonia should be entrusted with. Wasting no time, Saturninus sent him on his way with a cavalry escort that same night. On the road several hours later, Flavianus's party was met by a courier coming the other way. As it happened, the courier was carrying a letter from Vespasian for Flavianus. When Flavianus read it, he found that Vespasian had relieved him of his post—probably because he suspected Flavianus due to his family ties to Vitellius. With relief, Flavianus discontinued the trip to Egypt and went into hiding.

The following day, at noon, just as the troops at Verona were breaking for lunch, another demonstration broke out in their ranks. This time it was directed against the army's commander, General Saturninus. Copies of several letters had been circulating around the camp that morning, supposedly written in friendship by Saturninus to Vitellius at Rome. The letters were probably forgeries, and their sudden appearance was very convenient for General Primus. But Saturninus was so unpopular with the rank and file that the letters were immediately believed by many who read them. In a rage, hundreds of soldiers hurried to the Verona gardens where the commander in chief was relaxing. As the men surged into the gardens calling for Saturninus's death, General Primus again intervened, this time accompanied by two other well-liked officers, his cronies General Aponianus of the 3rd Gallica and Colonel Messalla of the 7th Claudia. While the three officers kept the men at bay, the old general was hustled into a hiding place in the garden—the furnace of a bathhouse currently out of commission.

After being sweet-talked by Primus, and unable to find the object of their anger, the troops eventually gave up their quest and went back to their duties. Saturninus, emerging blackened from head to toe from his hiding place, was scared witless. Gladly he gave up command, even gave up his twelve lictors so he would be inconspicuous, and quickly galloped back east to take refuge at Padova. Now that both lieutenant generals had departed the scene, the other senior officers—Brigadier Generals Aponianus of the 3rd Gallica, Lupus of the 8th Augusta, and Aquila of the 13th Gemina, Colonel Messalla of the 7th Claudia, and Procurator Fuscus—all agreed that General Primus should resume command of the army.

The rank and file were also, in the words of Tacitus, strongly biased in Primus's favor. Without hesitation, Primus once more took charge. Tacitus was to write that there would be those who believed that Primus had engineered the demonstrations against Flavianus and Saturninus. In the first instance, this may have been a case of mud sticking to the already stained reputation of Primus. But while the outburst against Flavianus may have been spontaneous, someone must have planted the Saturninus letters.

Now Primus had the command of five legions and a free hand to conduct the war against Vitellius as he saw fit, for now. He would have preferred to have also had the 11th Claudia Legion from Dalmatia in his force. He and his colleagues would have been asking where in the name of the gods the 11th had gotten to—it had much less ground to travel from Kistanje in Dalmatia than the three legions that had come all the way down from Moesia. The 11th should have reached the army days ahead of those units. Primus could wait for the 11th to arrive, to narrow the numbers gap between his army and Caecina's by another five thousand men. But, as Romans were wont to say, there is danger in delay. Primus knew there was the ever-present danger of reinforcements arriving for Caecina from Rome or the Rhine.

At the same time, as Cassius Dio was to point out, Primus held supreme command of a Roman army even though he hadn't been chosen by his emperor or the Senate of Rome. That power would last for only a limited time—General Mucianus and his army of more than twenty thousand men from the East were thought to be only days away. When Mucianus did arrive, he would take command of Primus's army and stop further offensive operations, to follow Vespasian's plan of forcing the other side into submission. Primus knew that if he was to bring on a decisive battle, it had to be now or never.

In his defense, it has to be said that Primus was motivated by more than the desire for personal glory and advancement. His troops were greedy for victory and for spoils. The talk in the ranks was all of making the opponents of Vespasian pay. Not only pay with their blood, but with their property. Having seen, over the past two days, how easily his rank and file could be motivated to riotous behavior and mutiny, Primus knew that it would not take much for them to desert Vespasian's cause for Vitellius if they thought it was worth their while. Primus knew that to keep his army loyal he had to give them a military victory, and spoils, soon. He ordered the army to prepare to march.

Cheers rang out through Verona as the news spread quickly—Primus's legions weren't going to sit on their backsides in the city; they were taking the war to Vitellius. In the camp of the 3rd Gallica Legion, Chief Centurion Varus and Centurions Gallus and Julius passed on the word to their men to prepare for action.

At the Hostilia camp of Vitellius's army, General Caecina received news; almost certainly it was news he had been waiting for. At Ravenna on the Adriatic coast of northeastern Italy, the forty thousand sailors, rowers, and marines of Rome's Adriatic Fleet had just changed sides, swearing allegiance to Vespasian. The fleet's commander, Admiral Bassus, had also come out in favor of Vespasian once his men had made their declaration. Many of those serving with the fleet were from Pannonia and Dalmatia, and they liked Fuscus, procurator of Pannonia. Knowing he was with General Primus's army, and having a good report of him, the men at Ravenna had voted for Fuscus to take over the fleet's command. An influential freedman in the employ of Vespasian named Hormus was then on the east coast. He now traveled to Verona to join the army of Vespasian, and it seems that he was the one who conveyed the offer of the fleet command to Fuscus.

Caecina now promptly called a secret meeting at his Hostilia praetorium. While the troops were busy with training, improving defenses, and guard duty, the chief centurions and leading men from Caecina's legions were discreetly summoned to meet with their general. And when they had assembled in Caecina's tent, he informed them that the Adriatic Fleet had changed sides, that they themselves were low on supplies, that Gaul and Spain had turned against Vitellius, and that there was no hope of receiving reinforcements or provisions from Rome. Then, after Caecina had extolled the worthiness of Vespasian, he led the men in the praetorium in swearing allegiance to Vespasian. Caecina then ordered them to pull down the statues of Vitellius in the camp and to remove the oval *imagos* of the emperor from their cohort standards. At the same time, Caecina sent envoys galloping to Verona to inform Primus that Vitellius's army was coming over to Vespasian.

When Caecina's troops returned from their duties at end of the day and saw the statues of Vitellius lying on the ground and the name of Vespasian painted on their cloth detachment banners in place of Vitellius's name, they were at first stunned. There was a gloomy silence in the camp for a time, but soon there were mutterings of dissent. Cassius Dio says that during the night there was an eclipse of the moon, with the moon going a bloody color, which Caecina's troops took as a bad omen. Deciding that they were not meant to desert Vitellius, the bolder men in the ranks of the 5th Alaudae Legion, men who were still loyal to Vitellius after serving under him in his Army of the Lower Rhine at Vetera, today's Xanten in Germany, began to speak out. They complained that Caecina was surrendering the mighty legions of the Rhine without a battle. They derided the legions of the other side as units they had defeated on these very plains, at Bedriacum, earlier in the year. The best of Otho's legions, the 14th Gemina and the 1st Adiutrix, weren't even here this time, they said, while those that were present were of no account. With growing anger, soldiers declared that Caecina and Bassus had received palaces, gardens, and gold from Vitellius for their service to him, and now in return they had robbed him of his fleet and were trying to rob him of his legions.

As the disquiet among the men of the 5th Alaudae spread to the other units, men of the Alaudae consulted their commander, Brigadier General Fabius Fabullus, on what to do. As a result, in the early hours of the morning, scores of officers and rank and file burst into the pavilion of General Caecina and hauled him from his bed, accusing him of being a traitor. Josephus says that several legionaries had their swords drawn and were prepared to kill Caecina on the spot, and that they relented only when the tribunes begged them to spare his life so he could be sent to Vitellius. Their emperor, the tribunes said, should be the one to decide the fate of such a highly placed traitor. The troops relented, and Caecina was clapped in irons. Come the dawn, when the troops of Caecina's army assembled, the statues of Vitellius had been set up again and Vespasian's name had been removed from their standards. At the assembly, the troops reaffirmed their allegiance to Vitellius and elected General Fabullus of the 5th Alaudae and Camp Prefect Cassius Longus as their new joint commanders.

Over the next twenty-four hours there was much debate in the Vitellianist camp on what to do, with all ranks contributing their views. Some voices were for immediately advancing on Verona. Others were for waiting for expected reinforcements from Rome and elsewhere. Still others wanted to abandon the camp and withdraw toward Cremona, to link with their forces there before taking on the other side. Toward the end of the second day of often heated debate it was decided to withdraw to Cremona. Orders were given for the army to prepare to march the next day. At the same time, a detachment was sent to break down a bridge on the road north of the camp's location, to impede pursuit by Primus's army.

Soon after, the bridge party was busy hacking at the woodwork when a column of 120 marines came marching up to them. Marines were considered the lowest class of Rome's soldiers. Recruited from the ranks of freedmen, marines served in the Roman military for twenty-six years, six years longer than legionaries and a year longer than auxiliaries. This contingent was made up of the marine complements of three Liburnians, or frigates, of the Adriatic Fleet. It seems they had just been recruited in northeastern Italy and were on their way to join their ships at Ravenna; Tacitus says they were entirely ignorant of the fact that the fleet had just gone over to Vespasian. The legionaries working on the bridge, enraged at the sight of men from the fleet who had turned against their emperor, fell on the unsuspecting marines, who considered themselves on the same side as the legionaries. Every one of the marines was slaughtered.

Two days earlier, General Primus had been digesting the news that Caecina was bringing his army over to Vespasian's side when an informant told him that Caecina had been arrested and the army had returned its allegiance to Vitellius. That information could only have come from a deserter. In addition to telling of Caecina's arrest, this source from inside the Vitellianist camp told Primus that General Fabius Valens, Vitellius's favorite commander, had recovered from his illness and had recently left the capital. Primus assumed that Valens was hastening north to take charge of Vitellius's forces. The informant also told Primus that Vitellius's army was expecting a vast number of Germans to join them by way of Rhaetia, and that at Rome Vitellius had lost his lethargy and summoned large numbers of legionary and auxiliary reinforcements from Britain, Gaul, and Spain.

Primus was not to know that those Germans would not materialize. Nor was he yet aware that the governor in Britain was unable to control his unruly troops, the commanders in the Spanish provinces were rethinking their support for Vitellius, and many tribes in Gaul were beginning to think about taking advantage of Rome's civil war to throw off Roman rule. As far as Primus was concerned, it was vital to swiftly bring Vitellius's army to battle while they were rent by internal strife and before they were joined by either Valens, considered a formidable general by Primus, or reinforcements. Now Primus conceived what had the potential to be a brilliant outflanking maneuver, one that could give him a swift victory and also satisfy the desire of his men for plunder.

Tacitus, who up to this point provided much detail about the conflict in northern Italy, does not tell us precisely what took place next. But from subsequent events it is possible to work out that it went as follows. Potentially there were three different routes from Verona to Cremona. Vitellius's army sat outside Hostilia astride the middle road, a diagonal route to Cremona from Verona. The most northerly route, which ran west almost to Brescia and then due south, was the longest. The third route, the southern route, was roughly ten miles longer than the middle route. This was the Via Postumia, which ran south to Mantova, then lanced due west to Cremona. Primus decided to take the southern route. While Vitellius's army sat in its camp with its men arguing over their best course of action, Primus would bypass them. Swinging south and then west, he would advance on Cremona, which he knew was defended by only the 1st Italica and 21st Rapax Legions and some cavalry. If he could draw those units into battle, his much larger force could destroy the two Vitellianist legions and then take the undefended city of Cremona, which he would allow his men to pillage. Then he could turn and either force Caecina's army to surrender for lack of supplies or crush it in a second battle.

Primus's army marched out of Verona that same day, as planned, but under orders to make as much speed as possible. Instead of heading down the road to Hostilia to confront the enemy, they now marched south, for Mantova. Camping overnight at Mantova, and after two days on the march, the army reached the village of Bedriacum, site of the surrender of Otho's army in April. In May, when Vitellius had visited the Bedriacum battlefield, Otho's dead still lay there. By the time that Primus's army reached Bedriacum, the locals had burned the rotting corpses of men and animals in piles, and buried the remains in mass graves. Tacitus says that with Cremona just a day's march to the west, as soon as they arrived at Bedriacum Primus's legions set about building a fortified camp.

The choice of Bedriacum by Primus for his camp was not so much symbolic as strategic. The village was not far from a junction of the middle route to Cremona and the southern route. Camped here, his troops were in a position to both advance on Cremona and counter the troops from Hostilia when and if they came marching down the middle route. But for now, as Primus's men dug, the main army of Vitellius was still in camp outside Hostilia, ignorant of the fact that their opponents had left Verona and skirted behind them.

At dawn assembly the next day, Primus ordered his legions to further fortify their camp and sent his auxiliaries forward to forage in the countryside east of Cremona for food and fodder. Cremona was strongly for Vitellius. Those soldiers in Primus's army who had surrendered after the Battle of Bedriacum would never forget that the people of Cremona had later covered the road to their city with ivy and rose petals to give Vitellius a red-carpet welcome when he arrived at their city. This countryside around Cremona, covered with fertile farms and vineyards, was controlled by Cremona. It was, in the view of Primus's troops, enemy territory. So, as Tacitus was to observe, Primus's order to forage was in reality a license to pillage, and the auxiliaries set off on their task with enthusiasm.

By the middle of the morning, some time after the auxiliaries had moved off, Primus himself left Bedriacum, to lead a cavalry reconnaissance in force along the road to Cremona and determine the disposition of enemy units. At this point he had no idea whether Caecina's army was still at Hostilia, as he hoped. He took the majority of his cavalry with him—four thousand troopers. Some of these were legion cavalry, but most were auxiliaries. These were men from Gaul, Spain, Illyricum, Holland, and Germany, wearing breeches and chain mail armor, each equipped with a long cavalry sword, a lance, throwing darts in a quiver, and a flat, oval shield. As Primus set off with the cavalry, he was accompanied by his friend Colonel Messalla of the 7th Claudia and Chief Centurion Varus of the 3rd Gallica.

With scouts out, Primus and his massive cavalry formation rode along the highway for eight miles, passing the intersection with the middle route to Verona. No travelers were encountered on the road—tidings of the approach of an army had quickly traveled ahead of the Vespasianist column. Tacitus says that just before eleven o'clock, an excited scout came galloping along the road from the west. Reining in his lathered horse, he informed General Primus that an enemy force was approaching from Cremona. Halting the column, Primus quizzed the scout for details. The trooper told of seeing a small mounted advance force and of hearing the noise of a much larger infantry force coming down the road not far behind. Pulses in Primus's force began to beat faster.

XXIII

THE BLOODBATH
OF CREMONA

G ray-haired Titus Manlius Valens was nervous as he rode in the vanguard of the column heading east. His richly embroidered scarlet cloak, the expensive helmet, the gold-inlaid breastplate, and the red ensign tied in a bow around his chest—these all signified that Valens was a brigadier general, the commander of a legion. Around him, young subordinate officers riding in full armor and white cloaks, men including Colonel Julius Calenus and Colonel Alpinius Montanus, were silent, grim-faced. The only sounds were those of horses' hooves on the paving stones and the rhythmical tramp-tramp-tramp of the marching feet of ten thousand men of the 1st Italica and 21st Rapax Legions and several thousand auxiliaries as they marched along the Via Postumia.

Civilians hurrying into Cremona that morning had brought the unbelievable story that Vespasian's entire army was just a day's march east. Somehow Vespasian's legions had bypassed General Caecina's army outside Verona, and now elderly General Valens—who was no relation to Fabius Valens, Vitellius's senior general—had the task of saving the day for his emperor.

At sixty-three years of age, the last thing Titus Valens had expected was the responsibility of salvaging Vitellius's cause in a civil war he wanted no part of. For a brigadier general, Valens was exceptionally old. Mostly, Roman brigadier generals were in their thirties. In fact, Valens was by far the oldest legion commander involved in the civil war on either side. He had the late emperor Galba to thank for his appointment to the command of the 1st Italica Legion the previous year. It had seemed a cushy job at the time, taking him to the relative peace of central Gaul. The 1st Italica had been raised by Nero in A.D. 66 to take part in his Caspian Gates operation. The first legion raised south of the Po River in Italy in more than a century, the Italica had been filled with healthy young men who were all at least six Roman feet tall—about five-foot-ten in our feet and inches. Calling the legion "the Phalanx of Alexander the Great," Nero had equipped the Italicans with spears twenty-one feet long and formed them into a Greek-style phalanx formation. As Alexander the Great's phalanxes had defeated every cavalry force sent against them, conceivably Nero's intention had been to use the 1st Italica to foil the Parthian cavalry his army would have encountered during the Caspian Gates operation.

For two years after the Jewish Revolt flared and the aborting of the Caspian operation, the 1st Italica had remained in Cisalpine Gaul, where it had trained. In March of A.D. 68, when Julius Vindex, governor of the province of Gallia Lugdunensis, revolted, the 1st Italica had been ordered to stand by to march for Gaul to combat Vindex's uprising. The Army of the Upper Rhine had swiftly quashed the Vindex Rebellion in May, after which its legions marched back to the Rhine. But the situation in Gallia Lugdunensis was still volatile. The people of the city of Vienne, in adjoining Gallia Narbonensis, were at the throats of their longtime rivals the people of Lugdunum, modern-day Lyons. Today Lyons is the third-largest city in France. Then it was the capital of the province of Gallia Lugdunensis. The people of Vienne and the Lyonese had supported different sides during the Vindex Revolt, and even after Vindex was executed, armed gangs from Vienne had continued to raid Lyons.

Founded in 43 B.C. as a colony of legion veterans, Lyons was not just any city. Seneca described it at this time as the showpiece of Gaul. The region had a high population, and Lyons had quickly grown into a handsome and prosperous city. Importantly, it housed the Imperial Mint, established by Augustus. The mint had a permanent guard of the fifteen hundred men of the 18th Cohort of Rome's City Guard, but the new governor of Gallia Lugdunensis, Junius Blaesus, had felt this force insufficient for the task in the troubled climate he found on his arrival. Besides, it seems that at least part of the 18th Cohort had served as Vindex's bodyguard. When Blaesus sent urgently to Rome for reinforcements, the Palatium ordered the 1st Italica Legion and the cavalrymen of the Taurine Horse regiment from Turin across the Alps to France.

By the time the 1st Italica had arrived in Lyons in June, Nero was no longer emperor. Galba had shortly after passed through the region on his march from Spain to Rome to take the imperial throne. Avoiding the usual candidates for high office, Galba had appointed many men with dubious records and questionable qualifications to senior positions. He also recalled a number from exile, including Antonius Primus, and gave them important posts, thinking that in their gratitude they would be especially loyal to him. In this atmosphere, Galba had left his friend and client Titus Valens in Lyons to take command of the 1st Italica Legion. Despite his age, Valens was fit—he had been particularly strong and healthy as a child. And he'd had experience leading a legion, although not the most inspiring experience—seventeen years earlier, as commander of the 20th Valeria Victrix Legion in Britain, he'd lost a number of officers and men in Wales in fighting with the Silure tribe, and as a result he'd lost his appointment. Valens had been living in obscurity and relative poverty ever since. It would have seemed to both Valens and Galba that there was no likelihood that Valens and his tall Italica spearmen would see any significant action at Lyons.

Lyons and Vienne are separated by the Rhône River, and while the Taurine Horse took up quarters at Lyons, the 1st Italica had camped between the two cities, on the Lyons side of the Rhône, to literally keep the people of the two cities apart. Before long, the Lyonese were urging the legionaries to raid Vienne, to repay the Viennese for their earlier raids. Supposedly to show their support for Galba, the people of Vienne then quickly raised a legion in their province, calling it the 1st Adiutrix—*adiutrix* means supporter, or assistant. Officially the new legion was intended to support the nearby 1st Italica. In reality, knowing that the people of Lyons were pushing it to attack Vienne, the Viennese created the legion to protect them from the 1st Italica. But as soon as it had been enrolled, Galba had taken the 1st Adiutrix away to Italy, to train at Ravenna.

The 1st Italica was still outside Lyons when Galba was assassinated the following January 15. Two weeks before, the 1st Italica and Governor Blaesus had received letters from the legions on the Rhine, urging them to swear allegiance to Aulus Vitellius, who had been appointed to command the Army of the Lower Rhine by Galba only the previous year. Encouraged by Governor Blaesus, the men of both the 1st Italica and the Taurine Horse had come out for Vitellius, and General Valens had gone along with them. As Vitellius readied two Rhine armies to march on Rome and overthrow Otho, he had sent orders to General Valens to march the 1st Italica to the passes of the Cottian Alps, between France and Italy. Their job had been to secure the passes for the force of thirty thousand men coming down from the Rhine under General Caecina.

As the 1st Italica was preparing to depart on that mission, the people of Lyons had come to them to make one last attempt to convince them to sack Vienne. The city was on their route, they said, telling the Italicans of all the valuable loot the Viennese possessed. By the time they reached Vienne, the men of the legion had warmed to the idea of pillaging the city, and began clamoring to be allowed to storm it. Old General Valens had to think fast if he was to save Vienne. The local dignitaries came out to Valens and begged him not to allow his men to run riot in Vienne, presenting him with a large bribe, which he reluctantly accepted. By distributing 300 sesterces to every man in the legion—the equivalent of four months' pay—he had been able to talk them out of looting Vienne.

As the legionaries had swung east and headed for the mountains with jangling purses, word of what had occurred at Vienne preceded them. The people of towns the 1st Italica had to pass by met them on the road and pressed more bribes on General Valens, which he again shared with his men. According to Tacitus, the impoverished Valens became rich almost overnight as a result of his tour of duty with the 1st Italica and that march to the mountains. By the time the legion reached the foot of the Alps at the town of Lucus Augusti, today's Luc-en-Diois, on the Drôme River, Valens had become accustomed to receiving bribe money. So when the townspeople there resisted the idea of parting with their money, he threatened to have his legionaries burn the town to the ground. The townspeople quickly changed their minds and paid up.

Valens had fought one battle for his new emperor—the men of the Italica had performed creditably in Vitellius's army at the Battle of Bedriacum. But that had been under the overall command of the dashing general Caecina. Valens would have been the first to admit he was no Caecina, who was now lodged in irons in the Cremona city prison after being sent back from Hostilia under heavy guard two days ago. Now old Valens had the task of stopping the entire Vespasianist advance into Italy—he was the senior Vitellianist officer at Cremona. With the 21st Rapax, Caecina's own legion, now commanded by its tribune, Colonel Calenus, Valens was the only general in the city. A year ago, all he had wanted had been a brigadier general's salary of a few hundred thousand sesterces a year, and a quiet posting. At his age, he would not have hankered for promotion to praetor, or even the top of the totem pole post of consul. A consulship would be nice, with its huge salary, the twelve lictors for life, the right to be first to speak in Senate debates, the place of honor at the theater, at banquets, in religious processions. And a consulship that gave his name to the year—each Roman year was identified by the names of the two first-appointed consuls for that year—that was the highest honor for a Roman. But that all added up to responsibility. And after years of being a nobody, with a career going nowhere, Valens lacked both the experience and the ambition for responsibility. Now it seemed that responsibility for the outcome of the entire civil war could rest on his shoulders, could depend on his decisions.

That morning, with the news that the army of Vespasian was approaching Cremona along the Via Postumia, Valens had sent dispatch riders galloping north to Caecina's former army at Hostilia less than forty miles away, urging its commanders there to bring their legions down to Cremona on the double. Valens could have remained inside the city and let the other side lay siege to it, but Cremona was crowded with tens of thousands of visitors. This was the week of the Cremona Fair, and craftsmen, merchants, and cashed-up buyers had come from throughout Italy and Gaul. With the news that a hostile army was approaching, none of the visitors was prepared to leave the safety of the city. Crowded with as many as a hundred thousand residents and visitors, Cremona would be difficult to defend from within. It would be even more difficult to feed so many people plus Valens's thirteen thousand troops for long. So the city fathers had convinced Valens to save the city by confronting the army of Vespasian in the field. In the meantime, they had reminded him, the longer he could stall the enemy, the more time he gave the legions from Hostilia to reach him.

Now, when Valens's column had traveled only a short distance from Cremona, a messenger came galloping hell for leather from the direction of his advance guard down the road to the east, bringing news that the enemy was near. Valens gave several orders. In response, the men of the Taurine Horse and his other cavalrymen went charging down the road to the east to support the advance guard. And the trumpets of the cohorts of the 1st Italica and 21st Rapax sounded "Battle Order." The standards of the legions and auxiliary cohorts inclined this way and that. The 1st Italica formed battle lines across the road, with the Italians' giant spears pointing skyward like a forest of dead trees. Colonel Calenus, a native of central France, led his Spanish legionaries of the conventionally armed 21st Rapax into the fields flanking the highway. There they formed their battle lines on one side of the Italica. The auxiliary units, including a Treveran light infantry cohort from today's Luxembourg, under Colonel Montanus, took up positions on the other side of the Italian legion.

Calmly, Valens dismounted, passed his horse to a groom who led it away to the rear, and accepted a shield from one of his attendants. Valens ordered "Advance at the March" sounded. Then, in silence, with the afternoon sun casting long shadows in front of them, Valens and his troops moved forward, each rank in step, keeping their positions, at the march, toward the unseen enemy.

In one of the senior cohorts of the 21st Rapax Legion beside the tall Italicans marched Legionary Julius Mansuetus, a swarthy Spaniard serving his second enlistment in the legion. After twenty-nine years with the famous Rapax, "the rapacious one," the legionary was at least forty-six years of age. He had no idea that in the enemy army marching toward him, serving in the 7th Galbiana Legion, was a young Spanish conscript just a year into his military service—his own son.

With the sun in his eyes, General Primus sat astride his horse on the road to Cremona. His four thousand cavalrymen massed behind him, waiting for the enemy. Knowing that taking cavalry against legions without infantry support invited disaster, he had sent Colonel Messalla and a number of junior officers hurrying back the way they had come. Messalla had orders to round up the auxiliaries who were busy looting farms in the vicinity, and to bring them up on the double to support the cavalry. Others rode back to Bedriacum to call the legions to arms.

The waiting was too much for Chief Centurion Arrius Varus of the 3rd Gallica Legion. Varus suddenly ordered the men behind him to follow at the charge. Kicking his horse into action, Varus went galloping toward Cremona with his standard bearers and trumpeter galloping close behind. The trumpeter was sounding "Charge." Tacitus doesn't identify the unit that followed Centurion Varus. He simply calls them the bravest among Primus's troopers. In all probability it was the 3rd Gallica's own cavalry squadron that went charging off with Varus. As, whooping with excitement, some 120 troopers galloped after Varus, General Primus, furious, had "Recall" sounded by his own trumpeter. But it was too late. Even if they could hear the call above the thunder of pounding hooves, Varus's troopers ignored it.

Cursing, Primus ordered his remaining troopers to spread out in their squadrons on either side of the road, leaving a space in the middle for Varus's men to pass through at speed. He had a feeling that Varus would be back soon, with company.

Centurion Varus's galloping squadron charged into General Valens's mounted advance force on the Via Postumia. Briefly, the Vitellianists stood their ground and fought at close quarters. Once several of their men toppled to the road with mortal wounds, the remainder fell back, with some of Varus's men giving chase. But just as Varus and his companions were congratulating themselves in their victory and watching as the enemy dead were stripped, the cavalry reinforcements sent by Valens came up at full speed, pursuing those of Varus's men who had been foolish enough to continue the chase toward Cremona. Caught flat-footed and outnumbered something like five to one, Varus's troopers turned and fled back toward General Primus and the main cavalry force, with the opposition troopers giving chase and cutting down stragglers who were too slow. Now, says Tacitus, those of Varus's men who had been the most eager in the chase found themselves last in the desperate flight.

Despite General Primus's preparations, Varus and his men rode straight into their waiting comrades. The Vitellianist cavalry then came up at a rush and attacked the entire waiting force, and Primus's neat squadrons were turned into a disorganized rabble, even though they outnumbered the Vitellianists. Scores of running fights broke out as Vitellius's troopers pushed the more numerous opposition force back down the road toward Bedriacum. With each man similarly outfitted, often the only way to tell friend from foe was by the unit motif on each oval cavalry shield. In Primus's ranks, confusion and panic set in. Large numbers of Primus's cav- alrymen were wounded. Pulling out of the fight, many rode off, down the road and across country, toward Bedriacum and the safety of their camp. As they rode, they collided with the auxiliaries who were coming across the fields to their support.

Primus was beside himself with rage. As a Roman saying went, anger is a brief madness. And, like a madman, Primus was in the thick of the fighting, pushing his horse into melees wherever the struggle was hardest to relieve his beleaguered men, without a thought for his own safety. With swirling sword he cut down enemy troopers left and right, yelling encour- agement and orders to all who would obey. When one of his retreating mounted standard-bearers refused his direct order to come back, Primus grabbed a lance from one of his own startled men and threw it at the retreating horseman. The lance transfixed the trooper. Galloping up, Primus leaned over and seized the dead rider's standard. Planting its sharp bottom end in the ground, Primus turned it toward the enemy. Calling to his men, he declared that this was the direction in which brave men should be heading.

Shamed by his words, one hundred troopers rallied to Primus on the highway. They formed up just west of a small wooden bridge that had been broken down by some of their fleeing colleagues to prevent further pursuit. The Vespasianist cavalry had by this stage been driven back a mile beyond the intersection with the Verona road, to where the Via Pos- tumia crossed a winding creek. The steep banks of the meandering waterway were like a wall. With that at their back, Primus and his hundred stood motionless in tight formation, horses flank to flank. Even if they had wanted to, riders could not have pulled out of line. With shields and lances raised, the riders waited to receive the enemy cavalry, which, in the flush of victory, came charging at them.

The opposition cavalry bounced off the immovable line. At Primus's urging, the line pushed forward. Driven back, it was the other side's turn to panic. The mayhem was compounded when Colonel Messalla reached the scene leading large numbers of auxiliaries from units that had been stationed with his 7th Claudia Legion in Moesia. From north and south of the highway, auxiliaries came on the run, and with loud battle cries they drove into the flanks of the tightly packed enemy cavalry formations. At close quarters, the light infantry jabbed at horses and riders with their spears. As many Vitellianist troopers were felled, large numbers of their comrades turned and fled. Primus and his men gave chase. Primus's hundred cheered triumphantly. And across the fields, more of Primus's cavalry came cantering back to rejoin the fight now that they saw the tables turning.

Vitellianist cavalry would stop and fight after several miles, then turn and flee again. In this stop-start way, General Valens's cavalry was driven back down the highway toward Cremona. Primus kept up the pressure as more and more of his troopers rejoined him. The auxiliaries were trotting in his wake, occasionally stopping to make prisoners of wounded men, to strip the dead of their weapons and equipment, and to commandeer the horses of the dead to carry their loot.

For two hours this skirmishing pursuit continued along the highway. Four miles from Cremona, the fleeing Vitellianist cavalry came upon General Titus Valens and his two legions and auxiliaries extended across their path in their battle lines. The bright sun, low in the west now, glinted on the golden eagles of the 1st Italica and 21st Rapax Legions. With General Primus and his thousands of troopers in hot pursuit, the bloodied men from Turin and the other Vitellianist cavalry expected their own infantry to let them pass through their lines. But General Valens, knowing such a movement could break up his legions, issued a command. Trumpets sounded. The long spears of the five thousand men of the 1st Italica came down from the horizontal and projected out in front of their line like the quills of a porcupine.

The Vitellianist cavalry found themselves caught between their own lines and Primus's cavalry. With nowhere to go, they were forced to either turn and fight or to flee off into the countryside to north or south. At this point, a confident commander, with twelve thousand infantry at his disposal, could have ordered his foot soldiers to advance and engage Primus and his cavalry at close quarters while they were without infantry support. But old General Valens knew only one tactic: defense. He called for his lines to hold their positions. Tacitus was to say that the men of the 21st Rapax and 1st Italica had never given bold, flamboyant General Caecina much credit for their success when he had commanded them. Only now, in his absence, did they realize the imprisoned Caecina's true value as a leader.

As the enemy cavalry in front of Primus thinned to reveal the stationary infantry of Valens's lines wavering under the impact of their own cavalry who tried to force a passage through them, Colonel Messalla came up with his auxiliaries. Seeing his opportunity to capitalize on the situation, General Primus charged Valens's front line where he could see weaknesses. Primus's cavalry punched several holes in the lines, and Messalla's auxiliaries poured through the gaps. The spearmen of the 1st Italica, while effective against cavalry, would prove particularly vulnerable to light infantry, who only had to push aside the long, unwieldy spears and close in with their swords. Soon individual cohorts of Valens's legions were being isolated. Tacitus says that the proximity of Cremona's walls was too tempting to the Vitellianists. As men began to stream away from his battle lines toward the safety of the city, Valens had no choice but to order retreat. In good order, individual cohorts of his legions pulled back toward Cremona.

With sunset approaching, and having fought now for the entire afternoon, General Primus signaled for his exhausted cavalry and enthusiastic auxiliaries to halt and not pursue the retreating enemy. In the twilight, with the warmth of the day quickly giving way to the chill of a late fall evening, all Primus's legions came marching along the highway from Bedriacum to join him. Tacitus says the new arrivals passed heaps of enemy dead. Pools of blood, severed limbs, and discarded weapons lay everywhere. Unhappy that they had been deprived of a chance to play a part in the fighting, men of the 3rd Gallica and Primus's other legions demanded to be allowed to advance all the way to Cremona. They wanted to either accept the surrender of the city, or, preferably, take it by storm and loot it.

Cremona was situated on level ground and would not be a hard nut to crack, said the legionaries. There was an old Roman saying; "The fortress that parleys speedily surrenders." The hope of many in the ranks was that they would be able to assault Cremona by night, before the city had a chance to parley the next day. The legionaries didn't want Cremona to surrender, because under the rules of plunder they would not be able to loot the city. They might receive praise in return for their wounds, they said, but the wealth of Cremona would go into the purses of their generals and colonels. If they took Cremona by storm, the spoils would be theirs.

Primus's tribunes and centurions tried to talk their troops out of a night assault, but the men, becoming more and more enamored with the idea of storming Cremona now, ignored them. To drown out their officers, the legionaries began to crash their javelins and swords against their shields. The dissention quickly spread throughout the ranks, until even the more disciplined men joined in. It became apparent to General Primus that he had to act personally. Striding into the heart of the army, he put up his hand for silence.

When his presence and personal authority had restored order, says Tacitus, Primus called, "I wouldn't snatch your deserved glory from you, but soldiers and generals have different duties. You are eager for battle, but generals serve the cause by thinking first, by taking advice, by delay— through prudence rather than fear." The difficulties of a night assault, he said, were obvious—the darkness, the unfamiliarity of the city's streets, the well-positioned enemy defenders on the city walls. "Even if the gates were wide open, we can't take the risk of entering the place without first reconnoitering it, and in daylight at that."

When soldiers responded that they were prepared to take that risk, Primus asked how they could possibly assault the city when the darkness prevented them from determining where to launch assaults, where to site artillery, where to build siege works. Legionaries countered that later in the evening the full moon would rise, and they would have moonlight to work by.

So, says Tacitus, Primus turned to an individual soldier. "Did you bring your ax and spade?" he demanded. The man shook his head no. Primus glared at another. "Did you?" He knew that the legions had left all their ancillary equipment back at the Bedriacum camp.

"No, Commander," the soldier acknowledged.

"Can you undermine or break through walls with your bare hands?" Primus asked another. "Or even with swords and lances? No!" He looked at the sea of shadowy faces around him. "And what happens if we have to throw up an embankment? Or if we need to build a mantlet to shelter beneath? Shall we stand baffled, like an empty-headed mob, marveling at the height of the enemy's walls and towers? Wouldn't it be smarter to wait one night, until our artillery and siege equipment arrive?"

Primus's logic prevailed, and, although not very happy at the pause, his men agreed to wait. The general dispatched the horse sutlers and mule drivers who had followed the legions to hurry back to Bedriacum and fetch back a baggage train containing the legions' artillery, ammunition, and siege equipment. To avoid the downed bridge, the wagons would have to take the Hostilia road to the Via Postumia intersection. As the noncombatants hurried away, the legions spread beside the road just before it rose in a causeway that stretched over the Po floodplain toward the west. There, without fires and camp equipment, the legionaries had to sup on whatever hardtack they had brought with them. But many men were still not happy at the delay in attacking Cremona, and their displeasure and impatience were growing when a detachment of cavalry that had harried General Valens's retreating troops all the way to the walls of Cremona returned to the army, herding several prisoners.

The prisoners, stragglers from Valens's force, were brought to General Primus for questioning, and men gathered around the general as he quizzed the captives. Not only did the prisoners talk, they boasted, telling Primus that the army formerly commanded by General Caecina had, during the day, made a forced march down from Hostilia to answer General Valens's plea for help. The army had crossed the plain, skirting to the north of the Via Postumia, and were now at Cremona. Not only had the men of six legions and various auxiliary units covered more than thirty miles in a day, said the prisoners, but Vitellius's army's baggage train was also coming up, bringing artillery and other important equipment. Primus asked the prisoners what those legions were doing now. They were, was the reply, preparing to march in the darkness to attack Primus's army tonight.

Primus immediately called his senior officers together for a council of war, and they agreed on the disposition of the legions to give Vitellius's army a hot reception. A good general always looked for rising ground on a potential battlefield, and sought to dominate it. The best thing on offer here was the raised causeway of the Via Postumia. Primus ordered General Aquila's 13th Gemina Legion, which had been depleted by about 20 percent by casualties at the Battle of Bedriacum in April, to occupy the causeway. Forming up shoulder to shoulder across its eighteen-foot width, the cohorts of the 13th lined up along the causeway, the men of the latter cohorts facing right and left to defend the raised roadway as if it were a small hill. General Lupus's 8th Augusta Legion was given the honored right wing, lining up facing west on open farmland on the plain, which stretched away to the northern horizon. General Apronianus and the 3rd Gallica were placed between the 8th Augusta and the causeway. The Gallica's line was broken at one point by thick, impenetrable brushwood; the cohorts on either side of the brushwood would have to operate independently of each other. Colonel Messalla and the 7th Galbiana formed up on flat, relatively clear ground to the immediate left of the causeway. Fellow Spanish legion the 7th Claudia stood on the Galbiana's outside, occupying the left wing. It had the advantage of an irrigation ditch running in front of it—the legion could let loose javelins from behind the ditch but was protected from a direct frontal assault.

The men of the Praetorian cohorts lined up immediately to the rear of the 3rd Gallica, in reserve, and this was where General Primus stationed himself. Half the auxiliary cohorts were assigned to each wing, while the cavalry was divided between each wing and the rear to prevent an out-flanking maneuver. Primus also retained the two German kings, Sido and Italicus, with their contingents of combined cavalry and infantry, in reserve at the rear, ready to be thrown into the battle wherever there was a hole to be plugged or an opportunity to be exploited. The moon would shine on the battlefield as the night grew older, but with both sides dressed and equipped identically, shield designs and watchwords would be the only ways to identify who was on your side and who wasn't. As Primus's troops took their positions, a new watchword chosen by their commander was passed among the units.

The army of Vitellius soon came marching up from Cremona, in battle formation. As the prisoners had claimed, the men from Hostilia had indeed force-marched to reach Cremona. Linking up with General Valens and his two bloodied legions, they now marched down the Via Postumia to confront Primus's army. As Tacitus was to write, a wise general would have allowed his weary troops to enjoy a hot meal, would have given them the night to rest before going against the army of Vespasian. But the army of Vitellius was not commanded by a general, wise or otherwise. Ever since General Caecina's arrest, this army had been commanded by a committee; a committee that reflected the views and wishes of the rank and file. And the consensus of the troops was that they should go against Vespasian's army without delay. Right now they outnumbered the other side by some fifty thousand men to forty-four thousand. Fearing that General Mucianus and his twenty thousand men from Syria could arrive at any moment to change the odds in favor of Vespasian, they had voted to act without delay.

Six of Vitellius's legions were at half strength or less. These legions were distributed evenly over the battle lines. The 4th Macedonica was on the right wing. The 5th Alaudae and the 15th Primigeneia were next to it; combined, these two legions could field only thirty-six hundred men. Some six thousand Evocati militia, made up of veterans of the 2nd Augusta, 9th Hispana, and 20th Valeria Victrix Legions who had served in Britain and been living in retirement on the Rhine prior to their recent recall by Vitellius, occupied the center. On the left stood four cohorts from the 1st Legion. A different legion from the 1st Italica, this 1st Legion had

once been Pompey the Great's most famous unit. Later awarded the title
1st Augusta before losing it for cowardice in Spain, it had then briefly carried the title 1st Germanica, for service under Germanicus Caesar, before
Tiberius frowned on that title's use. Fabius Valens, Vitellius's top general,
had been the 1st's commander on the Rhine; the four cohorts that had
come to Italy with Valens were probably led by Camp Prefect Longus.
Next to the 1st in the battle line were five cohorts from each of the 16th
Gallica and the 22nd Primigeneia Legions. The 16th's general was still on
the Rhine with the remainder of the legion, so it was led here by its tribune or camp prefect.

The 21st Rapax had its six cohorts here, led by their tribune. And the
1st Italica had all ten of its cohorts present. But because they had been
mauled and forced to retreat during the afternoon, both these units were
split, with centuries from each mingled with the other legions. This may
have increased the strength of those other legions, but it would have done
nothing for the morale of the men of the Italica and the Rapax. As an
indication of how command and control were now nonexistent in Vitellius's army, the auxiliaries and cavalry were permitted to choose where they
went in the battle line. Old General Valens was here, as were the elected
commanders of Vitellius's army, General Fabullus of the 5th Alaudae and
Camp Prefect Longus. But once the battle began, each legion would fight
independently. Just a single objective had been transmitted to Vitellius's
troops: gain control of the causeway.

As Primus and his troops stood, cold and hungry, waiting in the darkness for the other side to launch the battle, Chief Centurion Varus and his
comrades of the 3rd Gallica were impatient to prove that they, the con-
querors of the Roxolani, were the best legion on the field. They had the
added incentive of knowing that if Vitellius's army could be overcome
here, Cremona lay invitingly undefended and open to plunder.

At 9:00 P.M. the battle began as, with a roar, Vitellius's infantry charged.
Primus's front line stood firm and received the charge without a backward
step. In the darkness the conflict quickly deteriorated into a number of
unit-versus-unit battles. Tacitus says the fighting was indecisive yet fierce,
with first one side, then the other in one pocket and another having the
upper hand. For hour after hour it raged. Tacitus says that even if you were
the strongest, most courageous soldier and had the sharpest eyesight, it
made little difference—luck played more of a role in the darkness. As
both armies became mixed, a soldier, unable to identify a man opposite,
would demand the watchword from him. After this had occurred a few
times, both sides learned the other's watchword, making the watchwords

of both sides useless. Legionaries were trained to fight close to their standards, which stood above the heads of the crowd as rallying points. But in this confused battle, standards were being continually taken on both sides and hurried to the rear as trophies. In this chaos, where self-preservation was the rule of the day, men killed soldiers on their own side more than once.

On the Vitellianist right, the cohorts of the 4th, 5th, and 15th, being confronted by the ditch on the extreme left of Primus's line, had swung in toward the causeway, concentrating their forces against General Primus's own unit, the 7th Galbiana Legion, beside the causeway. In particular they went up against the Galbiana's 1st Cohort, aiming for the legion's golden eagle. As a result, the 7th Galbiana took fearsome casualties. Five first-rank centurions were among the early fatalities. The legion's eagle-bearer was killed and his eagle seized. Immediately, Chief Centurion Atilius Verus of the Galbiana killed the opposition soldier who'd taken the eagle, and regained it. Verus passed the eagle to other hands, then led its defense. The centurion killed a great many of the enemy as they tried desperately to again take the eagle, and was himself wounded time and again. He, too, died before the night was out. But the eagle of the 7th Galbiana was saved, and the legion's honor was preserved.

Among the Vitellianist troops throwing themselves at the 7th Galbiana was Legionary Julius Mansuetus; his senior 21st Rapax cohort had been mixed with the legions on his army's right wing. Mansuetus was brought to the ground by a blow from a teenage legionary of the 7th Galbiana. The young man was bending over the dying Spaniard to strip him of his gold and silver bravery decorations when Mansuetus recognized the face; it was almost as if he were looking at himself. Before he had been enrolled in the Rapax in Spain twenty-nine years before, Mansuetus had fathered a son, one he had not seen since. That son had grown to manhood and been drafted by Galba into his new 7th Legion the previous year.

Colonel Messalla, commander of the 7th Claudia Legion, recorded, in a story later repeated by Tacitus, that the son now recognized his father. Horror-stricken, the younger Mansuetus cradled his father in his arms until he died. According to Messalla, the boy cried aloud, being heard by many around him to say, "This guilt is shared by us all. How small a part does a single soldier play in a civil war?"

Young Mansuetus then used his bloodied sword to dig a grave, and buried his father there on the battlefield. Tacitus says that other men from the same families and the same towns also killed each other in this battle.

General Primus, seeing the 7th Galbiana line beside the causeway on his left begin to waver, led the Praetorian cohorts across from the right to bolster it. The Praetorians came charging through the Galbiana's line and pushed the enemy back. But then the other side regrouped and drove the Praetorians back. The status quo was regained, with neither side able to break through the line of the other.

Now large, rounded stones came whizzing out of the darkness to crash into the Vespasianist lines. Vitellius's artillery officers had managed to mount several catapults on the causeway west of the battle site. The smaller pieces were tending to fire too high, sending their stone missiles over heads and crashing into trees. But a particularly large catapult operated by the 15th Primigeneia Legion began to have devastating effect. For anti-personnel purposes, standard stone-throwing catapults fired stones about twice the size of a baseball. They were dangerous enough, able to take off heads and kill several people at once. But this 15th Legion monster was firing ammunition the size of bowling balls. The troops of Primus's 13th Gemina Legion were taking the brunt of this artillery fire, with its men being mowed down, literally like tenpins.

In the middle of the night, two legionaries, apparently from the 13th Gemina, decided to silence this artillery piece. Grabbing the shields of fallen Vitellianists of the 15th Primigeneia and disguised as soldiers of Vitellius, they made their way to where the giant catapult was in action. Then, tossing aside their shields, they killed the catapult's crew and hacked through the ropes and leather springs of the weapon with flashing swords. By the time enemy troops came running up, the pair had put the artillery piece entirely out of action. The two legionaries didn't survive to be decorated by their general. Both were cut down beside the catapult they had wrecked. The story of their brave deed would later be related by men from Vitellius's side, but the identities of the pair never became known.

In the early hours of the morning, the moon rose as expected—in the east, behind the army of Vespasian. This illuminated the men of Vitellius's army but put Primus's men in shadow. Aiming for the remaining Vitellianist artillery was made extremely difficult, says Tacitus; artillery officers misjudged the range because of the shadows.

With the dawn now not far away, General Primus, able to see the faces of his men in the moonlight, moved among his troops as the rear ranks held back from the fight or flopped exhausted on the ground after hours of fighting, with their wounded lying all around them. Even though they had taken the heaviest casualties so far, he berated the men of the 7th Galbiana and 13th Gemina at the left and center, respectively, of his line.

The 13th in particular received the brunt of his tirade—these northern Italians had fought and lost at Bedriacum, and Primus wasn't going to let them forget it.

"What are you doing here?" he yelled to them. "Why did you bother to take up arms against Vitellius again?" He pointed to the west. "Over there is the battlefield where you can erase the stain of your past disgrace and regain your honor."

As these troops who had come down from Pannonia loudly, angrily declared that they would indeed regain their honor this day, Primus moved on to the 7th Claudia and 8th Augusta. "You started this war!" he called to them. "But what is the point of challenging the Vitellianists with threats if you can't deal with their attacks or even their looks?" He left them roaring that they would show him that they could fight as well as boast. As the general moved on, the troops pulled themselves together and pushed back into the fray.

On the Vespasianist right, just as the first streaks of the new day were appearing in the eastern sky, Primus took a different tack with the men of the 3rd Gallica. He reminded them that their predecessors had fought under his namesake. "Remember how under Mark Antony the 3rd Gallica defeated the Parthians? Remember how, under General Corbulo, you whipped the Armenians? And how only last year you discomforted the Sarmatians?" This brought smiles from the men of the Gallica. Now Primus urged the men of the 3rd Gallica to get up and fight, to live up to their formidable reputation, and to show the rest of the legions how to fight. The Gallicans cheered. And Primus knew they would give him everything in another drive at the enemy.

The general was not so complimentary about the men of the Praetorian Guard who lounged with the Gallicans. "Clowns!" was how he described them, says Tacitus. "If you don't win today, what other general, what other camp will welcome you?" He pointed to their Praetorian standards, whose pointed ends stood planted in the ground, with shields and javelins stacked around them. "There are your standards, there are your weapons. You can do no worse than meet defeat and death, for you can't disgrace yourself any more than you have."

The shamed Praetorians found their anger and their voices. Responding that they were ready to regain their honor, they dragged themselves to their feet and again took up their weapons and their standards. As Primus addressed the Praetorians, the Syrians of the 3rd Gallica turned east, dropped to their knees, and prayed to the rising sun, the manifestation of their god Baal, as they did every morning. This morning they prayed for strength and victory. And as the golden orb rose above the horizon, they hailed Baal as loudly as they hailed any general. Then the men of the 3rd Gallica rose, once more took up their shields and javelins, let out a roar, and in the light of the new day prepared to go back into the battle with new energy, and a determination to live up to their fame.

Meanwhile, General Primus had spread a rumor through the ranks of the rest of his troops that General Mucianus had just arrived from the East with his army, and the roar they had heard from the Syrian legionaries had been the sound of the 3rd Gallica greeting them. In the light of the new day, and filled with fresh confidence and resolve, the remainder of his army launched into a new offensive. At the same time, General Primus led an attack along the causeway by chosen men of the 13th Gemina. This sudden rush at the center, complemented by a new drive on both wings, gave the other side the impression that the Vespasianists had received fresh troops. Word ran through Vitellius's army that General Mucianus had arrived from Syria with Vespasian's reinforcements.

The narrow Vitellianist line of militiamen on the causeway gave way in the face of Primus's charge, and the Evocati troops, men in their fifties and older, fell back on their own artillery and wagons. There was mayhem on the causeway as Primus and his assault troops drove past the artillery and just kept going. Seeing their center give way, the Vitellianist troops on the wings began to turn and run for the protection of Cremona.

Primus and the 13th Gemina drove the enemy before them all the way down the Via Postumia to Cremona, slaughtering any who tried to make a stand. Wheeling around to the north of the city, the 13th drove toward the north gate, which opened onto the Brescia road. But now they found a closed gate and an unexpected impediment. During the brief war with the emperor Otho, Vitellius's troops had built an entrenchment all the way around Cremona, setting out their camp between the city walls and the entrenchment line. As a result, Cremona was encircled by an outer wall of earth and by its original inner stone wall. As the troops of Vitellius flooded back from the battlefield with the 3rd Gallica and the other Vespasian legions hard on their heels, they swarmed through the three gateways in the entrenchments, and now the gates thudded shut.

Typically this outer entrenchment consisted of earthen walls ten feet high, with a trench ten feet deep and three feet across in front of it. The earthen walls were lined with wooden guard towers, and there were towers on either side of the gates—in this case gates in the southern, eastern, and northern walls. Wooden ramparts supporting defenders and artillery ran all the way around the inside of the walls. Thousands of Vitellianist

troops had been killed on the battlefield, but tens of thousands of survivors reached the entrenchments.

As all the legions came up to the city, General Primus, his fellow
brigadier generals and colonels, and Vespasian's influential freedman, Hormus, met to decide what to do next. Tacitus says they considered marching the army back to the safety of their camp outside Bedriacum, but this
was dismissed as too fatiguing. Building a new camp outside Cremona
would only invite sorties against the working legionaries by the other side.
Yet most of the officers felt their troops too exhausted by a day and a
night of fighting to contemplate an immediate assault on the Cremona
entrenchments.

These were all tactically sound, logical arguments. But as General Primus
pointed out to his colleagues, their troops weren't interested in either tactics or logic. They were only interested in plunder, and there was the danger that the commanders could lose control of the troops if they didn't let
them have their head. So it was agreed that an assault on the entrenchments should be launched as quickly as possible, while the Vespasianists
maintained the initiative. Primus now divided his legions among the three
gates in the entrenchment walls, encouraging competition among each
group, urging each to win the glory of being the first to break through. The
3rd Gallica Legion and the bloodied 7th Galbiana Legion were jointly
assigned the southern gate, on the Via Postumia. The 7th Claudia and the
8th Augusta were given the eastern gate, and the 13th Gemina the northern gate. While some legionaries prepared equipment and ammunition,
others were sent to range around the by now deserted farms in the district
to bring back spades, pickaxes, hooks, ladders, and building materials. By
midmorning the legions were ready to go against the walls. And the defenders were ready to defend them.

Primus's legions formed shield testudos and went into the attack. Once
they reached the gates, men sheltering beneath the shields held by comrades around them began to attack the woodwork with their tools. Those
against the wall wielded spades and pickaxes. On the wall above, defenders who didn't have to worry about taking cover from covering fire from
Primus's artillery, which still hadn't arrived from Bedriacum, hurled down
spears, and dropped massive stones onto the shields. Gaps appeared here
and there in the testudos, which began to totter drunkenly as men exposed by the gaps were wounded or killed. Others on the ramparts used
long poles to exploit the gaps and break up the testudos. Unable to maintain their formations, the damaged tortoises fell back, leaving large numbers of dead and mangled men at the base of the walls.

This reverse opened the eyes of the attackers to their exhaustion and their hunger—they hadn't eaten a proper meal since the day before last. As officers urged their men to re-form their testudos and renew the attack, there was hesitation in the ranks. Now, says Tacitus, the generals went among the troops and pointed to Cremona beyond the entrenchments, saying that if they wanted their spoils, the city, overflowing with gold and women, was theirs for the taking. Colonel Messalla, who was on the spot, would write that this was the idea of Hormus. Pliny the Elder, a friend of Vespasian and at this time serving as a procurator in Spain, would later blame General Primus for appealing to the basest instincts of his men, not Hormus.

Whoever sponsored the idea, it worked. The legions rediscovered their enthusiasm and re-formed their testudos, agreeing on new tactics for a fresh assault. Now, too, the stone-throwing catapults that had been abandoned by Vitellius's troops on the Via Postumia causeway were brought up and sighted against the southern wall. With a roar, Primus's legions went back against the walls. This time they ignored wounds and casualties. This time, too they formed a unique double testudo—men climbed up on the first roof of shields and formed a second testudo with their shields above it.

At the southern wall, the 3rd Gallica and 7th Galbiana were making the best progress. The Galbiana was using an effective wedge-shaped testudo against the wall, and the 3rd Gallica men were attacking the wooden gate with axes and swords. One tower above the gate was coming under accurate fire from the captured catapults now being used by Primus's artillerymen. In the other tower, the Vitellianist gunners manning a Scorpio quick-firer cursed as their arrows simply glanced off the top row of shields below them. Finally, out of ammunition, the exasperated artillerymen pushed their Scorpio from the tower. With an almighty crash, the artillery piece fell on part of the Gallica's testudo, crushing men beneath it.

But in its fall, the Scorpio had taken the top of the rampart with it. At the same time, a supporting strut of the tower on the other side of the gate took a direct hit from a stone-throwing catapult; the strut gave way, and with screams from its occupants the tower collapsed inside the wall, spilling men all around it. Encouraged by this, the men of the 7th Galbiana increased the pitch of their work, determined to undermine the wall where it had been damaged by the falling artillery piece. Next to them, the men of the 3rd Gallica, not to be outdone, hacked feverishly at the wooden gate. General Primus, seeing that real progress was being made here, hurried forward with handpicked auxiliaries and joined the 3rd Gallica in the assault at the southern gate.

Suddenly there was a cheer from the Gallicans. The Via Postumia gate was giving way. Legionary Gaius Volusius of the 3rd Gallica was the first man through a gap in the gate. Moments later the gate gave way entirely under the pressure of the attackers. The 3rd Gallica swept in the gateway like a torrent at the flood. Legionary Volusius climbed the rampart beside the gate and waved to the troops of Vespasian outside, urging them to join him and his comrades inside.

"Come on, boys!" Volusius yelled excitedly. "The camp is taken! The camp is taken!" For being the first man to cross the enemy's wall, Legionary Volusius earned the Mural Crown, a crown of gold, the second most prestigious Roman military bravery award.

Seeing the gate breached and Vespasian's troops flooding into their camp, the Vitellianists on the southern wall jumped down from their battlements and ran back to the city gates and into Cremona itself. The defenders on the other walls, seeing what had taken place at the Via Postumia gate, also deserted their positions and fled back to the city. Cremona had massive inner gates of wood and outer gates of iron bars. Defenders manning the gate towers cut the ropes that kept them suspended. They all came crashing down. Those too slow to reach the gates were left trapped outside, to be cut down by the 3rd Gallica. And then there was silence, broken only by the groans of the wounded among the dead lying outside the entrenchments and all the way to the city walls.

Primus had all three outer gates opened to permit his troops to now surround the city itself. It was the middle of the day. The fighting had been going on now for twenty-four hours, virtually without stop. As his wounded were taken away and his troops looted the Vitellianist camp and the city buildings outside the city walls, Primus surveyed the situation. The city walls were high—much higher than the ramparts his troops had just stormed. They had formidable stone towers in them, and were lined with artillery and defenders. But like most cities of the day, 286-year-old Cremona had long ago overflowed its old walls. Some of its finest buildings were outside those walls, and were now in Primus's hands. A number of those buildings, near the city walls, were taller than the walls, and Primus had troops detailed to occupy their upper floors, to pull them apart and rain down roof beams, tiles, and flaming arrows on the defenders on the adjacent wall. At the same time, Primus had some of the buildings in the captured zone put to the torch, to show the people of Cremona what would happen to the entire city if they continued to resist. The 13th Gemina Legion was delighted to be able to set fire to the wooden amphitheater they'd been forced to build here for Vitellius in April and May.

Now, too, as flames gained hold and palls of smoke began to rise at various points outside the city, Primus had captured Vitellianist artillery pieces brought up from the outer walls, and opened fire on the defenders on the battlements. His legions then began to prepare a giant testudo for a concerted assault against one part of the stone wall.

On the ramparts, watching all this, the surviving tribunes and centurions of Vitellius's army began to dread what would happen to them if Vespasian's army succeeded in storming the city itself. They knew that the Vespasianists would go on a killing rampage, and they would be at the top of the killing list. The officers quickly had the name and images of Vitellius removed from all the military standards in the city and then approached Generals Fabullus and Valens and advised them to surrender Cremona—now, while there was still time. And it was agreed that General Caecina, who had changed his loyalty to Vespasian, would be an ideal envoy on their behalf.

General Caecina was swiftly released from his chains and brought from his prison cell to the generals who had previously answered to him. His official consular robes and his twelve lictors were returned to him. And, many of them in tears, the generals and tribunes and centurions begged Caecina to go out to Vespasian's army and negotiate an honorable surrender, one that guaranteed them their lives. Caecina folded his arms, shook his head, and steadfastly refused to become involved on their behalf. These men had made their bed by going against him; now they could lie in it.

Soon after, General Primus's men saw olive branches being displayed around the walls of Cremona—the white flags of the day. Cremona had surrendered unconditionally. After Primus ordered his artillery to cease firing, one of the city gates opened, and the standard-bearers of the eight legions of Vitellius represented in Cremona came marching out with all the eagles and other standards of their units, and handed them to Primus. Behind the standard-bearers came the generals and unarmed officers of the legions. Trooping after them, most of their men, eyes to the ground, looking dismal, shattered, and fearful of their fate, followed in a long line. Primus's troops formed an avenue for the surrendered troops to pass through. And as the thousands of surrendered men shuffled along that avenue, the victors admonished them for fighting in the cause of Vitellius, and threatened them with their weapons, implying that they weren't yet out of hot water.

The noise died away, but then General Caecina came down the avenue, clad in his official robes and escorted by his lictors. Now Primus's troops howled and catcalled, calling Caecina a cruel tyrant for siding with Vitellius and causing the death of Otho's men at Bedriacum, including relatives and friends of soldiers in Primus's ranks. They even accused him of betraying Vitellius, the man he had made emperor. But General Primus respected Caecina. Giving him an escort, he sent him to Vespasian in Egypt. The surrendered troops were escorted down the Bedriacum road for three miles. There, at the roadside, they were told to set up a prisoner-of-war camp. But on Primus's orders their standards were returned to them, and they were told to maintain their unit structures.

Primus then summoned his own men to an assembly outside Cremona. From the tribunal he praised individual soldiers such as Legionary Volusius of the 3rd Gallica, and the army as a whole for the great victory. But, he reminded them, the defeated troops were their fellow Romans and deserved forgiveness. He also told them that they could elect their own centurions from their ranks to replace those who had died in the fighting. Saying nothing about the fate of the people of Cremona, Primus then entered the city with an escort. At the city baths he stripped off his grimy, bloodied armor and uniform and settled into a bath. Outside, Primus's forty thousand surviving troops and even more noncombatants from his army flooded into Cremona to exact the price of victory on the city and its occupants. Once they had pillaged a house or a temple, the looters would toss in a lighted torch and move on to the next building. Before long, smoke rose across the city.

General Primus knew exactly what was happening beyond the walls of the bathhouse. This was the reward his men had sought and had been promised. Primus didn't like it, but he knew that even if he had forbidden the army to plunder Cremona they would have ignored him and gone ahead anyway; and in the process he would have lost all authority over them. The civil war was not yet over. Vitellius still had tens of thousands of troops at Rome, and the able general Fabius Valens. Primus needed his troops; he knew it, and they knew it. And it made him as irritable as a bear with a toothache. Sourly he moved from cold bath to tepid bath to hot bath.

"The water is not warm enough," he complained as he lounged in the last bath.

Tacitus says that a bathhouse slave was overheard by a member of the general's staff to say, with a nod toward the now burning city, "It will soon be warm enough."

XXIV

STORMING ROME

F or four days, more than eighty thousand soldiers and noncombatants plundered Cremona. It was a rich city at any time, but packed as it was with merchants and buyers who had come for the Cremona Fair, it was one giant treasure chest. Primus's legionaries had no compunction in treating the people of Cremona brutally. Fellow Romans the Cremonans might be, but the men of the 3rd Gallica were Syrians, and those of the two 7th Legions and the 8th were all Spaniards. None felt any connections with the Cremonans, people who had actively supported Vitellius's troops against them. And while the soldiers of the 13th Gemina were themselves from northern Italy, they hated the Cremonans for the humiliation they had suffered here in the spring.

Thousands of people were killed by the plunderers. Tacitus says that a number of Vitellius's soldiers had refused to give themselves up when their officers surrendered their army, and had gone into hiding in the city. Every one was tracked down by Primus's troops and killed. Any civilian who tried to protect his or her property or loved ones was put to the sword. Women and girls were raped; pretty male youths were subjected to homosexual rape. The healthiest, most handsome residents were rounded up, to be sold as slaves. And when there was no more gold to find, noncombatants fought over loot with auxiliaries, and auxiliaries fought with legionaries. All the while, the city burned. In the end, just a single building remained standing, the Temple of Mephitis, outside the walls.

On the fifth day since the city's surrender, as an early winter rain began to fall, dousing the last smoldering embers, Primus marched his glutted legions away, to the camp three miles to the east where the prisoners were being held. Before he left Cremona, Primus issued an edict making it unlawful to retain a citizen of Cremona in captivity. This was supported by cities throughout Italy that declared their refusal to allow the purchase as a slave of any resident of Cremona. In response, some of Primus's men killed their captives, before it was realized that there was profit to be had in ransoming the more valuable prisoners back to their wealthy families.

According to Cassius Dio, between the battle outside Cremona and the subsequent rape of the city, 50,000 people died. Josephus says that General Primus lost 4,500 men in the two days of fighting and that 34,200 troops in Vitellius's army died at Cremona. By combining the two figures, it would appear that more than 11,000 civilians were killed.

Primus had already sent messengers hurrying to Britain and Spain with the news that Vitellius's army had been totally defeated, and urging the provinces' legions to declare for Vespasian. Now, too, he freed two colonels from the other side, sending the Gallic tribune Julius Calenus and the Trevean auxiliary prefect Alpinius Montanus back to their native lands as living proof that Vitellius's army no longer existed.

In early November, at the Via Postumia camp, Primus's army was joined at last by the 11th Claudia Legion from Dalmatia. Tacitus gives "hesitation" as the reason for the 11th Claudia taking so long to get here. But from numismatic evidence we know that the 11th had quickly sworn for Vespasian—its pay had been minted in October bearing Vespasian's image, not Vitellius's. And the other illuminating thing about the 11th Claudia's pay in A.D. 69 was that it was minted not in Dalmatia, but up at Castra Batavor in Noricum, modern-day Passau in Bavaria, hundreds of miles to the north. Castra Batavor was an auxiliary base at the junction of the Danube, Inn, and Ilz rivers. On the northern boundary of the province of Noricum, it faced Germany and sat astride a potential route for reinforcements for Vitellius. It seems that Governor Pompeius Silvanus of Dalmatia had taken it on himself to march the 11th Claudia and six thousand raw auxiliary recruits he'd quickly levied in Dalmatia up to Passau instead of hurrying to join Primus in Italy. Either that or he had received a plea for support from Procurator Felix of Noricum. Either way, once at Passau, Silvanus had come under pressure from the commander of the 11th, Brigadier General Annius Bassus—who, says Tacitus, was now increasingly manipulating his superior—to march to join Primus in Italy. And now here they were outside Cremona after marching all the way down from Bavaria.

Primus now learned that Field Marshal Mucianus's army had been sidetracked on the way to Italy by the need to counter a sudden Dacian invasion of the now lightly defended province of Moesia, with the Dacians having wiped out Roman auxiliary units and occupying both banks of the Danube. Freed of the need to keep one step ahead of Mucianus, Primus made his dispositions for the march on Rome, to take the throne from Vitellius. Having required the survivors from the surrendered opposition units to swear allegiance to Vespasian, he now sent seven of the eight greatly depleted Vitellianist legions marching off to camps in Dalmatia, where they could serve as reinforcements to Mucianus in Moesia if necessary. It seems that General Bassus of the 11th Claudia talked his boss, Lieutenant General Silvanus, governor of Dalmatia, into leading these men back to his province. Of Vitellius's former units, the 21st Rapax apparently came out of the Battle of Cremona with the least casualties, for this legion was ordered by Primus to remain at the Via Postumia camp with a number of auxiliaries in case he needed them.

Primus decided that as the 11th Claudia had not yet seen action it should head the column making for the capital. He then handpicked legionaries from his own legions to take to Rome with him. Chief Centurion Arrius Varus had redeemed himself since his rash cavalry charge on the first day of the battle, leading his men of the 3rd Gallica in breaking down the gate in the entrenchments, and Primus chose both Varus and the 3rd Gallica to march south with him. He sent his wounded and those men he considered superfluous back to Verona. The six thousand Dalmatian levies he sent to Ravenna. The newly installed pro-Vespasian commander there, his friend Admiral Festus, had sent Primus a message to say that the most elite marines at Ravenna were clamoring to join the drive to the capital, so Primus swapped the green Dalmatians for six thousand tough marines.

Accompanied by the marines, the 11th Claudia Legion, chosen auxiliaries, and the best men from the 3rd Gallica and his other legions, General Primus crossed the Po River as rain continued to fall and entered Italy proper, heading down Italy's east coast. As he marched south with some thirty thousand troops, it was with the knowledge that Vitellius could now call on only the men of the Praetorian Guard, City Guard, German Guard, and Night Watch. In numbers, these units roughly equaled his force. But with news of the total defeat of Vitellius's legions at Cremona now circulating in Rome, Primus was hopeful that these men would fail to fight.

The march south was not easy. First, the heavy, persistent rain flooded the Padus River in Primus's path. As the legions struggled to cross, Primus, impatient to advance on Rome before the snows came, left most of his troops to follow as best they could, and pressed on with just the cavalry and auxiliary light infantry. He hurried to Rimini, junction of the Aemilian Way from the west and the Flaminian Way, the road to Rome. Here, news reached him that General Fabius Valens, Vitellius's last real hope, had been captured on board a ship off Marseilles after he had unsuccessfully tried to rally support for his emperor in the south of France. In the end, Valens had been deserted by all except four bodyguards from the emperor's German Guard, three centurions, and three close friends.

Before long there were reports that the Tyrrhenian Fleet at Micenum south of Rome also had deserted to Vespasian, and with each passing day as he advanced toward the capital Primus heard stories that this town and that town in Campania south of Rome had sworn allegiance to Vespasian. At Tarracina in Campania, a force made up of a City Guard cohort and gladiators sent by Vitellius to stop this tide of defections had themselves gone over to Vespasian. This was all good news for Primus, but Vitellius still ruled in Rome, and Primus's force was suffering from the cold and becoming desperately low on supplies as it pushed south.

Soon Primus began to have trouble with his cold, hungry men. They were demanding the bonus that was traditionally paid to the members of the Roman army by each new emperor. To make light of it, they called the money they claimed their *clavarium*—literally, money to buy shoe nails. But pin money or not, Primus had no cash to give them. One legion cavalryman even claimed payment for killing his own brother on the other side at the Battle of Cremona. Antonius put the men off with promises of big rewards once they reached Rome. It was all he had to give them.

All the while, letters were flowing between Field Marshal Mucianus and Primus, with Mucianus urging him to slow down and wait for him before entering Rome. Although Primus suspected that Mucianus only wanted the glory of entering Rome for himself, he did pause, deciding that he might need the full force of his army to take the capital after all. As his cavalry scouted the roads of Umbria ahead, he sent back to Verona for the remainder of his able-bodied troops. While he waited, he penned a vitriolic letter to Vespasian in Egypt, declaring that he was the one winning the war for him while others tried to grab the glory that was rightfully his.

"The upset of Vitellius's divided and scattered legions by a fierce cavalry charge," he wrote to his emperor, according to Tacitus, "followed by the unrelenting strength of the infantry in a conflict that lasted a day and a night, was a glorious achievement, and it was all my work." He also claimed credit for the fact that the legions in Spain and Britain were now coming out for Vespasian, and dismissed the destruction of Cremona as the price of civil war. He added, without naming Mucianus but clearly referring to him, "My efforts will be wasted if those who have not shared the dangers win the rewards."

As December arrived, Primus was inspired by news that fourteen cohorts of Vitellius's Praetorian Guard—fourteen thousand men—were marching north with all Vitellius's cavalry to intercept him in the Apennine Mountains, which run down the center of Italy. Not far behind the Praetorian column came a legion hastily created by Vitellius by arming sailors from the fleet at Ostia—much as Nero had done eighteen months before. Urged by his colleague Centurion Varus to strike quickly, Primus led his now grumbling troops southwest and occupied the town of Bevagna, old Mevania, without waiting for his legions to catch up.

The weather worsened as Primus continued his advance over the Apennines. As his advance force crossed the mountains, they were hit by snowstorms. Slowly, unhappily, his troops trudged on to the village of Carsulae, ten miles north of Narnia, which Vitellius's Praetorians had occupied. Here at Carsulae, Primus was met by Major General Quintus Petilius Cerialis, who was married to Vespasian's cousin. The redheaded Cerialis, who had commanded the 9th Hispana Legion in Britain at the time of Queen Boudicca's Revolt nine years before, had escaped from the capital disguised as a farmer. Primus immediately admitted Cerialis to his council of war, and quizzed him on the state of affairs at Rome.

In the meantime, Vitellius withdrew five Praetorian cohorts and five hundred cavalry from Narnia, calling them back to march to Campania under his inept brother Lucius, in an attempt to restore Vitellius's control there now that almost every Campanian town had gone over to Vespasian.

Centurion Varus, who was by this time receiving personal letters from Field Marshal Mucianus, joined Primus, Cerialis, and the other senior officers as they discussed organizing a peace conference with Vitellius's troops at Narnia. But as soon as word leaked out about this, their troops protested—they wanted to advance on Rome right away and seal this whole affair with steel, not negotiate a surrender. Primus had to call an assembly to calm down the troops. There, he reminded them that as long as he led them there would not be another Cremona, that if they could win Rome without bloodshed it would do them far more credit. The remaining men of the 3rd Gallica and the rest of Primus's legions now came marching in through the snow from Verona, bringing a long baggage train and welcome supplies. For the first time in weeks, the men of Primus's advance force ate well that night.

At Narnia, news of this massive troop buildup just up the road soon weakened the resolve of Vitellius's troops. The final straw for Vitellius's men came the next day, when Centurion Varus led a light force in a lightning raid on a camp containing four hundred cavalry at Interamna, outside Narnia. Varus's sortie caused panic—at that camp and at Narnia. Most of the troopers, almost certainly Germans of the Singularian Horse, the new Praetorian cavalry regiment, surrendered to the 3rd Gallica centurion.

Word now reached both sides, too, that General Fabius Valens, Vitellius's captured chief general, had been executed by Vespasianists in the south of France. Officers of the Praetorian Guard at Narnia began to openly discuss going over to the other side, and several tribunes and centurions soon deserted. The fate of the force was sealed when Vitellius's two Praetorian prefects, Julius Priscus, until recently a centurion, and Alfrenius Varus, the former camp prefect of the 5th Alaudae Legion, slipped out of camp that night and rode back to Rome to tell their emperor that all was lost. The next day, Primus's entire army, now more than fifty thousand strong, came down from Carsulae and formed up in battle order on the plain below Narnia. The Vitellianist troops in the town marched out to them behind their standards and surrendered—nine Praetorian cohorts, the legion of seamen, and the remaining cavalry, totaling more than fourteen thousand men.

At Rome, as the army of Vespasian drew daily closer, the emperor Vitellius executed men who had brought him bad news from the north. Desperately he tried to raise a new army, levying every able-bodied man in the city into service, including slaves. Units were formed and equipped with military standards, even though there weren't enough arms to go around or officers to lead them.

Then, seemingly coming to grips with his increasingly dire situation, Vitellius invited Vespasian's elder brother Flavius Sabinus, the City Prefect, to enter into talks at the Palatium. Sabinus, at least sixty-two years of age and probably several years older, had led the 14th Gemina Victrix Legion in Claudius's invasion of Britain and fought alongside his brother Vespasian in that campaign. A former consul, he'd been governor of Moesia for seven years, then City Prefect for twelve years in two stints during the reign of Nero, before being removed by Galba. After Otho took the throne in January, the Praetorian Guard had elected their own tribunes and also had selected their own prefect of the city, calling back General Sabinus. Plutarch says the guardsmen made their choice either in honor of the memory of Nero, whom Sabinus had served faithfully for so many years, or with an eye to Sabinus's powerful brother Vespasian, then commander in chief in Judea.

Sabinus had gone north with Otho in March as Vitellius's two armies entered Italy, but had seen no combat. He'd been in command of a body of gladiators at the Po River when Otho's army fought and lost the Battle of Bedriacum in April. Returning to the capital, he'd resumed his City Prefect's duties and led the troops of the City Guard and Night Watch in swearing loyalty to Vitellius as their new emperor, subsequently keeping the city under control as he and it waited for the victorious Vitellius to arrive.

Vespasian's brother did not personally go to the palace for the meetings initiated by Vitellius—that would have immediately caused rumors to spread through the capital. Instead, as his go-between in the delicate negotiations, Sabinus used ex-consul Rubrius Gallus, whom Vitellius knew and trusted. In the course of the discussions the mild-mannered Sabinus advised the emperor that his best course, for himself and for Rome, was to abdicate. His envoy Gallus passed over letters from Field Marshal Mucianus and General Primus guaranteeing that if Vitellius did step down he could live in peaceful retirement in a secluded villa on the Campanian coast.

Vitellius, apparently accepting the inevitable, began discussing suitable retirement houses with his staff. Then, in the sacred precincts of the Temple of Apollo and in the presence of witnesses, Vitellius ratified an agreement with Sabinus and vowed to step down. As the emperor returned to the Palatium to prepare to depart Rome, Sabinus sent orders to the tribunes of the two City Guard cohorts still in the city and the commanders of the seven Night Watch cohorts, instructing them to keep their men under strict control during the forthcoming transition of power.

But as soon as word leaked out about the agreement, Vitellius was surrounded by men he'd appointed to positions of power, who warned him not to trust Vespasian. They assured him that just as he had executed Valens, Vitellius's best general, he would execute Vitellius himself. And they played on his fears for the safety of his family. But eventually, after much soul-searching, and reminded by members of his staff that he had given his oath to step down, Vitellius saw no other course but abdication. Late in the morning of December 18, after hearing of the surrender at Narnia from the two Praetorian colonels, the emperor left the Palatium surrounded by distraught staff, and convened a meeting of his family and supporters in the heart of the city. Tall, florid, with a substantial paunch and a treble chin, the fifty-four-year-old emperor stood on the rostrum, looking out over the people who'd gathered in the Forum to hear him. With the men of his German Guard personal protection detail watching in disbelief and with staff and family members in tears, Vitellius announced that he was stepping down from the throne.

"For the sake of peace, for the sake of the country," he said. In tears himself by this point, he offered his ornate official dagger, symbol of his imperial power over life and death, to Consul Caecilius Simplex, to formalize his relinquishment of power. But Consul Simplex would not accept it. With the boisterous crowd calling for him to change his mind, Vitellius tried to make his way to the house of his brother Lucius, who was commanding Praetorians in Campania, rather than return to the Palatium. But Vitellius found his path barred by the now angry throng. Only one street was open to him, the Sacred Way, which led back to the Palatium. So he hurried back to the comparative safety of the palace.

Word quickly spread through the city that Vitellius had abdicated. It seemed that his last act as emperor had been his noblest. In a celebratory mood, a vast crowd of supporters of Vespasian gathered outside the house of Flavius Sabinus, among them many senators and knights. When he emerged, Sabinus found that men of the Night Watch had assembled spontaneously outside his door, and with them providing an escort, he moved down into the center of the city, followed by his delighted supporters. It seems he intended to convene a sitting of the Senate and to then propose that his fellow senators vote for a smooth and peaceful transition of power from Vitellius to Vespasian, thereby putting the final official seal on the change of government.

It was midafternoon as the crowd moved down past Lake Fundanus. Ahead, an opposing crowd of Vitellius supporters formed in their path, among them cohorts from the German Guard, the emperor's bodyguard unit, who were armed only with swords, as the law required. There was a lot of pushing and shoving from both sides, and the tall, bearded Germans drew their swords. Seeing many in his escort waver, and considering discretion the better part of valor, Sabinus hastily withdrew to the buildings on the adjacent Capitoline Hill, which housed the most sacred temples of Rome.

His supporters scattered. Some ran to their homes. Some of the nobles, notably former colonels and retired generals, joined Sabinus in the Capitoline complex. Among this group were women, including Verulana Gratilla, one of the leading ladies of Rome. Sabinus's most prominent supporter was one of the two current consuls, Gaius Quintius Atticus. None of these people was armed, but men of the Night Watch stayed with Sabinus, their commander—they were armed, and there were some seven thousand of them. The heathen German Guardsmen, uncertain about the propriety of storming the home of Rome's gods, surrounded the Capitoline Hill but didn't venture to go in after the revolutionaries.

As night fell, it began to rain. The large numbers of members of the public who had gathered around the Capitoline to see what would happen went home, and the German Guards, after leaving a few sentries stationed around the hill, went back to their quarters at the Palatium. In the middle of the chilly night, as the rain drummed down, reducing visibility and forcing the German sentries to huddle under distant colonnades, Sabinus was able to send soldiers of the Night Watch to his house to fetch his children, including his son Flavius Clemens. The Night Watch troops also located Sabinus's nephew Titus Flavius Domitian, the eighteen-year-old youngest son of Vespasian, at Vespasian's house on Pomegranate Street in the 6th Precinct. Domitian was included in the little rescue party that returned to the Capitoline.

Sabinus and his supporters could have escaped from the city that night, as both Field Marshal Mucianus and General Primus had been urging him to do for weeks in secret letters smuggled in, tied to the legs of poultry being brought to market. Previously, Sabinus had said he was too old and unwell to leave, but now he stayed as a matter of principle. He was sure that Vitellius would abide by his word, that the German Guard had acted without authority, and that the situation would correct itself in the morning. Just to be on the safe side, he sent a mounted messenger to General Primus at Narnia to tell him that he, Domitian, and their supporters were under siege on the Capitol, and urging him to send troops as quickly as possible.

Before dawn, Sabinus sent a first-rank centurion of the Night Watch, Cornelius Martialis, to confer with Vitellius at the Palatium and find out what was going on. The emperor agreed to see Centurion Martialis, and, apparently embarrassed, assured him when they met that the troops of his bodyguard were determined not to let him vacate the throne and would neither obey him nor let him leave.

"I no longer have the power to command or forbid the German Guard to do anything," the emperor said with a shrug before letting Centurion Martialis out of the palace by a side door so he wasn't intercepted by German sentries outside.

After the centurion slipped back to the Capitol in the light of the dawn and passed on a gloomy report of his meeting with Vitellius, Sabinus and his supporters heard warning shouts from their lookouts, followed by the sound of hobnailed army boots on the paving stones outside. Three cohorts of the German Guard had marched on the double from the Palatium to finish what they had begun the day before. Each cohort of the German Guard was 480 men strong. These 1,440 Germans had come without their senior officers. Fearing what might happen to them if Vespasian came to power, and remembering how Vitellius had disbanded Otho's German Guard without any benefits, the rank and file were determined to keep their emperor on the throne and so keep themselves in a job.

After halting and forming into a line, the Germans advanced up the lower slope of the hill to the Capitol's outer gates. Spurning other weapons or siege equipment, each tall soldier of the bodyguard had come armed only with his sword, his normal armament for Palatium duty. They were outnumbered by the defenders of the Capitol, but the very size of the men of the German Guard would have sent shivers down the spines of Sabinus's soldiers of the Night Watch. Former slaves, the Night Watch men were nothing more than policemen and firemen, and had never seen active service, as these Germans had. Frantic now that they realized how serious the Germans were, the Night Watch troops overturned statues and furniture and piled it all in barricades at the Capitol entrances, knowing they would have to fight for their lives.

It was the Saturnalia, the seven-day annual Festival of Saturn, which ran from December 17, a religious and gift-giving festival that became the Christian Christmas. For the duration of this, the merriest festival on the calendar, Romans did no work and enjoyed the liberties that the Saturnalia brought with it, including the freedom to legally gamble. A day's march from Rome, General Primus was allowing the men of the 3rd Gallica and his other units to enjoy the Saturnalia holiday at leisure in their marching camp. He'd moved on a little way from Narnia, leaving some of the surrendered troops there under guard, bringing others with him, halting at Ocriculum on the Flaminian Way.

Field Marshal Mucianus had smashed the Dacian invasion of Moesia with the 6th Ferrata and his other troops, and now, after a forced march, was not far away from Primus's army. Marching down through eastern Italy now, he continued to send Primus dispatches urging him not to enter Rome, but to wait outside and give Vitellius a chance to leave the throne voluntarily, enabling the city and the organs of government to survive intact. Primus was taking the field marshal's advice. With the shame of the sack of Cremona hanging over him like a dark cloud, there was no way he wanted a repeat of that affair. He knew there were plenty of soldiers in his army who would sack Rome without a moment's hesitation if he gave them the word—the Syrian legionaries of the 3rd Gallica in particular. Gritty, determined, greedy for victory, they were without question his best troops. They were also greedy for spoils, and now that they'd had a taste of loot at Cremona, they wanted more. For the moment, Primus was able to placate his men by saying there was time enough to take Rome once the Saturnalia ended.

When the messenger from Flavius Sabinus arrived from Rome, seeking urgent military aid, Primus was taken completely by surprise. To occupy Capitoline Hill while Vitellius still had troops in the city loyal to him would have seemed provocative, if not insane. It must have crossed Primus's mind that with Sabinus out of the way there would be more opportunity for his own career advancement. But it also would have occurred to him that if Vespasian's son Domitian was killed in Rome while Primus stood idly by outside the city with fifty thousand men, he could kiss his career aspirations good-bye.

Primus quickly summoned General Cerialis, Vespasian's cousin by marriage. Assigning a thousand cavalrymen to Cerialis, among them troopers who had come over from Vitellius's side at Narnia only days before, he told him to ride like the wind to save the Vespasianists at the Capitol. At the same time, the general ordered the rest of the army to prepare to march. As trumpets sounded throughout the camp, Cerialis galloped south with his cavalry force, determined to save his relatives. At a crossroads north of the city he diverted from the Flaminian Way to the Salarian Way. Everyone in Rome knew by now that Vespasian's army was coming down the Flaminian Way. Swinging around to the northeast via this route, Cerialis at least stood the chance of bursting into the city unexpectedly via the Colline Gate.

At the Capitol, the men of the German Guard were pressing home their attack. Their first sally against the front gates had been beaten off by defenders on the roof of a colonnade beside the gateway, who rained stones and roof tiles on the attackers. The Germans had then set alight the roof of the colonnade, and the fire had partly burned the front gate, but a barricade behind the gate held, and the fire died away. The Germans then transferred the assault to the opposite side of the hill, and were pushing the defenders back when someone on one side or the other started a fire in the roof of one of the buildings lining the outside of the Capitoline complex. This fire quickly spread. Dry rafters hundreds of years old and Roman eagles carved in wood supporting pediments were soon alight. Before long, all of the sacred Capitoline Hill was ablaze.

On the other side of the city, General Cerialis and his mounted relief force were in trouble. They'd been spotted coming down the Salarian Way, and before they could even reach the city's Colline Gate they were intercepted by a mounted detachment supported by infantry—probably troops of the City Guard cohorts still in Rome. As smoke billowed like a distress beacon in the distance from the growing conflagration on Capitoline Hill, Cerialis and his cavalry found themselves ambushed among buildings, gardens, and winding lanes unfamiliar to them. Most of the cavalrymen who'd come over to Vespasian's side at Narnia lost their nerve when the decurion Tullius Flavianus, the commander of a squadron, was taken prisoner by Vitellius's troops. They turned around and rode back the way they had come as fast as they could go. General Cerialis and those troopers who remained with him tried to fight on but were eventually driven back down the Salarian Way. The Vitellianists pursued them a little way, then withdrew victoriously into the city. At the village of Fidenae, Cerialis tried to regroup.

At the Capitol, the German Guards, ignoring the choking smoke, burst in on the last stronghold of the defenders. Many men of the Night Watch simply gave up. They didn't have as strong a motive for fighting as the Germans did, and neither did they have the combat experience. Their officers loyally fought to the end around Flavius Sabinus and Consul Atticus. Four of them, including Centurion Cornelius Martialis, were cut down by the Germans before Sabinus and Atticus were captured alive. A number of people managed to escape from the Capitol. Some disguised themselves as slaves; others overheard the men of the guard exchanging their watchword in the smoke and used it themselves to get by. Vespasian's son Domitian and Sabinus's son Flavius Clemens, Domitian's cousin, hid for a while in the quarters of a servant of the Capitoline Temple of Isis. Dressed as priests of the Isis order, the pair was allowed to leave by the Germans and subsequently hid at the home of a client of Vespasian in the city.

The men of the German Guard chained Sabinus and Consul Atticus and dragged them across the city to the Golden House. The emperor, looking lost, met them on the steps of the palace. All around him, German Guard soldiers demanded the right to execute the pair, and payment for the deed. Trying to speak on Sabinus's behalf, Vitellius was shouted down. The matter was quickly resolved. Every soldier within striking distance put a sword into Sabinus there in front of Vitellius. With a guttural Germanic cheer his head was then cut off. The mutilated body of Vespasian's brother was dragged away to the Gemonian Stairs and cast down the steps, the fate of convicted traitors.

This bloodletting seemed to satisfy the Germans for the time being—killing the brother of the pretender to the throne was the cause of some satisfaction to them, so they agreed to Vitellius's plea to spare the life of Consul Atticus. As the sun went down and the ruins of the Capitol continued to smolder, people of the city, free men and slaves, began to arm themselves against the army they knew was now only a few miles away. They had been given confidence by the two successes of the emperor's troops at the Capitol and outside the Colline Gate. An uneasy, unreal calm settled over the city.

Meanwhile, General Primus had marched his army well into the night as he tried to reach the city and save Sabinus. He called a halt only when messengers arrived from inside the city with devastating news. The temples on the Capitol had been razed. The three thousand brass tablets on which the laws of Rome, going back hundreds of years, were inscribed had been destroyed. And Vespasian's brother Sabinus was dead.

The next day, envoys came from the city seeking a peace agreement. Those who went to General Cerialis at Fidenae received a rude reception from his chastened troopers. The envoy's attendant was killed and the envoy himself wounded. General Primus was more receptive, but he sent back the message that the murder of Vespasian's brother meant that all peace negotiations were now terminated. Primus then called an assembly of his army.

The men of the 3rd Gallica and Primus's other troops were chafing to get on with the business they had come here for. Primus, anxious to prevent another event like the sack of Cremona, managed to quiet the soldiers long enough to say that for now they would move to the outskirts of the city and establish a camp beside the Tiber River at the Mulvian Bridge. He was probably hopeful that the sight of his army outside the city would make the Vitellianists surrender unconditionally. He told his troops that next day they would go against the capital. But they clamored for immediate action. Eventually, worried that his men would storm the city anyway and go on an unrestrained rampage even worse than Cremona, he gave in to them. He passed on instructions for the order of the advance, then gave the command to prepare to march.

Primus's army advanced on Rome in three columns. We don't know in which column the men of the 3rd Gallica marched. But Chief Centurion Varus was at their head, and Centurions Gallus and Julius, if they had survived the Battle of Cremona, were here with their men. The attack proceeded quickly. One column continued straight down the Flaminian Way. Another marched along the bank of the winding Tiber. The third swung east, linked up with General Cerialis's re-formed cavalry, and advanced down the Salarian Way. As they approached the city, Primus's troops could see the standards of various Vitellianist units displayed on the hills of

Rome, but they knew that most of these represented hastily drafted citizen-soldiers who had few arms and no training.

Thousands of city residents with a few swords, sticks, and shields flooded out to bar the army's progress beyond the suburbs. A charge by General Primus's cavalry quickly scattered them. Now three groups of professional soldiers loyal to Vitellius tried to counter each of the three prongs of the advance. The German Guard was prominent, as were three thousand men of the City Guard. They were all vastly outnumbered. Limited resistance was put up before Vitellius's troops withdrew into the city. They were subsequently able to slow the advance several times. On one occasion it was at the Gardens of Sallust in the northeastern suburbs of the city, where the defenders stood on the garden walls raining rocks and javelins onto the legionaries. General Cerialis's cavalry soon drove the defenders from the gardens, then pushed on and forced their way through the still open Colline Gate. In the northwest of the city a brief delay was experienced by one of the three Vespasianist columns when an opposition defensive line formed in their path on the Field of Mars. After brief fighting, the outnumbered Vitellianist cohorts fell back. Finally, by the afternoon, the city's last organized defenders had been driven into the castlelike Praetorian Guards' barracks, the Castra Praetoria, in the 4th Precinct.

That afternoon, in the city streets, residents who favored neither side in the war or were certain that Vespasian had as good as won it, still frequented taverns and baths as if it were an ordinary day. Straggling defenders were hunted down in stores and private homes as passersby pointed them out to the advancing troops of Vespasian. Prostitutes went about their trade, ignoring the corpses of fallen soldiers lying in the street.

The end was inevitable. Only the Praetorian barracks remained to be dealt with. Here, surrounding the tall walls and solid guard towers, the best legions, especially the 3rd Gallica, were in their element. They brought up their artillery, formed their testudos, and went to work at the two main gates with fire and steel. Eventually the gates, which had been built to hold out the public but not an army, gave way. The disciplined cohorts drove in through the two high, arched gateways in their tight formations and slaughtered the defenders who bravely stood against them inside. Many defenders preferred death to surrender. Rome was taken in a day. Cassius Dio was to say that fifty thousand died in the assault, although this may have been an inflated figure.

When Vitellius heard that Vespasian's troops had entered the city, and while the assault on the Praetorian barracks was still consuming the attention of the invaders, Vitellius slipped out the backdoor of the Palatium. With vague plans to escape the city and join his brother's troops in Campania, he was carried in a litter to his wife's house on the Aventine Way. Then he changed his mind and had himself returned to the palace. On his return, he found that his servants had fled. Not a single bodyguard remained with him. In his eight months in office, Vitellius had squandered an estimated 900 million sesterces. One of his banquets alone, according to Suetonius, had cost the taxpayers 400,000 sesterces. Now no amount of gold would buy Vitellius safety.

Alone in the vast palace, he tried to close massive doors but couldn't. Changing into a servant's clothing, he hid in the servants' quarters. Before long, Vitellius was dragged from his hiding place by Colonel Julius Placidus, a tribune with either the Night Watch or the City Guard. To win favor with Vespasian's army, Colonel Placidus and the men with him decided to publicly execute Vitellius. They roughly bound his hands behind his back, then led him from the palace. He was surrounded by Night Watch troops and civilians who jeered him and made fun of his limp—his hip had been injured after he'd been run over in a chariot race with the emperor Caligula in his younger days.

On the way to the Forum, a member of the German Guard stepped into the party's path. As the German drew his sword, the members of the escort didn't know whether he was planning to kill Vitellius or save him. Then he struck, at Colonel Placidus. The bareheaded Placidus tried to duck out of the way of the German's blow, but wasn't quick enough. The blade sliced off his ear. Recovering from their surprise, Placidus's soldiers cut down the German.

The now bloodied procession continued to the Forum. When Vitellius's treble chins dropped onto his chest, he was forced to look up, at swordpoint, and take in the spot where the emperor Galba, one of his recent predecessors, had been murdered. All around them, a noisy crowd was gathering. The same mob that had urged Vitellius to stay on as their emperor now pulled down his statues and called him names. At the Gemonian Stairs, where Sabinus's headless body had been displayed, a tribune heaped insults on Vitellius, to the pleasure of the mob.

Vitellius, stunned more than frightened, looked around their hate-filled faces and said, shaking his head, "Yet, I was your emperor."

Before he could say another word, swords were thrust into him from every quarter, and he fell dead in front of the cheering crowd.

Rome had fallen. Still the men of the 3rd Gallica roamed the streets, looting the homes of known Vitellius sympathizers and cutting down anyone who looked like a Vitellianist soldier disguised in civilian dress.

The men of the detachment led by Centurion Julius who had escorted Paul of Tarsus to Rome almost ten years earlier would have noticed much change in the city. In some places there was still-blackened rubble from the Great Fire five years back, but much reconstruction had been undertaken since the fire had leveled three of Rome's fourteen precincts and destroyed much in another seven. Nero's new building regulations had resulted in wider streets, in height restrictions, in new buildings constructed all of stone, in the use of open spaces, in colonnades as fire barriers, and in increased access to piped water for firefighting.

The 3rd Gallica soldiers saw the Colossus, the giant statue of Nero, 120 feet tall, that he'd erected outside the Golden House. And if they stopped looting long enough, they would have noticed that the nearby housing block on the Triumphant Way was now occupied by an ornamental fish pond, the Stagnum Neronus, also created by Nero. There had stood the house Paul of Tarsus had occupied for two years under house arrest. Like all the properties on that block, the apostle's residence had been destroyed in the fire.

General Primus, even though he personally looted the Palatium of money and slaves, wanted to get his troops out of the city quickly, before they did too much damage. The last thing his reputation needed was another Cremona. He had a good excuse: Lucius Vitellius, the dead emperor's brother, was still on the loose in Campania with a force of six thousand Praetorian infantry and five hundred cavalry. Appointing Centurion Varus of the 3rd Gallica to the powerful post of Prefect of the Praetorian Guard—in effect, police chief of Rome—and leaving a detachment of auxiliary troops with him to secure the capital, Primus marched his legions out of the city to deal with the last of the Vitellianist forces.

Within days, Lucius Vitellius and his troops surrendered in Campania. Closely guarded by Primus's legions, the haughty Praetorians were marched back along the road to Rome in a long, drawn-out line, silent, and defiant despite their situation. Lucius Vitellius himself was thrown into the city prison, and was executed shortly thereafter. His disarmed Praetorians were dismissed from the army, without retirement benefits.

The day after Rome was taken, Field Marshal Mucianus arrived with the 6th Ferrata Legion and the rest of his troops from Syria. With the civil war now over, the Senate met on December 21 and unanimously declared Vespasian the new emperor of Rome, after which he took the title Caesar Vespasianus Flavianus. They also declared a Triumph for Field Marshal Mucianus, as Vespasian's commander in chief. Officially, a Triumph could not be granted for a victory over Roman citizens, so the ingratiating Senate announced that the award was for Mucianus's successful action against the

Dacian raiders in Moesia on his way to Rome. To General Primus the Senate awarded consular rank—the brigadier general was now a lieutenant general. They awarded Chief Centurion Arrius Varus of the 3rd Gallica Legion praetor status—the equivalent of promotion from captain to major general. And they stripped Major General Tettius Julianus, the commander of the 7th Claudia Legion who had gone into hiding in Pannonia, of his rank.

As Vespasian's forces were ordered into winter quarters, every man was awarded a victory bonus—a measly 100 sesterces each. Field Marshal Mucianus promptly sent Primus's own unit, the 7th Galbiana Legion, back to its station in Pannonia. For other troops, it was tents on the Field of Mars outside Rome. But one legion received special treatment. The 3rd Gallica was sent south to Capua, in Campania. This beautiful little city had supported Vitellius to the very end. A favorite resort of the wealthy nobles of Rome, it was filled with expensive villas, which were filled with valuable contents. This was like sending a kleptomaniac into an unattended department store. The 3rd Gallica marched down to Capua, set up camp, and, as the winter dragged by, its legionaries looted the nearby properties with regularity. In Rome, the new administration turned a deaf ear to complaints from Capua about the Gallicans. At least, down there, the Syrian legionaries weren't up to their greedy tricks in the capital, and weren't leading other troops astray.

Field Marshal Mucianus quickly took control at Rome on Vespasian's behalf. To begin with, there was a major revolt on the Rhine to deal with. The Batavian Julius Civilis had taken General Primus's suggestion to heart and created a "demonstration" on the Rhine. Thousands of auxiliaries from Batavia, Trier, and elsewhere had risen in revolt under Civilis, with the aim of creating their own empire in Gaul. They had wiped out the cohorts of several legions based on the Rhine, killed several Roman generals, and had compelled the remaining legionaries of the Armies of the Lower Rhine and Upper Rhine to join the revolt. Every Roman legion base from the North Sea to Switzerland had been taken. Mucianus now dispatched Vespasian's cousin Major General Cerialis and an old retired lieutenant general, Annius Gallus, to lead an army to put down the Civilis Revolt. Seven legions, including the 8th Augusta from General Primus's victorious army, would soon converge on the Rhine. While gout-ridden old General Gallus traveled slowly north in a litter, General Cerialis, anxious to redeem his reputation after failing to rescue the emperor's brother, galloped north with the Singularian Horse. Outside Cremona he picked up the six cohorts of the 21st Rapax Legion left there by General Primus, along with a number of auxiliaries, and headed for the Alps and the Rhine.

Soon Field Marshal Mucianus would depart for Lyons in France to coordinate operations on the Rhine, taking the young prince Domitian with him. But before he did that, Mucianus set in train a number of legion transfers. One involved a new assignment for the 3rd Gallica. But the legion's destination was not to be the Rhine.

XXV

THANKS TO THE
3RD GALLICA

hile most of the cohorts of the 3rd Gallica Legion were leading the overthrow of the emperor Vitellius at Rome, a lone cohort from the legion had remained behind the walls of Ascalon, on the Mediterranean coast south of Jerusalem. In Egypt, the man the Gallicans had chosen as their emperor, Vespasian, had by late December learned of the defeat of Vitellius's army at Cremona. He knew that either via abdication or force Vitellius himself would soon be removed from power, as both Primus's and Mucianus's armies closed in on Rome. Vespasian was still unaware that on December 21 the Senate had officially proclaimed him emperor, when he bade farewell to his son Titus, who, on his orders, was to march from Egypt to take charge of Roman forces in Judea. Titus, who would turn thirty on December 30, had been instructed by his father to take Jerusalem from the Jewish rebels and bring the three-year-old Jewish Revolt to an end.

In the last days of A.D. 69, Titus left his father in Alexandria, taking his troops by sea to the far side of the Nile before commencing the overland march. As his chief of staff he took with him the astute Tiberius Alexander, Prefect of Egypt. Another officer on Titus's staff was the tribune Heternius Fronto, an old friend—the pair had served together as auxiliary cohort commanders attached to the 2nd Augusta Legion in Britain earlier in their careers. Colonel Fronto led the four cohorts of the 18th Legion that had been levied in Libya before being stranded in Egypt by the Jewish uprising. Titus also added to his column auxiliaries and Evocati militia veterans who had retired in Egypt.

From Egypt, Titus marched his eclectic force up the Mediterranean coast of Idumaea. At Ascalon he brought the 3rd Gallica cohort into his force, leaving auxiliaries to take their place as the garrison of Ascalon. Titus continued north to Caesarea, passing through the blackened town of Joppa, which had been raided in A.D. 66 and again in 67 and now had a permanent garrison of Roman auxiliaries in a hilltop fort. Already in camp at the Judean capital when Titus reached it were the 15th Apollonaris Legion and large numbers of auxiliaries and allied troops.

At the start of the spring of A.D. 70, the 12th Fulminata Legion marched down from Laodicea in Syria to join the buildup, bringing three thousand auxiliary troops with it from the Euphrates for rear-echelon duties. At his operational headquarters in Caesarea, young Titus, until recently a mere colonel but now vested with all the powers of a field marshal, gathered his staff around him and commenced planning for a final, decisive Judean offensive.

The coordinated advance began in the middle of spring—the 12th and 15th Legions set out from Caesarea accompanied by the men of the 18th Legion and the single cohort of the 3rd Gallica. The 10th Legion advanced on Jerusalem from its camp at Jericho, and the 5th Macedonica set off from its camp at Emmaus, just northwest of Jerusalem. By early May, Titus had surrounded Jerusalem and begun his assault on the city.

In Italy, the six 3rd Gallica cohorts at Capua received their marching orders. Field Marshal Mucianus had rapidly consolidated his control, easing the instruments of power away from General Primus and his colleague Arrius Varus of the 3rd Gallica, the men chiefly responsible for bringing Vitellius down. Apart from his promotion to lieutenant general, Primus received no official appointment. And immediately following the fall of Rome in the third week of December, Primus's own legion, the 7th Galbiana, had been sent back to Pannonia by Mucianus, to be stationed at Carnuntum. There, in A.D. 70–71, the legion, which had suffered heavy casualties at the Battle of Cremona, would be combined with survivors from the 18th Legion to create the new 7th Gemina Legion.

In the spring of A.D. 70, Mucianus, acting on behalf of Vespasian, removed Arrius Varus, the former 3rd Gallica centurion, from his brief tenure as Prefect of the Praetorian Guard. He gave him a new appointment at Rome, Commissioner of the Grain Supply. This was still an important post, but it lacked the military power of the colonelcy of the Guard. At the same time, the men of the 3rd Gallica at Capua, "the former troops of Varus," as Tacitus describes them, were ordered to march back to Syria. Their new base was to be at Raphanaea, in the south of the province. Some would see this as a reward for the legion, but in reality Mucianus was moving the Gallicans out of reach of Varus and Primus, to whom they could be expected to show their first loyalty. After all, the 3rd Gallica had been the legion that had inspired and led the movement for Vespasian in the West. Rome had now experienced four emperors within twelve months. With all four having gained the throne of the Caesars through the efforts of the military, Mucianus was removing from conceited but popular Primus both the temptations and the tools for a tilt of his own at the throne.

When the six cohorts of the 3rd Gallica Legion marched out of Italy for the long journey back to Syria, they took with them moneybags bulging with gold. Who would have thought, after the way the legion had been savaged in the early stages of the Jewish Revolt, that this would turn out to be the most profitable enlistment in the legion's history? In two memorable years they had stripped the Roxolani and had sacked Cremona, Rome, and Capua.

By the time the legion reached their new Syrian station in the summer, its "lost" cohort was heavily engaged in the siege of Jerusalem. In July, two months into the siege, when the 5th Macedonica Legion encountered difficulties in its sector during the assault on the Antonia fortress, Legionary Sabinus of the 3rd Gallica rose to prominence. Titus had broken through Jerusalem's Third Wall, its outer defense. He had subsequently built his own wall of circumvallation around the city to cut it off from the outside world. He then concentrated on the Second Wall, which incorporated the Temple and the Antonia Fortress, with each of his four main legions assigned a different operational sector.

On July 20, Moesian legionaries of the 5th Macedonica Legion had attacked the Antonia with siege towers and battering rams, without success. Another party, using a testudo, had removed four large stones from the wall using crowbars, before being forced to retreat. In the night, part of the wall gave way. But the next morning, Rome's legionaries saw that inside the Antonia's outer wall the Jewish defenders had built another high wall from rubble. This meant that the attackers would have to start all over again.

Addressing a special morning assembly of his best troops, Titus called for volunteers to scale the new wall. It was now that Legionary Sabinus of the 3rd Gallica stepped up. He was a small, slender man with dark, shrunken skin who looked anything but a soldier, according to Josephus. The Syrian legionary volunteered to scale the wall, and eleven other men from various legions followed his example. The twelve volunteers moved into position. A little before 11:00 A.M., with his shield raised over his head and his sword drawn, Sabinus moved forward to the pile of rubble.

The other men followed close behind as, from their lines, thousands of their comrades roared encouragement.

As the Jewish defenders rained javelins, arrows, and stones on him, Sabinus seemed to be charmed—nothing touched him as he clambered up the pile of stones at amazing speed. Behind him, three men fell back, wounded. The other eight, inspired by Sabinus, kept climbing, slipping, and stumbling on the rocks as they tried to ward off missiles coming down at them while they scaled the wall. The partisans on top of the wall could not believe what they were seeing. Sabinus seemed unstoppable. Ignoring missiles coming his way, he climbed with the sureness and rapidity of a monkey. As he mounted the top of the wall, the defenders turned and fled, thinking he must be some sort of superman. Sabinus turned and, grinning, waved his sword triumphantly to his lines, from where Titus and the rest of the army were watching. The Romans cheered.

Then Sabinus lost his footing and fell headlong into the midst of the Jewish defenses. He landed with a clatter of his segmented metal armor. The noise caused the fleeing Jews to turn around. Seeing the "superman" lying in the dust, they found new courage and rushed back. Sabinus put up a valiant fight, but eventually, with a roar of victory, his attackers at last ended the life of the plucky Syrian legionary from the 3rd Gallica. Three more Roman volunteers who reached the top of the wall also were killed. Although this particular attack failed, the Antonia Fortress was taken two days later.

As the siege continued, Syrian troops in Titus's army were guilty of murdering prisoners, in the quest for gold. It became known that some Jews who had escaped the city and given themselves up to the Roman army had swallowed gold coins, to hide them. Syrian troops and Arab auxiliaries began slitting open prisoners' bellies, looking for the treasure. According to Josephus, both legionaries and auxiliaries were involved, implicating men of the 3rd Gallica cohort. Titus called a meeting of the legion and auxiliary commanders and issued a strict order forbidding any repeat of such barbarous activity, on pain of death.

By the end of September, Jerusalem had fallen to the Roman army. According to Josephus, 1.1 million Jews had died during the siege and 97,000 were taken prisoner. As Titus departed, the 10th Legion was commencing the wholesale destruction of the Jewish Temple and the city, on his orders. The other Roman units were sent to new postings. And for the first time since the spring of A.D. 68, the 3rd Gallica's "lost" cohort was reunited with the remainder of the legion when it marched into Raphanaea.

The 3rd Gallica Legion saw no more combat during its enlistment. The next decade consisted of boring garrison duty in Syria. By the time the 3rd Gallica underwent its twenty-year discharge in A.D. 80, Titus was their new emperor—Vespasian had died, of natural causes, the previous year. Many Gallicans took their discharge and went into wealthy retirement in Syria that year. They went to fifty-acre land grants with their booty from twenty years in military service, plus their 12,000-sesterce retirement bonus. A new enlistment of young Syrians brought the legion back to full strength for the first time since the beginning of the Jewish Revolt.

In A.D. 81, Titus officially opened a new stone amphitheater at Rome. Called the Hunting Theater, it was designed for wild-beast hunts, and replaced the wooden 29 B.C. Theater of Taurus, destroyed in the Great Fire of A.D. 64. The site of the Hunting Theater was Nero's fishpond. It had been drained, and in A.D. 72 Vespasian had personally turned the first sod at the construction site. The emperor Trajan would relocate the giant statue of Nero, the Colossus, to stand outside the Hunting Theater, and as a result the theater acquired a new name: the Colosseum. When Titus died, again of natural causes, in the same year the Colosseum opened, Vespasian's youngest son, Domitian, took the throne. Domitian gave the legions their first pay raise in 150 years, increasing their annual salary from 900 sesterces to 1,200 sesterces.

From their Syrian base, the men of the Gallica learned how the fates of men linked to the legion played out with varying endings over these years. They were to never again hear of General Marcus Antonius Primus, or of Arrius Varus, the former 3rd Gallica centurion. As for Aulus Caecina, Vitellius's former flamboyant general, Vespasian not only pardoned him but also made him a consul. But in A.D. 79 Titus, who had become his father's Prefect of the Praetorian Guard, executed Caecina at a banquet at Rome after he had been implicated in a plot against Vespasian.

Vespasian's cousin General Cerialis put down the Civilis Revolt by the end of A.D. 70, and all the Rhine bases returned to Roman control. Vespasian abolished several of the legions that had gone over to Civilis, including the 1st. Cerialis, made a consul by Vespasian, then went to Britain as governor and conquered Brigantia, today's Yorkshire, expanding Roman control farther north in Britain.

Cornelius Fuscus, the Procurator of Pannonia who had worked closely with Primus to initiate the pro-Vespasian movement in Pannonia and who later became admiral of the Adriatic Fleet, was made Prefect of the Praetorian Guard by Domitian. In A.D. 86, leading an army into Dacia, Fuscus was killed. During this campaign one of his legions, the 21st Rapax, lost its eagle and was wiped out, apparently on the march. The Rapax was never re-formed. In this battle, the curved Dacian sword, the scimitar, proved to possess, like the curved Japanese samurai sword, incredible cutting power. It had sliced through Roman helmets, splitting open the heads of legionaries of the Rapax. As a result, all Roman helmets soon received a cruciform metal reinforcement on top, to provide better protection.

Tettius Julianus, former disgraced commander of the 7th Claudia Legion, regained favor and rank under Domitian. Leading another Roman force into Dacia in A.D. 89, General Julianus defeated a Dacian army under their leading general, Vezinas, at Tapae, before withdrawing to Moesia.

And then there was Titus Manlius Valens, the elderly brigadier general of the 1st Italica Legion at the Battle of Cremona. General Valens not only survived the Cremona battle, he lived to age ninety. During his twilight years he was made a praetor by one of the Flavian emperors. And in A.D. 96, when Valens was ninety, Domitian appointed him consul. Consul Valens died in office, but he had achieved the great distinction of having his name attached to the year. The reviled emperor Domitian was assassinated later that same year, to be replaced on the throne by the elderly senator Nerva.

Joining the 3rd Gallica at its Raphanaea base in A.D. 87 as a tribune was Gaius Plinius, who would become famous as the letter-writer Pliny the Younger. While with the 3rd Gallica he undertook an audit of the books of the auxiliary units attached to the legion and found a number of irregularities. The conscientious Pliny went on to become a consul, and by A.D. 111 he was governor of the province of Bithynia-Pontus. There he threw himself into the task of rubbing out the growing Christian sect that had been planted in the province by the apostle Paul in the previous century. Describing Christianity as "a degenerate sort of cult carried to extravagant lengths," Pliny rounded up suspects and asked each thee times if they were Christians. If they denied Christ and sacrificed to the emperor Trajan, they were set free. Many displayed "unshakable obstinacy" in Pliny's own words, and would not deny their faith. Roman citizens among them were sent to Rome for trial. Most were not citizens, and they suffered crucifixion or death in the arena. Pliny also had some noncitizens tortured to obtain confessions, among them two female deacons of the church in Bithynia-Pontus.

The emperor Trajan, Nerva's successor, wrote to Pliny that the punishment of admitted Christians was correct. Roman citizens who confessed to a belief in the divinity of Jesus of Nazareth should be, he told Pliny, "sent in chains to the officers in charge of my Praetorian cohorts." But the emperor urged his governor to ignore anonymous pamphlets then circulating that accused people by name of being Christians. Such accusatory pamphlets were, Trajan said, "quite out of keeping with our age."

The 3rd Gallica Legion served in the Second Jewish Revolt in Judea in A.D. 132–135, a bloody conflict that resulted in the emperor Hadrian banning Jews from Judea. In the reign of Septimius Severus, Syria was divided into several provinces, with the 3rd Gallica's home becoming the province of Syria Phoenicia. By the fourth century, the legion was stationed at Danaba, a legion base on the Palmyra road outside Damascus. During these later centuries the 3rd Gallica was involved in Roman pushes east. They took part in battles against the Sassanid Persians, who superseded the Parthians and several times defeated Roman armies, and in internal and internecine wars when emperors and pretenders fought for the throne of Rome as the empire began its decline.

Little of the activities of the legion in these later times was recorded. But nothing could compare to the exploits of the 3rd Gallica during the first centuries B.C. and A.D. Thanks to the 3rd Gallica Legion, Rome had defeated the dashing prince Pacorus and the opportunistic Quintus Labienus, and retrieved Syria and Cilicia from the Parthians. Thanks to the 3rd Gallica, King Herod was able to secure his throne in Judea. Thanks to the 3rd Gallica, Mark Antony had survived his botched campaign against the Parthians. Thanks to the 3rd Gallica, Corbulo had regained Armenia for Rome. Thanks to the 3rd Gallica, the Roxolani Sarmatians did not again attempt to cross the Danube until the following century. Thanks to the 3rd Gallica, two Jewish revolts were put down. Thanks to the 3rd Gallica, Vespasian became emperor of Rome and restored the empire's stability and prosperity.

But there is one other great achievement of the 3rd Gallica Legion, one for which it has not been given credit by history. Not once, not twice, but three times between A.D. 58 and A.D. 60, officers and men of the 3rd Gallica Legion saved the life of the Christian apostle Paul, and gave him as many as nine more years for his ministry. First they saved him at the Temple, then in the night dash from Jerusalem to Caesarea, then on the Maltese shore. Had Paul died on any of these occasions, he would not have reached Rome, would not have nurtured the Christian church there that blossomed following his death. And he would not have continued his work, which saw more congregations grow in both the East and the West.

It was at Rome, center of the ancient world, that Christianity took firm root following Paul's death. After A.D. 70, and the death of more than a million Jews in Vespasian's and Titus's methodical completion of the Judean offensive, Jerusalem was no longer the center of the Christian church, and most of the Jewish leaders of that church were dead. The Christian movement founded by Paul in the eastern provinces and promoted at Rome, the church of the Gentiles, survived to become the Christian church of today. Without Paul, and his work at Rome and elsewhere, Christianity itself may have died.

In the lifetime of the first Christian Roman emperor, Constantine, in the fourth century, Rome possessed a large congregation, an influential bishop, and the first major Christian cathedrals, of Saint Peter and the Basilica of Constantine—now Saint Giovanni in Laterano. Only through the emperor's patronage was it possible to integrate Christianity with pagan practices and eventually supersede them. Without that patronage, a Christian complexion could not have successfully been given to pagan religious festivals and observances, Christian patron saints would not have replaced pagan patron deities, roadside pagan shrines would not have been replaced by Christian variants.

If Constantine had not converted to Christianity and supported the Christian church during his lifetime, it is quite probable that Christianity would not exist today as we know it. Or perhaps it would not exist at all. And if we accept that Paul personally founded the Christian church in Spain following his two years at Rome, there is good reason to contend that Constantine would not have converted to Christianity, because some scholars believe that the Spanish bishop Hosius, who is known to be Constantine's spiritual adviser in later years, may have been the one to convert Constantine to Christianity in the first place. No Paul, no Christian church in Spain, and no Bishop Hosius.

Would the Christian church at Rome have survived, or grown, if Paul had not spent several years there? Would the church have developed in Spain without Paul's influence? Who knows? Two things are certain. The last decade of Paul's life, as celebrated in his New Testament letters, was his most influential. And the 3rd Gallica Legion gave him that last decade.

This has been their story. Centurion Julius and Prefect Lysias, the apostle Paul's saviors. Centurion Varus, veteran of Armenia, the Roxolani battle, and the Battles of Cremona and Rome. Camp Prefect Metilius of the doomed Jerusalem garrison. Centurion Antonius, victor at Ascalon, victim at Jefat. Centurion Gallus, who hid with his men in the rafters at Gamala. Legionary Volusius, winner of the Mural Crown at Cremona. Legionary Sabinus, who perished before he could receive a golden crown at Jerusalem. And thousands of other nameless Gallic conscripts and greedy sun-worshipping Syrians who marched and fought and died in the ranks of the 3rd Gallica Legion.

The Gallicans made a king, they made an emperor, using their muscle to install Herod the Great and Caesar Vespasian on their thrones. They made Rome's enemies from one side of the empire to the other dread their legion's name, and not a few of their fellow Romans besides. They made their names as the fearless servants of two Mark Antonys—saving the skin of Cleopatra's lover and making possible the meteoric career of Mark Antony Primus. They truly had been Mark Antony's heroes.

APPENDIX A

IMPERIAL ROMAN MILITARY RANKS AND THEIR MODERN-DAY EQUIVALENTS
(IN ORDER OF PRECEDENCE)

Army

Rank	Description	Equivalent
Miles gregarius	Literally, a "common soldier" of the legion.	Private
Signifer	Standard-bearer for legion cohort and maniple. No real authority. Unit banker.	Corporal
Aquilifer	Eagle-bearer of the legion. Most prestigious post for a standard-bearer.	Corporal
Tesserarius	Orderly sergeant; sergeant of the guard.	Sergeant
Optio	Second-in-command of a century and of a cavalry squadron. Unit training, administration, and records officer.	Sergeant major
Decurio	Decurion. Cavalry officer, commanding a squadron of cavalry. Several grades, based on length of service.	Second lieutenant
Centurio	Centurion. Officer commanding a century, maniple, and cohort. Sixty to a legion, including six *primi ordines*. Eleven grades, including *primi ordines* and *primus pilus*. Seniority usually determined by length of service.	First lieutenant
Primi ordines	Six most senior "first rank" centurions of a legion, serving in the first, double cohort.	Captain

Primus pilus	Literally the "first spear," a legion's most senior centurion, one of the *primi ordines*.	Captain
Praefectus castrorium	Camp prefect. A former centurion, the third in command of a legion; quartermaster, and officer in charge of major derachments separated from the legion.	Lieutenant colonel
Tribunus angusticlavius	Tribune of the thin stripe, a staff officer serving a six-month officer cadetship.	Lieutenant colonel
Praefectus	Commander of an auxiliary cohort or wing.	Colonel
Tribunus laticlavius	Tribune of the broad stripe, second in command of a legion, and commander of Praetorian Guard/City Guard cohorts. Also called military tribune. Had first to serve as prefect of auxiliaries. Because of limited positions, Claudius began appointing "supernumerary" tribunes, who didn't serve but still moved up the promotional ladder.	Colonel
Praefectus praetoria	One of two commanders of the Praetorian Guard, of equal rank. While nominally prefects of the guard held the rank of colonel, some rose through the ranks and were former centurions, while others were ex-generals. On occasion they commanded field armies.	Colonel
Legatus legionis	Legate of the legion. Legion commander. Of senatorial rank.	Brigadier general
Praetor	A senior magistrate at Rome, second only to the consuls. Praetors and former praetors could command a legion and armies in the field.	Major general
Consul	The highest official at Rome after the emperor. The two consuls for the year shared the presidency of the Senate and gave their names to the year. Consuls or former consuls normally commanded Roman field armies. Seniority was determined by the number of consulships held and when.	Lieutenant general
Propraetor	Governor of an imperial province. A former consul. (See GLOSSARY for details.)	Lieutenant general
Proconsul	Governor of a Senatorial province. A former consul. (See GLOSSARY for details.)	Lieutenant general

Navy

Miles classicus	A soldier in the Marine Corps.	Enlisted marine
Centurio classicus	Centurion of marines.	Lieutenant
Navarchus	Commander of a warship in the Roman navy.	Captain (naval)
Praefectus classicus	Commander of a Roman navy squadron or fleet.	Admiral

APPENDIX B

THE GERMAN GUARD

Down through the ages military autocrats have created special units to serve as their personal bodyguard. Napoleon had his Gendarmerie d'Élite, Hitler the SS Leibestandarte. Julius Caesar used a handpicked group of German cavalrymen. For his part, Augustus instituted the German Guard as the bodyguard of the emperors of Rome.

Variously called "the Bodyguard," "the German Cohorts," "the Imperial Guard," and "the German Guard" by classical and later historical writers, the Cohortes Germanor comprised an elite auxiliary unit that served as the personal bodyguard of the emperor, and was quite separate from the Praetorian Guard. Unlike the Praetorians, the men of the German Guard were not Roman citizens, and for that reason their unit, like most auxiliary units, was little documented by classical authors.

From Suetonius we know that during the reign of Caligula, in about A.D. 40, at least one cohort of the German Guard was made up of Batavians. It's likely that men for the unit were recruited from areas in modern Germany, Holland, Luxembourg, Belgium, and Switzerland.

Augustus formed the unit after he came to power in 30 B.C., influenced, no doubt, by the fact that Julius Caesar had used German cavalrymen as his personal bodyguards during the Gallic War and the civil war. Augustus briefly lost faith in his bodyguard in A.D. 9 after Arminius, or Hermann, wiped out Varus's three legions in the Teutoburg Forest. According to Suetonius, suddenly suspicious of all Germans, Augustus had the men of the German Guard assigned to various Italian islands for a time, until the German scare passed and the paranoia dissolved. And even when he allowed the German Guard back into Rome, he abolished one of their cohorts.

Members of this unit stood some four inches taller than legionaries. Their principal armament was the German-style spear, up to twelve feet long, with sidearms of a dagger and a long sword like that used by most German fighting men and all Roman cavalry, with a blunt, rounded end.

251

Their shield was large, flat, and oval, like that of other auxiliary infantry units, and decorated with a spiral Celtic motif. While on duty at Rome, spear and shield were stored away in an arsenal, as troops in the city were permitted to be armed with swords only. Like all auxiliary units, the German Guard wore breeches—calf-length trousers—and each cohort marched behind a square cloth banner, a *vexillum*, rather than a legion-style standard.

There is only one instance of the German Guard serving outside Rome other than as the bodyguard of the emperor, when in A.D. 14, shortly after the death of Augustus, Tiberius sent picked men of the unit with his son Drusus to bolster two Praetorian cohorts assigned to putting down the mutiny of three legions in Pannonia, a task they achieved with brutal efficiency.

According to Josephus (*Antiquities*), the German Guard was of legion strength: ten cohorts, each of 480 men. But unlike a legion, each cohort would have been commanded by a prefect. Suetonius says that Augustus allowed only three cohorts of the German Guard to be on duty in Rome at any one time, and that other cohorts of the unit were quartered on rotation in towns near Rome. Almost certainly this included the well-fortified Alba Fucens, the modern Albe, famous in the first century B.C. as a garrison and prison town and by the third century the permanent station of one legion. Suetonius also stated that the German Guard had no separate barracks in the city—apparently the duty cohorts were quartered at the Palatium. During the war of succession following the death of Nero, three German Guard cohorts stormed the Capitol in December A.D. 69.

One of the tasks of the German Guard was to search all persons for weapons, irrespective of rank, age, or sex, before they entered the emperor's presence. This practice was inaugurated by Augustus when reducing the Senate, but discontinued by Vespasian when he came to power. Suetonius indicates that Claudius was the first emperor to have armed German Guards on duty at his banquets, a practice applied through many later imperial reigns.

During the arrests and investigations that Nero instigated after the discovery of the Piso plot against his life in A.D. 65, men of the German Guard were included in all detachments of soldiers sent throughout city and countryside in search of suspects. Tacitus says that Nero felt he could count on the loyalty of the Germans because they were foreigners. They went along to ensure that the Praetorians did their job.

Yet, for all their impressive appearance, the men of the German Guard weren't all that successful at their job as bodyguards, with many emperors being murdered right under their noses. The long list of failures began in A.D. 41, when they were unable to protect Caligula from their own commander, Cornelius Sabinus, and Cassius Chaerea, Prefect of the Praetorian Guard. Following Caligula's murder the German Guard was in disarray. Dio and Suetonius say they went on an indiscriminate rampage, killing innocent people, including several senators. They then began fighting among themselves.

According to Josephus, the three cohorts of the German Guard on duty in Rome at the time of Caligula's murder seized the Capitol and Senate House, on Senate orders. With Claudius under the protection of the Praetorian Guard at their barracks, the Senate, protected by the German Guard, next day met to discuss a suitable successor to Caligula, ignoring the fact that the Praetorians had already chosen Claudius as emperor. As the debate continued, says Josephus, it became clear to the men of the German Guard that the Senate expected them to fight the Praetorians to remove Claudius, whom the senators did not consider suitable for the throne. The commander of the German Guard contingent at the Senate House led his men out, declaring that they had nothing against Claudius as emperor and saw no reason to fight the Praetorians, with whom they had "the closest ties" after years of serving side by side at Rome. The German Guard cohorts marched to the Praetorian barracks and joined forces with the Praetorians, forcing the senators to hurry to the barracks and hail Claudius as emperor.

The commander of the German Guard, who reported directly to the emperor, was a prefect, of colonel rank, like the commander of the Praetorian Guard. In A.D. 31 Tiberius appointed Naevius Sertorius Macro to command the German Guard, with a secret brief to overthrow Sejanus, the powerful Prefect of the Praetorian Guard, after which Macro took the executed Sejanus's job as Praetorian prefect.

Caligula appointed gladiators of the Thracian school as the officers of the German Guard. Caligula's Prefect of the German Guard, Colonel Sabinus, would later become a lover of Valeria Messalina, infamous third wife of the emperor Claudius. Not surprisingly, Colonel Sabinus lost his job following the murder of Caligula—but not his life. One account has him falling on his sword after Caligula's assassination, but he survived, with declining fortunes—he had to return to the gladiatorial arena. Fighting in a contest in front of Claudius and Messalina in the Circus Maximus in A.D. 46, when well into his forties, he lost the bout. Unpopular with commoners and nobility, apparently for his arrogance when commander of the bodyguard, Sabinus's fate seemed sealed when the crowd called for him to be killed by the victor of the contest. But Messalina had his life spared, causing a great scandal. Sabinus later committed suicide.

The Prefect of the German Guard in the latter part of the reign of Nero was Colonel Scipulus. Dio says that when the Praetorian Guard convinced the German Guard to join them in deserting Nero in the summer of A.D. 68, the Germans murdered Scipulus before vacating the Palatium and joining the Praetorians at their barracks. According to Suetonius, Galba found men of the German Guard looking lost and wandering around Nero's Golden House when he arrived at Rome, and immediately ordered the unit disbanded. He says Galba repatriated them to Germany, refusing to pay their retirement bonuses because they had been loyal to his opponents.

Otho, who replaced Galba, re-formed the unit. Together with cohorts of the Praetorian Guard and Praetorian cavalry, they accompanied Otho when he withdrew to Brixellum to allow his brother and senior generals to fight his last battle for him at Bedriacum in April A.D. 69. They were guarding Otho's camp when he took his own life, but swore allegiance to the new emperor, Vitellius. This didn't prevent Vitellius from disbanding the existing German Guard and replacing it with his own German auxiliaries.

Soldiers sent by Vitellius to the legions in eastern Europe and the Middle East in A.D. 69 to announce his seizure of Otho's throne are described as having a superior attitude and speaking Latin with coarse accents, and were probably from his German Guard.

Men of the German Guard at Rome were among the last troops to remain loyal to Vitellius. Three cohorts determinedly stormed the Capitol when it was occupied by Vespasian's elder brother Flavius Sabinus, before taking part in the last stand of Vitellius's troops at the Praetorian barracks on December 20, A.D. 69. A lone soldier of the German Guard struck a blow at the leader of Vitellius's execution squad.

It is probable that the German Guard was disbanded by Field Marshal Mucianus on behalf of the emperor Vespasian in December A.D. 69. The unit had been fiercely loyal to Vitellius and had murdered Vespasian's brother. Mucianus, Vespasian's right-hand man, was a pragmatic and efficient manager. There is likely to have been a palace guard to serve Vespasian, built around the force of bodyguards that Vespasian brought with him from the East, many of whom were Germans. But it's unlikely that new recruits were brought into the unit from German auxiliary units, because these units were siding with the Batavian rebel Civilis in his revolt on the Rhine at that time.

The emperor Vespasian shunned a close personal guard. His Palatium at Rome stood open day and night and was unguarded. And he abolished the routine established by Claudius of every person coming into his presence being searched by bodyguards.

There are references to German troops serving as the bodyguards of various later emperors. Vespasian's son Domitian may have re-formed the German Guard. He took a major if inexpert interest in military affairs and did much to ingratiate himself with the Roman army, including giving the legions a pay raise. And he was a man with many enemies. If anyone needed a fierce and fearsome bodyguard unit, it was Domitian. And the reputation of the German auxiliary troops on Rome's payroll filled both criteria.

Cassius Dio says that the emperor Caracalla, who was assassinated by his own officers in A.D. 217, used a bodyguard of Germans and Scythians, free men and slaves, raising them to centurion status and granting them the title "Lions." The Lions seem to have been dissolved after Caracalla's death, for Dio makes no reference to it, nor to the old German Guard, when listing the units of the Roman army of about A.D. 233.

As a former consul and imperial governor, Dio had intimate knowledge of the emperor's bodyguard. But he mentions just one auxiliary unit, the Batavian Horse, successor to the Singularian Horse as household cavalry. Dio doesn't mention the Night Watch or Marine Corps, either, which were recruited from ex-slaves. And the Evocati, the militia of retired legionaries, rates a brief mention, as Dio confesses he had no idea of its strength. So lack of mention of the German Guard is no guarantee it no longer existed.

Later writers say that in A.D. 238 a German Guard was indeed still in existence as the emperor's bodyguard unit, and in that year they failed to save the lives of the joint emperors Balbinus and Maximus, elderly senators only recently appointed by the Senate on the death of the emperor Maximinus. The pair was said to have been dragged naked from the Palatium by the Praetorian Guard and hauled through the streets. Fear of the imminent arrival of cohorts of the German Guard forced the Praetorians to cut short their torture of the pair and put them out of their misery.

Did the German Guard outlast the Praetorian Guard, which was abolished by Constantine in A.D. 312? It's impossible to say. By the fifth century, following the sack of Rome, emperors of the eastern empire were using eunuchs as bodyguards.

All in all, the German Guard did not prove to be a particularly effective imperial bodyguard unit. The best that can be said of it is that its commander rid the world of Caligula and its rank and file were responsible for his uncle Claudius becoming emperor.

APPENDIX C

SOURCES

Primary Sources

The books in this series are based primarily on classical texts, inscriptions, and coins. Some epigraphic material is on stone monuments small and large. Some source material comes from documents inscribed on metal, vellum, and papyrus.

Inscriptions and written records can generally be taken at face value, even if some inscriptions raise more questions than they answer. In the late first century B.C., for example, a number of former legionaries had honorific names inscribed on their tombstones relating to the legions in which they had served, but frequently those honorifics were neither official nor in widespread use and often swiftly disappeared. Classical coins can be an invaluable guide to the stations and movements of Roman legions. The men of the legions were paid with coins minted with the name of their legion and sufficient information to determine the year and location of the minting.

In the more than thirty years of research and writing that went into this book, the many classical and contemporary written sources listed below were consulted. Primarily, this work was made possible by the following classical sources, listed alphabetically.

Acts of the Apostles and the letters of Paul in the **Holy Bible** provide a contemporary insight and an on-the-spot account, from a layman's point of view, of several aspects of legion activity during the first century A.D. Acts gives a detailed account of Paul's arrest in Judea, his rescue by Roman troops, and his later journey to Rome under escort.

Appian. Born in about A.D. 95 at Alexandria, of Greek stock, Appian was an advocate in the courts at Rome and later served as a financial administrator in the provinces. In the middle of the second century he wrote a number of books on Roman history, including his *Civil Wars*. He is the least well regarded of the classical historians of the Roman Empire.

257

Recommended English translations: *Appian: Roman History*, trans. H. White (1889), rev. for Loeb series by I. Robinson (London: Loeb, 1913); and *Appian: The Civil Wars*, trans. J. Carter (London: Penguin, 1996).

Julius Caesar. *The Gallic War* and *The Civil War*, together with *The Alexandrian War, The African War, and The Spanish War* by other hands. The first volumes of Caesar's *Commentaries* deal with his 58–51 B.C. conquest of Gaul and were published in his lifetime. He was still working on his account of the civil war, which leaves off after the Battle of Pharsalus, when he was murdered in 44 B.C. At the urging of Caesar's former chief of staff Lucius Cornelius Balbus, Caesar's staff officer Aulus Hirtius combined Caesar's writings with additional material, some of which he wrote himself, the rest apparently penned by officers involved in the last battles of the civil war, and the collection was published by Balbus. Despite errors, deletions, and propagandist overtones, they provide a fascinating insight into one of history's most brilliant generals.

One of Caesar's loyal generals, Gaius Asinius Pollio, himself a successful author, is quoted by Suetonius as saying that Caesar's memoirs showed signs of carelessness and inaccuracy. He added that Caesar didn't always check the truth of reports that came in, and he had been either disingenuous or forgetful in describing his own actions.

Recommended English translations: Among the best are *The Commentaries of Caesar*, trans. W. Duncan (London: Dodsley, 1779); *Caesar: Commentaries on the Gallic and Civil Wars*, trans. W. A. M'Devitte and W. S. Bohm (London: Bell, 1890); *Caesar: The Gallic War and the Civil War*, trans. T. Rice Holmes, Loeb series (London: 1914–1955); *Caesar: The Conquest of Gaul*, trans. S. A. Handford (1951), rev. J. F. Gardner (1967) (London: Penguin, 1967); and *Caesar: The Civil War*, trans. J. F. Gardner (London: Penguin, 1967).

Cicero. Marcus Tullius Cicero (106–43 B.C.) was one of the most noted orators of his day. A leading senator and famous defense counsel, he was a prodigious author. His collected letters are of most interest when it comes to the legions.

Recommended English translations of his correspondence include: *Cicero: Letters to Atticus*, trans. O. E. Winstedt, Loeb series (Cambridge, Mass.: Harvard University Press, 1912–1958); *Cicero: Letters to His Friends*, trans. W. Glynn Williams, M. Cary, and M. Henderson, Loeb series (Cambridge, Mass.: Harvard University Press, 1912–1958); *Letters of Cicero*, trans. L. P. Wilkinson (London: Hutchinson, 1949); and *Cicero: Selected Letters*, trans. D. R. Shackleton Bailey (London: Penguin, 1986).

Cassius Dio. Also referred to as Dio Cassius and Dion Cassius; his full name was Cassius Dio Cocceianus. Born in Bithynia in about A.D. 150, son of a proconsul, he joined the Senate under the emperor Commodus. Twice a consul, and governor of Africa, Dalmatia, and Upper Pannonia, he had extensive military experience. He wrote a history of the Roman Empire in eighty books in the years leading up to his death in 235. Despite frequent bias and sometime glaring errors, Dio is still a valuable source.

Recommended English translations: *Dio's Roman History*, trans. E. Cary, Loeb series (London: 1914–1927); and *Cassius Dio, the Roman History: The Reign of Augustus*, trans. I. Scott-Kilvert (London: Penguin, 1987).

Josephus. Born in about A.D. 37, Joseph ben Matthias was a young Jewish general who commanded Galilee for the partisans during the first year of the Jewish Revolt of A.D. 66–70 and who later took the Roman name Flavius Josephus after being captured at Jefat in A.D. 67 and becoming a Roman collaborator. He wrote extensively under the patronage of all three Flavian emperors. His *Jewish War*, *Life* (of Josephus), and *Jewish Antiquities* include rare verbatim quotations from letters of Mark Antony and provide great detail on the causes and events of the Jewish Revolt. He died in A.D. 92–93 or 100.

Recommended English translations: *The Jewish War*, trans. H. St. John Thackery, R. Marcus, and L. H. Feldman (London: Loeb, 1926); also, the trans. of G. A. Williamson (London: Penguin, 1959, rev. 1970); *The Complete Works of Josephus*, which includes *Jewish Antiquities*, trans. W. Whiston (1737; repub. as *The New Complete Works of Josephus* [Grand Rapids, Mich.: Kregel, 1999]).

Pliny the Younger. Gaius Plinius Caecilius Secundus, nephew and heir of Pliny the Elder. Second-in-command of the 3rd Gallica Legion at one time, he became a consul in A.D. 100 and governor of Bithynia-Pontus, A.D. 111–113. His correspondence is enlightening.

Recommended English translations: *The Letters of Pliny the Consul*, trans. W. Melmoth (1746; rev. W. M. Hutchinson [London: Loeb, 1915]); *Pliny's Letters*, trans. A. J. Church and W. A. Brodribb (Edinburgh: Blackwood, 1872); and *The Letters of the Younger Pliny*, trans. B. Radice (London: Penguin, 1963).

Plutarch. Plutarchos (A.D. 46–c.120) was a Greek scholar who wrote in the reigns of Roman emperors Nerva, Trajan, and Hadrian. Shakespeare used Plutarch's *Parallel Lives* as the basis for his plays *Julius Caesar* and *Antony and Cleopatra*. This, Plutarch's great work, gives short biographies of numerous historical figures and is a major source on the life of Mark Antony. It also provides background material on key players in the history of the legions: Sulla, Marius, Lucullus, Sertorius, Cato the Younger, Crassus, Pompey the Great, Julius Caesar, Brutus, Cassius, Cicero, and the emperors Galba and Otho.

Recommended English translations: Sir Thomas North's 1579 translation—the one used by Shakespeare—can be heavy going with its Tudor English, but can present a different picture than later versions. Easier reads are John Dryden's *The Lives of the Noble Grecians and Romans* (1683–1686; reprint, Chicago: Encyclopaedia Britannica, 1952); *Plutarch's Lives of Illustrious Men*, trans. J. and W. Lanhome (London: Chatto & Windus, 1875); and *Plutarch's Lives*, trans. B. Perrin, Loeb series (London: Loeb, 1914–1926).

Polybius. This Greek statesman and historian lived between 200 and 118 B.C. Traveling widely, Polybius wrote his *History of Rome* after returning to Greece in 150 B.C. With broad experience of Roman political and military matters he wrote with intelligence and authority about the Roman army of the mid-second century B.C.

Recommended English translations: *The Histories of Polybius*, trans. E. Shuckburgh (London: Macmillan, 1889); *Polybius: Histories*, trans. W. R. Paton (London: Loeb, 1922–1927); and *Polybius: The Rise of the Roman Empire*, trans. I. Scott-Kilvert (London: Penguin, 1979).

Suetonius. Biographer Gaius Suetonius Tranquillus was born in A.D. 69, in the middle of the war of succession that followed Nero's demise. At the time, Suetonius's father was serving as second-in-command of the 13th Gemina Legion. Briefly in charge of the imperial archives and later senior correspondence secretary to the emperor Hadrian, he was fired about A.D. 123 for disrespect to the empress Sabina while Hadrian was away. His subsequent book *Lives of the Caesars* is full of gossip and salted with errors but nonetheless makes interesting reading.

Recommended English translations: *Lives of the Twelve Caesars*, trans. P. Holland (1606; reprint, New York: Limited Editions Club) (1963; rev. trans., London: F. Etchells and H. Macdonald, 1931). A 1796 translation by A. Thompson, Robinson, reprint, Williamstown, Mass.: Corner House (1978); Loeb series, trans J. C. Rolfe (London, 1914); and *The Twelve Caesars*, trans. R. Graves (1957; rev. M. Grant [London: Penguin, 1979]).

Tacitus. Publius Cornelius Tacitus (A.D. 55–117) was the king of Roman historians. His *Annals* and *Histories* and, to a lesser extent, his *Agricola* and *Germania* are treasure troves of information about Rome and her empire in the first century A.D. He was consul in A.D. 97 and governor of Asia in A.D. 112. His books abound with facts and figures taken directly from official records and lost works of other writers, including Pliny the Elder and serving soldiers such as Vipstanus Messalla, deputy commander of the 7th Claudia Legion during the crucial war of succession battles of A.D. 69.

Recommended English translations: *Annals & Histories*, trans. A. J. Church and W. J. Brodribb, London (1869–1872); reprint, Chicago: Encyclopaedia Britannica (1952); also trans. W. Peterson, Loeb series (1914–1937); reprint, Franklin, Pa.: Franklin Library, 1982; *Annals*, trans. M. Grant (London: Penguin, 1966); *Annals*, trans. D. R. Dudley (New York: Mentor, 1966); *History*, trans. A. Murphy (London: Dent, 1900); *The Agricola and The Germania*, trans. A. J. Church and W. J. Brodribb (London: Macmillan, 1869–1872); *Tacitus*; trans. H. Mattingly and S. A. Handford (London: Penguin, 1948); *Tacitus*, a combination of all his works, trans. C. H. Moore and J. Jackson (London: Heinemann/Putnam, 1931).

Virgil. Revered poet Publius Virgilius Maro was a farmer's son. Born in 70 B.C., he was tutored at Rome by Epidius, whose pupils also included Mark Antony and Octavian.

Among the many English translations available: *The Poems of Virgil*, trans. James Rhoades (Chicago: Encyclopedia Britannica, 1952); and H. R. Fairclough's translation for the Loeb series (Cambridge, Mass.: Harvard University Press, 1935).

Additional Sources: A Selected Bibliography

Abbott, F. F., and A. C. Johnson. *Municipal Administration in the Roman Empire*. Princeton, N.J.: Princeton University Press, 1926.

Arrian. *History of Alexander, and Indica*. Translated by P. Brunt. Loeb series. Cambridge, Mass: Harvard University Press, 1976.

Aurelius, M. *Meditations*. Translated by G. Long. Chicago: Encyclopaedia Britannica, 1952.

Azzaroli, A. *An Early History of Horsemanship*. London: E. J. Brill, 1985.

Birley, A. *Marcus Aurelius*. London: Eyre & Spottiswoode, 1966.

Birley, E. *Roman Britain and the Roman Army*. Kendal, U.K.: Titus Wilson, 1953.

Boardman, J., J. Griffin, and O. Murray. *The Oxford History of the Classical World*. Oxford, U.K.: Oxford University Press, 1986.

Bouchier, E. S. *Spain under the Roman Empire*. Oxford, U.K: B. H. Blackwell, 1914.

Boyne, W., with H. Stuart Jones. *A Manual of Roman Coins*. Chicago: Ammon, 1968.

Brogen, O. *Roman Gaul*. London: Bell, 1953.

Broughton, T. R. S. *The Romanization of Africa Proconsularis*. New York: Greenwood, 1968.

Bryant, A. *The Age of Elegance*. London: Collins, 1954.

Buchan, J. *Augustus*. London: Hodder & Stoughton, 1937.

Caracalla. *Historia Augusta*. Loeb series. Cambridge, Mass.: Harvard University Press, 1923.

Carcopino, J. *Daily Life in Ancient Rome*. London: Pelican, 1956.

Casson, L. *Ancient Egypt*. Alexandria, Va.: Time-Life, 1965.

Cave, W. *Lives, Acts, and Martyrdoms of the Holy Apostles*. London: Hatchard, 1836.

Chevalier, R. *Roman Roads*. Translated by N. H. Field. London: Batsford, 1976.

Church, A. J. *Roman Life in the Days of Cicero*. London: Seeley, 1923.

Clausewitz, C. P. G. von. *On War*. Translated by J. J. Graham. New York: Penguin, 1968.

Colledge, M. A. R. *The Parthians*. Leiden: E. J. Brill, 1986.

Collingwood, R. C. *Roman Britain*. Oxford, U.K.: Oxford University Press, 1932.

Cottrell, L. *Enemy of Rome*. London: Pan, 1962.

————. *The Great Invasion*. London: Evans, 1958.

Cowell, F. R. *Cicero and the Roman Republic*. Harmondsworth, U.K.: Penguin, 1956.

Croft, P. *Roman Mythology*. London: Octopus, 1974.

Cunliffe, B. *The Celtic World*. London: Bodley Head, 1979.

———. *The Roman Baths at Bath*. Bath, U.K.: Bath Archeological Trust, 1993.

———. *Rome and Her Empire*. Maidenhead, U.K.: McGraw-Hill, 1978.

Delbruck, H. *History of the Art of War*. Translated by J. Walter Renfroe Jr. Lincoln: University of Nebraska Press, Bison Books, 1990.

Divine, A. *Secrets and Stories of the War: Miracle at Dunkirk*. London: Reader's Digest Association, 1963.

Duff, J. D. *Lucan*. Cambridge, Mass.: Harvard University Press, 1977.

Dupuy, R. E., and T. N. Dupuy. *The Encyclopedia of Military History: From 3500 B.C. to the Present*. London: Military Book Society, 1970.

Emile, T. *Roman Life under the Caesars*. New York: Putnam, 1908.

Forestier, A. *The Roman Soldier*. London: A. & C. Black, 1928.

Frank, T., ed. *An Economic Survey of Ancient Rome*. Paterson, N.J.: Pageant, 1959.

Frere, S. S. *Britannia: A History of Roman Britain*. London: Routledge & Kegan Paul, 1987.

Frontinus, S. J. *Stratagems & Aqueducts*. Translated by C. E. Bennet and M. B. McElwain. London: Loeb, 1969.

Fuller, J. *Julius Caesar: Man, Soldier, and Tyrant*. London: Eyre & Spottiswoode, 1965.

Furneaux, R. *The Roman Siege of Jerusalem*. London: Rupert Hart-Davis, 1973.

Gardner, J. F. *Family and Familia in Roman Law and Life*. Oxford, U.K.: Oxford University Press, 1998.

Gibbon, E. *The Decline and Fall of the Roman Empire*. Chicago: Encyclopaedia Britannica, 1932.

Grant, M. *The Army of the Caesars*. Harmondsworth, U.K.: Penguin, 1974.

———. *Cleopatra*. Harmondsworth, U.K.: Penguin, 1972.

———. *Gladiators*. Harmondsworth, U.K.: Penguin, 1967.

———. *History of Rome*. Harmondsworth, U.K.: Penguin, 1978.

———. *The Jews of the Roman World*. Harmondsworth, U.K.: Penguin, 1973.

———. *Julius Caesar*. Harmondsworth, U.K.: Penguin, 1969.

———. *The Roman Emperors*. Harmondsworth, U.K.: Penguin, 1985.

———. *Roman History from Coins*. New York: Barnes & Noble, 1995.

Graves, R. *I, Claudius*. London: Arthur Barker, 1934.

Haywood, R. M. *Ancient Greece and the Near East*. London: Vision, 1964.

———. *Ancient Rome*. London: Vision, 1967.

Highet, G. *Juvenal the Satirist*. Oxford, U.K.: Clarendon, 1954.

Hill, W. T. *Buried London*. London: Phoenix House, 1955.

Home, G. C. *Roman London*. London: Eyre & Spottiswoode, 1948.

Horace. *Satires, Epistles, Ars Poetica*. Translated by H. R. Fairclough. London: Heinemann, 1955.

Jimenez, R. *Caesar against the Celts*. Conshohocken, Pa.: Sarpedon, 1996.

Jones, A. H. M. *Augustus*. New York: W. W. Norton, 1972.

Keppie, L. *Colonisation and Veteran Settlement in Italy, 47–14* B.C. London: British School at Rome, 1983.

――――. *The Making of the Roman Army: From Republic to Empire*. Totowa, N.J.: Barnes & Noble, 1984.

――――. *Roman Inscribed and Sculpted Stones in the Huntorian Museum University of Glasgow*. London: Society for Promotion of Roman Studies, 1999.

Ker, W. C. A. *Martial*. London: Loeb, 1919–1920.

Laking, G. F. *A Record of European Armour and Arms through Seven Centuries*. New York: A.M.S., 1934.

Leach, J. *Pompey the Great*. New York: Croom Helm, 1978.

Livy. *The War with Hannibal*. Translated by E. de Selincourt. Harmondsworth, U.K.: Penguin, 1965.

MacArthur, B., ed. *The Penguin Book of Twentieth-Century Speeches*. London: Penguin, 1992.

MacMullen, R. *Soldier and Civilian in the Later Roman Empire*. Cambridge, Mass.: Harvard University Press, 1967.

Mannix, D. P. *Those about to Die*. London: Mayflower, 1960.

Margary, I. D. *Roman Roads in Britain*. London: Phoenix House, 1957.

Marsden, E. W. *Greek and Roman Artillery*. Oxford, U.K.: Oxford University Press, 1969.

Mattingly, H. *Roman Coins from the Earliest Times to the Fall of the Western Empire*. London: Methuen, 1927.

Merrifield, R. *London: City of the Romans*. London: Batsford, 1983.

Mommsen, T. *The Provinces of the Roman Empire*. Edited by T. R. S. Broughton. Chicago: University of Chicago Press, Phoenix Books, 1968.

Morton, H. V. *In the Steps of the Master*. London: Rich & Cowan, 1934.

Mothersole, J. *In Roman Scotland*. London: John Lane the Bodley Head, 1927.

Napthali, L. *Life in Egypt under Roman Rule*. Oxford, U.K.: Clarendon, 1983.

Parker, H. D. M. *The Roman Legions*. New York: Barnes & Noble, 1958.

Payne-Gallwey, Sir R. *The Crossbow: Mediaeval and Modern, with a Treatise on the Ballista and Catapults of the Ancients*. 1903. Reprint, London: Holland Press, 1995.

Peterson, D. *The Roman Legions Re-created in Color*. London: Windrow & Greene, 1992.

Petronius Arbiter, G. *The Satyricon*. Translated by M. Heseltine. London: Loeb, 1913.

Philo Judaeus. *The Works of Philo*. Translated by C. D. Yonge. Peabody, Mass.: Hendrickson, 1993.

Plato. *The Dialogues*. Translated by B. Jowlett. Reprint, Chicago: Encyclopaedia Britannica, 1952.

Pliny the Elder. *Natural History*. Edited and translated by H. Rackman. London: Loeb, 1938–1963.

Raven, S. *Rome in Africa.* London: Longman, 1969.

Robertson, D. S. *Greek and Roman Architecture.* Cambridge, U.K.: Cambridge University Press, 1943.

Robinson, H. R. *The Armour of Imperial Rome.* Oxford, U.K.: Oxford University Press, 1975.

Romer, J. *Testament: The Bible and History.* London: Michael O'Mara, 1988.

Rossi, L. *Trajan's Column and the Dacian Wars.* London: Thames & Hudson, 1974.

Rostovtzeff, M. I. *The Social and Economic History of the Roman Empire.* New York: Biblio & Tannen, 1957.

Ryan, C. *The Longest Day.* London: Victor Gollancz, 1959.

Salway, P. *Roman Britain.* Oxford, U.K.: Oxford University Press, 1981.

Seager, R. *Tiberius.* London: Eyre Methuen, 1972.

Seneca. *Letters from a Stoic.* Translated by R. Campbell. Harmondsworth, U.K.: Penguin, 1969.

Sherwin-White, A. N. *The Roman Citizenship.* Oxford, U.K.: Oxford University Press, 1939.

Simkins, M. *Warriors of Rome.* London: Blandford, 1988.

Smith, F. E. *Waterloo.* London: Pan, 1970.

Starr, C. G. *Roman Imperial Navy, 31 B.C.–A.D. 324.* Ithaca, N.Y.: Cornell University Press, 1941.

Statius. *Collected Works.* Translated by J. H. Mozley. Cambridge, Mass.: Loeb, 1928.

Strabo. *The Geography of Strabo.* Translated by H. L. Jones. Cambridge, Mass.: Loeb, 1924.

Sulimirski, T. *The Sarmatians.* New York: Praeger, 1970.

Syme, R. *Ammianus and the Historia Augusta.* Oxford, U.K.: Oxford University Press, 1968.

———. *Historia Augusta Papers.* Oxford, U.K.: Clarendon, 1983.

———. *History in Ovid.* Oxford, U.K.: Oxford University Press, 1979.

Times (London). *Concise Atlas of World History.* London: Times, 1982.

Todd, M. *The Northern Barbarians, 1000 B.C.–A.D. 300.* New York: Blackwell, 1987.

———. *The Early Germans.* Oxford, U.K.: Blackwell, 1992.

Trench, C. C. *A History of Horsemanship.* Garden City, N.Y.: Doubleday, 1970.

[U.K.] War Office, General Staff. *Field Service Regulations.* London: H. M. Stationery Office, 1914.

[U.S.] Department of the Army. *US Army Survival Manual: FM 21-76.* New York: Dorset, 1991.

Utley, R. M. *The Lance and the Shield.* New York: Henry Holt, 1993.

Vernam, G. R. *Man on Horseback.* Garden City, N.Y.: Doubleday, 1964.

Waldeck, C. *Secrets and Stories of the War.* London: Reader's Digest Association, 1963.

Wallace, L. *Ben Hur.* London: Ward, Lock, 1890.

Ward, G. C., with R. and K. Burns. *The Civil War*. New York: Alfred A. Knopf, 1991.

Warmington, E. H. *Nero*. Harmondsworth, U.K.: Penguin. 1969.

Warry, J. *Warfare in the Classical World*. London: Salamander, 1989.

Watson, G. R. *The Roman Soldier*. Ithaca, N.Y.: Cornell University Press, 1969.

Webster, G., and D. R. Dudley. *The Rebellion of Boudicca*. New York: Barnes & Noble, 1962.

————. *The Roman Conquest of Britain*. London: Pan, 1973.

Webster's New Twentieth-Century Dictionary of the English Language. Cleveland: World, 1953.

Weigall, A. *Nero, Emperor of Rome*. London: Butterworth, 1930.

Wheeler, R. M. *Rome beyond the Imperial Frontiers*. London: Bell, 1954.

White, K. D. *Greek and Roman Technology*. Ithaca, N.Y.: Cornell University Press, 1983.

Wightman, E. M. *Roman Trier and the Treveri*. New York: Praeger, 1970.

Wiseman, F. J. *Roman Spain*. New York: Bell, 1956.

Yadin, Y. *Masada: Herod's Fortress and the Zealots' Last Stand*. New York: Grosset & Dunlap, 1966.

GLOSSARY

ACTA DIURNIA   Rome's *Daily News*, world's first newspaper. Handwritten daily by the Palatium at Rome and sent around the empire. Founded by Julius Caesar in 59 B.C.

AQUILIFER   Standard-bearer who carried the *aquila*, the legion's eagle. Eagle-bearer.

AUXILIARY   Noncitizen serving in Roman army. Light infantry and cavalry. Recruited throughout empire. In Imperial times served twenty-five years. Paid less than legionary. From the first century A.D., granted Roman citizenship on discharge. Commanded by prefects.

CAMP PREFECT   *Campus praefectus*. Imperial legion officer, third-in-command after commander and senior tribune. Promoted from centurion. Quartermaster, commander of major legion detachments. Took over the role filled by quaestors in republican armies.

CAMPAIGNING SEASON   Traditionally, early March to Festival of the October Horse on October 19, when legions conducted military campaigns, after which they went into winter quarters. Terms "seasoned campaigner" and "seasoned soldier" derive from this.

CENTURION   Legion, Praetorian/City Guard and Marines officer, sixty to a republican legion, in eleven grades. Equivalent to first lieutenant and captain. Enlisted man promoted from ranks, although there were some Equestrian Order centurions in late republic/early empire.

CENTURY   Legion subunit made up of ten squads. In republican times, of a hundred men. In imperial times, of eighty men. Commanded by a centurion.

CHIEF CENTURION   *Primus pilus* (first spear). Legion's most senior centurion.

CIVIC CROWN   Crown of oak leaves, military bravery award for saving the life of a Roman citizen in battle. Rarely awarded, highly prized. Julius Caesar was a recipient.

CLAVARIUM   Allowance to legionaries to buy shoe nails.

COHORT   Battalion. Ten to a legion. In Caesar's time, of 600 men. In imperial times, cohorts 10 through 2 had 480 men, the senior first cohort, 800.

COLONEL   See TRIBUNE and PREFECT.

CONQUISITOR   Roman army recruiting officer.

CONSUL   Highest official at Rome; president of Senate. Two held office annually. Also commanded Roman armies, with equivalent rank of lieutenant general. The minimum age in the republic, 42; in the imperial era the minimum age was thirty-seven, except for members of the imperial family.

CONTUBERNIUM   Legion subunit; the squad. In the republic, of ten men. In the empire, of eight men.

CURSUS PUBLICUS   Imperial courier service founded by Augustus with runners. Expanded to wheeled vehicles and mounted couriers. Way stations every six to ten miles. Covered up to 170 miles per day. It was a capital offense to interfere with cursus publicus couriers or their load.

DECIMATION   Literally, to reduce by a tenth. Legions punished for mutiny or cowardice by one man in ten being clubbed to death by their comrades after drawing lots. Ordered to be carried out by both Caesar and Antony on units under their command.

DECUMAN GATE   The main gate of legion camp, it faced away from the enemy.

DECURION   Equivalent of second lieutenant. Four to each legion cavalry squadron.

EAGLE   The aquila, sacred standard of a legion; originally silver, later gold.

EQUESTRIAN   Member of Roman order of knighthood. Qualified for posts as tribune, prefect, procurator, and Senate membership. Required net worth of 400,000 sesterces. In the imperial era served mandatory six-month legion cadetship as junior tribune at age eighteen or nineteen.

EQUITATAE   Imperial auxiliary units combining cavalry and infantry; usually "German."

EVOCATI   In republican times, the general term for legion veterans. In the imperial era, a militia corps of retired legion veterans, serving behind their old standards in emergencies and controlled by their provincial governor. Cassius Dio described them as "the recalled," because they were from time to time recalled to military duty.

FASCES   Symbol of Roman magistrate's power to punish and execute, an ax head protruding from a bundle of wooden rods. Carried by lictors. Denoted rank: quaestors had one, legates five, praetors six, consuls and most emperors twelve, dictator and some emperors twenty-four.

FIRST-RANK CENTURIONS   Primi ordines; legion's six most senior centurions.

FREEDMAN   Former slave, officially granted freedom.

FURLOUGH FEES   Payment allowing one legionary in four in camp to take leave.

GEMINA LEGION   "Twin" legion formed by merger of two existing legions.

GERMAN GUARD   Elite bodyguard unit of a Roman emperor, made up of hand-picked German auxiliaries. Instituted by Augustus. (SEE APPENDIX B.)

GLADIUS   Roman legionary sword, twenty inches long, double-edged, with pointed end.

IMPERATOR   Title. Literally, "chief" or "master." Highest honor for general. Became reserved for emperors after their armies' victories. Title "emperor" grew from *imperator*.

IMPERIAL   Relating to the period of Roman history from 27 B.C. to the fall of the empire.

IMPERIAL PROVINCE   In the imperial era, an "armed" province bordering unfriendly states. Garrisoned by at least 2 legions plus auxiliaries. Governed by a propraetor, a former consul whose appointment, by the emperor, was open-ended. A propraetor commanded all troops in his province, could wear a sword and uniform and levy recruits, and had capital punishment power.

LEGION   Regiment. Main operational unit of the Roman army. From *legio* (levy, or draft). In ten cohorts. Republican legion nominal strength, 6,000 men; imperial, 5,181 enlisted men and 71 officers, including own cavalry unit of 124 officers and men. At the beginning of the 1st century A.D. there were 28 legions; by A.D. 102, 30; and in A.D. 233, 33.

LEGIONARY   Soldier of a legion. Mostly a draftee. A Roman citizen. Most recruited outside Italy in the imperial era. Republican military age, seventeen to forty-six, served sixteen years; imperial, average age twenty, served twenty years from late in Augustus's reign.

LICTORS   Unarmed attendants of Roman magistrates, carrying their fasces.

LUSTRATION   The Lustration Exercise, religious ceremony performed by legions in March. Standards were purified with perfumes and garlands prior to each new campaign.

MANIPLE   Company. Legion subunit, of 200 men in the republic, 160 in imperial times.

MANTLET   Wooden shed, on wheels, used in siege works.

MARCHING CAMP   Fortified camp built by legions at the end of every day's march.

MARINE   Soldier with Roman navy. Freedman. Served twenty-six years, paid less than an auxiliary. Commanded by centurions. Organized by cohorts; unit titles unknown.

MURAL CROWN　Crown of gold awarded to first Roman soldier over an enemy city wall.

NUNTIUS　Literally, "announcer." Adjutant to Roman general, announcer of Daily Orders at assemblies.

OPTIO　Sergeant major. Deputy to centurion and decurion. Unit records and training officer. One to a century, four to legion cavalry units.

ORBIS　The ring, the Roman legion's circular formation of last resort.

OVATION　Lesser form of Triumph. Celebrant rode on horseback through Rome.

PALATIUM　Origin of the word "palace." Residence and military headquarters of emperors at Rome. First established by Augustus on Palatine Hill, from which its name derived. All emperors' headquarters were thereafter called the Palatium, even when new palaces were built.

PALUDAMENTUM　Roman general's cloak. Scarlet in republican times. In imperial times, legion commanders wore a scarlet cloak, commanders in chief, a purple cloak.

PILUM　A Roman legionary's javelin. Metal-tipped, weighted end, six to seven feet long.

PRAETOR　Senior magistrate and major general. Sixteen appointed annually once Caesar came to power. Could command legions and armies.

PRAETORIAN GATE　Gate of a legion camp that faced the enemy.

PRAETORIAN GUARD　Elite unit founded in the republic to guard Rome. Re-formed by Mark Antony immediately following the murder of Caesar in 44 B.C. with recently retired legion veterans. Elite imperial military police force under Octavian/Augustus.

PRAETORIUM　Headquarters in a legion camp.

PREFECT　Commander of auxiliary units, Praetorian Guard, City Guard, and naval fleets. A citizen of Equestrian Order status. Prefects governed Egypt and, between A.D. 6 and 41, Judea.

PROCONSUL　Literally, "as good as a consul." See SENATORIAL PROVINCE.

PROCURATOR　Provincial official of Equestrian Order rank, superior to prefect. Financial administrator and tax gatherer. Sometimes governed small provinces and subprovinces (e.g., Macedonia and Judea). Had capital punishment power.

PROPRAETOR　Literally, "as good as a praetor." See IMPERIAL PROVINCE.

QUADRIGA　Roman chariot drawn by four horses. A golden quadriga was used in Triumphs.

QUAESTOR Most junior Roman magistrate, entitled to one lictor. Assisted consuls on treasury matters and provincial governors with finance, military recruiting, etc. Mark Antony served as Caesar's quaestor in Gaul.

SALARIUM Annual allowance to legionaries to buy salt. (Origin of word "salary.")

SATURNALIA Festival of Saturn. Originally on December 17, extended to four days, then five, then seven. Slaves could dress like their masters, dice playing was legal, and patrons gave their clients gifts. Origin of Christian Christmas festival and of Christmas gift-giving.

SCORPION *Scorpio*, quick-firing artillery piece using metal-tipped bolts. Each legion was equipped with fifty of them, plus ten heavy stone-throwing catapults.

SECOND ENLISTMENT MEN Legionaries who voluntarily served another sixteen- or twenty-year enlistment with their legion when their first enlistment expired.

SEGMENTIA LORICA Segmented metal armor worn by legionaries from the first century A.D.

SENATE Rome's most powerful elected body. Members, needing a net worth of 1 million sesterces, qualified for legion commands, praetorships, and consulships. Minimum age thirty in imperial times. In Caesar's time, 350 to 400 members, increased by him to 900. At the start of the reign of Augustus, 1,000 members; he subsequently limited it to 600 members.

SENATORIAL PROVINCE In the imperial era, a province with a governor appointed by the Senate for a year, by lot, from its members. With the rank of proconsul (lieutenant general) the governor had capital punishment power but couldn't wear a uniform or sword or levy troops. Garrison of auxiliaries (except in Africa, where one legion was stationed).

SIGNIFER Literally, a signaler; the standard-bearer of legion subunits.

SPATHA Roman cavalry sword. It had a round end and was longer than the *gladius*.

TESSERA A small wax sheet on which was inscribed the legion's watchword for the day.

TESSERARIUS Legion guard/orderly sergeant. Distributed the *tessera* to his men.

TESTUDO "Tortoise" formation. Legionaries locked shields over their heads and at their sides.

THIRD ENLISTMENT MEN Legionaries voluntarily serving a third enlistment.

TORQUE Neck chain of twisted gold. Among the Roman army's highest bravery awards.

TRIBUNAL Reviewing stand in a legion camp; built in front of tribunes' quarters.

TRIBUNE (MILITARY)   Legion, Praetorian Guard, and City Guard officer. Six of equal rank in republican legions shared command. In imperial legion, a "thin stripe" junior tribune was an officer-cadet serving mandatory six months; five to a legion. One "broad stripe" senior (military) tribune per legion was a full colonel and legion second in command. Senior tribunes commanded Praetorian Guard and City Guard cohorts. From the reign of Claudius, twenty-five were appointed annually.

TRIBUNE OF THE PLEBEIANS   Ten tribunes elected to the Senate. In the republic they had the power of veto over Senate votes. This power was absorbed by the emperor.

TRIUMPH   Parade through Rome in a gold *quadriga* by a victorious general, followed by his soldiers, prisoners, and spoils. He also received T.D.s and a large cash prize. Initially granted by the Senate, later by emperors, and usually only to generals of consular rank.

TRIUMPHAL DECORATIONS (T.D.S)   A crimson cloak, crown of bay leaves, laurel branch, and statue in the Forum for generals celebrating a Triumph.

TRIUMPHATOR   Roman general celebrating a Triumph.

TRIUMVIRS   Members of the 43–33 B.C. Board of Three for the Ordering of State— Octavian, Antony, and Lepidus. Prior to that, unofficially, Caesar, Pompey, and Crassus.

VEXILLUM   Square cloth banner of auxiliary units and legion detachments.

WATCH   Time in Roman military camps was divided into watches of 3 hours, at the end of which sentries changed, on a trumpet call. The officer of the watch was a tribune.

WATCHWORD   Password in Roman military camp. At sunset, the tribune of the watch presented the most senior officer in camp with a register of men fit for duty and received the watchword for the next twenty-four hours. This was distributed to the sentries by guard cohort's *tesserarii*. The tribune of the Praetorian Guard obtained the guard's watchword directly from the emperor.

WINTER CAMP   A permanent base where a legion usually spent October to March.

INDEX